SMALL PRESS GUIDE
1997

A DETAILED GUIDE TO POETRY

AND

SMALL PRESS MAGAZINES

2ND EDITION

© Writer's Bookshop 1997
ISBN 0 9529119 0 6

First published by Writers' Bookshop, 7-11 Kensington High Street,
London W8 5NP

Edited by Ian Walton

Acknowledgements

A big thank you to all of the Magazine Editors whose publications are
listed for providing detailed information on time!
Thanks to Peter Finch for his thorough - in-depth introduction.

Thanks to Andy Cox of Zene Magazine for his invaluable help at the
inception of the 'Small Press Guide'.

A note from the Publisher

This is the second edition of a "smaller" magazines guide which we hope will be of invaluable help both to magazine editors and writers wishing to submit work for publication.

The information used has been supplied by the magazine editors and published at face value.

Where full information was not available to us prior to publication, we have listed those magazines after the main listings.

Should you wish to submit to them it would be wise to write to the magazine concerned (enclosing a stamped address envelope) asking for their guidelines.

This guide will be updated annually. If you feel we have omitted valuable information or that the guide could be developed further, we would like to hear from you.

Good Luck!

A Guide to Poetry and Small Press Magazines

Introduction
Peter Finch

The first thing you notice about little magazines is their sheer variety. Everything from sonnets to poesie sonore and from romanticism to rebellion. The field is as wide as it can be. Anyone can take part. Thousands do.

The little magazine as a vehicle for self-expression, self-aggrandisement, self-congratulation, performance, perverseness, glory, wonder, delusion, magnificence, fun, fabulosity, fantasy and faith has been on the rise since the establishment of *The Germ* in 1850. Regarded by many as the first, genuine little mag this Pre-Raphaelite invention paid neither its editor nor its contributors. Five hundred copies were printed out of which forty were sold. It ran for four issues and then folded in a state of financial loss. As a model for small literary magazines it has been followed, to greater and lesser degrees, ever since.

Let's start a magazine
to hell with literature
we want something redblooded
e.e. cummings

Little magazines are so easy. Collect a few poems, print them up and go. Estimates vary but by my calculations there are some five hundred or so little mags published in the British Isles. About half this number devote most of their pages to poetry. You'll find entries on the majority of them here. As institutions they change like the wind. Few last more than a dozen issues with most folding after far less. Their editors move house, give up, pass the project on. The names and addresses given here have all been checked with the individual publishers and were correct on the day when the directory was printed. I can't speak for the day after that.

Little magazines differ from their commercial counterparts in a number of significant ways. To begin with they lack the shiny slickness of the mass market journal. They do not have the advertisers. They need not conform to the standard distributor - required shape. They lack the large financial base. Commercial magazines come into being because entrepreneurs see a gap in the existing market and take steps to fill it. *Practical Boat Owner*, for example, came into existence because people with boats as a hobby wanted something to read. The income from potential sales alone is enough to turn a profit. Literary magazines, on the other hand, start up because poets need places to publish their work. They are begun because the writers need them, not because there are readers out there with time on their hands. This is art, not capitalism. The consumer is by no means king.

Little magazines are often at the cutting edge of literature. Unrestrained by taste, readership or advertisers they are able to promote the unpromotable. They provide bolt holes for the forgotten, the beginner, the neglected, the outsider, the specialist, the difficult, the hermetic, and the arcane. The unfashionable get published here as often as the new. There are no shareholders to please. Little magazines can do what they want.

Circulations are usually low. Run on shoe strings out of back bedrooms, lofts and basements little mags often never print more than three hundred copies. Those with grants from their arts board or local authority manage a few more. Only the half a dozen or so national magazines have circulations into four figures. Sales are not achieved, as most of you will have noticed, from the shelves of local branches of W.H. Smith (who regard such poetic ephemera as unshiftable nuisances). They happen when individual buyers try their luck by post, through subscriptions (send £15 and get three issues annually, if you are lucky) or as a result of hand-to-hand pushing at poetry readings, writers' workshops and literary clubs. Selling is the toughest part. The contributors get free copies. Finding other individuals willing to buy copies for the genuine joy of reading their contents is a struggle.

At one time the well-heeled little mag could readily be told from the upstart by the look of the production. The hobbyists used hard-to-read, scruffy mimeo and set their poems on a typewriter. The grant recipient used professional typesetters and proper printing: letterpress, offset litho. But today, with the advent of serious home word processors, desk top publishing packages and perfect plain paper photocopying it is much harder to spot the mag with resource. The new technology has a million advantages. Published poetry has no excuse anywhere for not looking good. At least half the poets in the business of publishing their work now own decent word processors and submit clear, crisply prepared manuscripts. It is the brave magazine that prints them looking less so.

British little magazines split into at least three main types. At the top of the pyramid comes the small group of magazines with some claim to providing a total overview of poetry in the UK. The best in the literary field appears here. These magazines are usually (but not always) in receipt of subsidy and are run by teams rather than an individual editor. Circulations are in the low thousands. Copies are occasionally seen on the shelves of newsagents. Libraries hold them. This is serious territory. Probably the best known is the magazine of the London based Poetry Society *The Poetry Review*. This is a well-printed, spine-bound compilation of new verse, news, views and reviews. It was begun as long ago as 1909, has published everyone from Ezra Pound to Ted Hughes and sees itself as the centre of poetry in Britain. Others will disagree, no doubt. Fellow national magazines include the arty and often experimental *Ambit*, Michael Schmidt's solid Carcanet produced *PN Review*, Jon Silkin's northern *Stand*, the all new poetry *The Rialto, Orbis, Outposts* and *Agenda* along with Forward Press's own high flyer *Poetry Now*. Other magazines may have aspirations - notably *Staple, Smiths Knoll, Scratch, The North, Envoi, Acumen* and *Iron* - but few come into the circulation range of the leading batch.

After these UK nationals come the regional mags and the genre specialists. Regional magazines concentrate on work from specific parts of the British Isles and Ireland. Many of their names make this obvious. *Poetry Wales* is Welsh, *Poetry Durham* is from the north east, *The Edinburgh Review* concentrates on Scotland, *Poetry Ireland* is the Irish national mag. The regional aspects of other magazines are often harder to discern. *HU* in earlier, less politically correct days was known as the *Honest Ulsterman, Otter* concentrates on new Devonshire poetry, *Planet* is the Welsh internationalist. *Doors* runs the subtitle *Into and Out of Dorset, Lines Review* and *Chapman* slug it out for the prize of being Scotland's best.

Genre specialists concentrate on the work of a specific form, type or style. *Haiku Quarterly, Blithe Spirit* and *Presence* specialise in Haiku and other eastern forms, *Global Tapestry Journal* and *Barfly* stay with the beat generation, *Psychopoetica* uses psychologically based material, *Parataxis*, and *Angel Exhaust*, *First Offence* and *Object Permanence* handle modernism and language-based texts. *Writing Women* sticks to that sex.

Below these groupings are the places where risks are taken, ideas tried out and dogmas expounded. Small mags begun because the editor was interested in poetry, because a local writing group wanted an outlet, because it seemed a good idea at the time. Little magazines so varied in style, shape, size and content that the British library system fails to contain them all. Many live for an issue or two then fade. Their names can be wonderful. You want to subscribe just to get that title on the shelf. *A Doctor's Dilemma, Strange Faces, Strength Before Bingo* and the much sought after *Bollocks To Uncle Jeffrey,* gone now, just yellow paper. But we do still have *Fatchance, The Printer's Devil, Thumbscrew, Rustic Rub, First Time* and *Dimentia.* Plenty of idiosyncracity there.

If you manage to appear in any of these magazines do not expect to get paid much. It is an illusion that money can be made from poetry. Maybe Roger McGough can make a bit when he writes for television and Ted Hughes when he sells his latest to a Sunday national. Here in the world of magazines most of the time the best you will get is a free copy of the magazine that carries your work. Occasionally generous editors offer a free subscription to contributors or even a small handful of copies but the small mag that pays has to be in receipt of subsidy. At the top end you may get £30 for a page, very occasionally more but real poetry is carried out for what it is. You want to make cash? Sell double glazing.

Basic Submission Rules

* Research your market. Do not submit your work to the first magazine name that takes your fancy. Have a look at it first. Send for a sample back copy. This will cost you a pound or so but it will not be that much. Study the market before you mail anything out. You can greatly increase your chances of acceptance by selecting magazines that will be sympathetic to your style. *Object Permanence*, for example, will not be that keen on seeing your tight, traditional sonnets. On the other hand *Rhyme Arrival* will not want to view your concrete poems.

* Learn a bit about the shape of the contemporary poetry world. Read anthologies of new poetry. Read widely and look into areas that at first do not appeal to you. Visit your library and your local bookshop. Keep up to date.

* Word process, type or otherwise set your poems single-spaced, laid out exactly as you would like to see them printed. Hand written texts are ignored by most publishers. Use white A4 paper. Print on one side of the paper only. Include your name and address either at the beginning or the end. Give your poem a title, even if this is its first line or title the work "poem". Staple multiple sheets together, top left.

* Keep a record of what you write, to where you submit it, when and the reaction you got. You may imagine you will be able to remember this kind of information. After a time, believe me, you will not.

* Enclose a stamped addressed envelope in sufficient size to carry your poems (if necessary) and the editor's reply back. Submission without s.a.e.s get binned.

* Expect to wait. Replies from some magazines come instantly. Others take weeks. It is not unusual to be kept waiting for a month or so. Longer than that write to enquire what is going on.

* Try to avoid submitting the same material to more than one magazine simultaneously. If the piece gets accepted by both you could be in embarrassing trouble.

There are enough magazines around of differing standards and different styles for everyone to get published. So long as you have a modicum of talent, persistence and an ability to follow both the rules and your nose you will get published. You may never become famous, nor rich but you will get your name in print. The depression of constantly returning rejected poetry can be alleviated by always having some work, out there, being considered. Submit to groups of magazines rather than concentrating on a single one. Rejection does not necessarily mean that your work is bad. It could well be simply unsuited, submitted at the wrong time or sent to a magazine that is already full.

Short Fiction

More around than there used to be. More magazines testing the water and a positive boom in those using dark fiction - gothic fantasy, strange worlds. *Ace of Rods, Alternative Worlds, Back Brain Recluse, Raw Nerve, The Third Alternative, Urban Fantasy.* Don't expect payment here either. The rules are the same as for poetry.

So many writers around. Be inventive rather than imitative. Plot can beat style. Be new. Make sure you provide what the market requires. Read as much as you can.

Prose, of course, takes up much more space than poetry. It takes longer to read, costs more to send. Expect, perhaps, to wait a little longer for replies and don't inundate magazines with more than an example or two of your work each time. Expect a higher rejection rate. There are far fewer slots waiting to be filled. Expect to find it takes much longer if you choose to revise a piece following an editor's comments.

Prose fiction should be submitted double-spaced, single side on A4 sheets, stapled to left hand corner, clearly titled. Put your name and address on the final sheet. Show extent (i.e.: 2500 words). Number pages (1 of 8 being the best style).

And keep your eyes open. New magazines start all the time. Check the listings published in the back pages of most titles for news of new arrivals. Do it now.

A RIOT OF EMOTIONS

Frequency:	Once or twice yearly
Subscription Cost:	No subs. yet
Single Issue:	£1 post paid
Back issue price:	90 pence, post paid
Cheques/PO Payable to:	Andrew Cocker
Overseas subs:	$2 per issue Europe, $3 rest of world
Payment Details:	Cash only US dollars

Description

ARTWORK: Black & White illustrations only SIZE: Maximum finished area should not exceed 14 x 20 cm / 5.5 x 8 inches. For aesthetic reasons all full page pieces must be portrait not landscape. Smaller pieces of any size are acceptable. All artwork should be camera ready (as you would wish to see it printed) including any photographic work which must be screened or photocopied. Submissions of words and art combined, e.g.. comic strips, illustrated poems / text are also acceptable. WRITTEN WORK: All text must be typed or neatly hand-written, and punctuated as you would wish to see it appear in print. All hand-written submissions will be typed by the editor unless it alters the presentation of the work. I am mainly interested in publishing poetry and short pieces of prose / fiction. I will consider short stories also, maximum 2000 words. SUBJECT MATTER: There are no real restrictions, but I favour the bizarre / weird / esoteric / imaginative and experimental. Selection of work is made purely on the basis of what I personally like. I do not judge whether contributions are 'good' or 'bad' according to any literary criteria or artistic rules. I am not interested in publishing anything racist, sexist, homophobic or otherwise discriminatory nature; apart from these few restrictions, an editorial policy of no censorship means that I do sometimes publish work of a shocking or confrontational nature, and pieces which contain strong language or 'swearing' provided it is for reasons of self expression and not merely gratuitous offences. Anyone easily offended should consider this fair warning. Opinions expressed by the contributors are not necessarily shared by the editor. REVIEWS: Reviews of small press publications: zines, books, pamphlets, mail are projects etc. are included in every issue. A free copy of the issue in which the review appears.

Addresses
Editorial: PO Box HK31, Leeds, West Yorkshire LS11 9XN

Reviews: As above
Subscriptions: As above
Payment terms
to contributors: One free copy to all contributors
Accept/Rejection
approximate times: Usually 2 weeks - 1 month
Inserts accepted: No
Price per 1000:
Circulation: 1000 copies.

A.L.I. (Avon Literary Intelligencer)

Frequency:	Quarterly
Subscription Cost:	£3 yearly
Single Issue:	£1
Back issue price:	£2
Cheques/PO Payable to:	Avon Literary Intelligencer
Overseas subs:	£61 yearly
Payment Details:	Sterling or International money order

Description

Poetry, fictions, criticism, news. Contributions are invited from people with something to communicate. People who just want a publication are welcome to add A.L.I. to their C.V.s (and save postage). A.L.I. is a sweet smelling yellow eyed alley cat quarterly literary jumped up newsletter.

Addresses

Editorial:	20 Byron Place, Clifton, Bristol BS8 1JT Electronic Submissions welcome:DSR @ Maths. Bath. AC. U.K.
Reviews:	As above
Subscriptions:	As above
Payment terms to contributors:	1 Copy A.L.I.
Accept/Rejection approximate times:	6 weeks
Inserts accepted:	Yes
Price per 1000:	Price per 200: £5
Circulation:	200

ABRAXAS

Frequency:	Quarterly
Subscription Cost:	£12 a year
Single Issue:	£3
Back issue price:	£3
Cheques/PO Payable to:	Paul Newman
Overseas subs:	£15 Europe/America
Payment Details:	IMO, cheque in sterling, postal order, foreign currencies must allow for exchange

Description

Abraxas (founded 1991) features lead articles by Colin Wilson on such subjects as philopsophy, literature and ideas, plus supplementary items; poems, surrealist, traditional and arcane; stories, gnomic, oblique, Abraxas has featured translations of Pable Palacio and Jose de Cuadra; reviews of heavy weight stories and articles of denizens of literary backwaters: J.C Powys, David Lindsay, Harold Visiak. Magazine offers contemporary Colin Wilson booklist offering signing and inscription service.

Addresses

Editorial:	57 Eastbourne Road, St Austell, Cornwall, PL25 4SU
Reviews:	Same as above
Subscriptions:	Same as above
Payment terms to contributors:	Free copy of magazine
Accept/Rejection approximate times:	About one in fifty acceptances usually subscribers or those who`ve studied magazine.
Inserts accepted:	Yes
Price per 1000:	£1.50
Circulation:	Increasing

ACE OF RODS

Frequency: 8 times a year
Subscription cost: £7.50
Single issue: £1.00 plus a postage stamp
                         (or all in stamps)
Back issue price:
Cheques/PO Payable to: Acca and Adda
Overseas subs:
Payment details:

Description
Ace of Rods is a contact magazine for those interested in paganism/wicca craft and is run as a non profit making venture. Diary events are mentioned, advertising is free to subscribers but commercial ventures are advised to study the advertising rates. The magazine is run cheaply and therefore the magazine cannot pay for contributions. The magazine aims to include extra features such as news, articles, reviews, letters (please specify letter is for publication) where space permits. All material should be of interest to pagans and may include folklore, magic, nature, crafts, tradition as well as reviews of books, events and music. Illustrations may be seasonal, magical, mythological but in all cases enquiries should be accompanied by a stamp and manuscripts clearly marked with a return address and sufficient postage. Contributors are advised to see the magazine.

Addresses
Editorial: Acca and Adda, BCM, Academia, London WC1N 3XX
Reviews: As above
Subscription: As above
Payment terms
to contributors: N/A
Accept/Rejection
approximate times:
Inserts accepted:
Price per 1000:   N/A
Circulation:

ACUMEN

Frequency:	3 times per year
Subscription Cost:	£10 for 3 issues UK; £12.50 Europe or USA sterling
Single Issue:	£3.50 UK Euro plus 45p
Back issue price:	Various
Cheques/PO Payable to:	ACUMEN
Overseas subs:	Details above
Payment Details:	Free copy or negotiable

Description

Acumen is a literary magazine with an emphasis on poetry. It seeks to please the intelligent reader with high-quality, well-written prose and poetry. In addition it has an extensive reviews section devoted mostly to poetry publications; and a recent innovation has been the issue of a free focus sheet and poster combined that provides a sampler of the poetry of an individual poet. Its overall aim is to emphasis the continuity of English poetry and literature into the present age.

Addresses

Editorial:	Patricia Oxley, 6 The Mount, Higher Furzeham, Brixham, S. Devon, PQ5 8QY
Reviews:	Glyn Pursglove, 25 St, Albans Road, Brynmill, Swansea, SA2 0BP
Subscriptions:	6 The Mount, Higher Furzeham, Brixman, S. Devon, TQ5 8QY
Payment terms to contributors:	Free copy or negotiable
Accept/Rejection approximate times:	Outright rejections within 2 weeks; shortlisting of possible acceptances for up to 3 months
Inserts accepted:	Yes
Price per 1000:	£100
Circulation:	600

AGENDA

Frequency: Quarterly, but often one double issue a year
Subscription Cost: £20
Single Issue: £5
Back issue price: £5 (but more for double issues)
Cheques/PO Payable to: Agenda
Overseas subs: £22 - $44
Payment Details: Visa & Mastercard

Description
We look for poems with 'more than usual emotion, more than usual order', and we are interested in work that can be lived with over years rather than poetry with immediate impact. We publish special issues on particular poems and themes and international numbers devoted to poetry in translation - Chinese, German, etc. Next issue is devoted to 'Dauto & the Contemporary Poet'. A Spanish number will appear next summer.

Addresses
Editorial: William Cookson, Agenda, 5 Cranbourne Court, Albert Bridge Road, London SW11 4PE
Reviews: As above
Subscriptions: As above
Payment terms
to contributors: Varies £10 - £15 per page prose.
Accept/Rejection
approximate times: 1 - 2 months
Inserts accepted: Yes
Price per 1000:   £100
Circulation: 1000 - 1500

AH POOK IS HERE

Frequency:	Monthly
Subscription Cost:	Free
Single Issue:	Free
Back issue price:	N/A
Cheques/PO Payable to:	N/A
Overseas subs:	Free
Payment Details:	N/A

Description

The best poetry and words and music and things and pictures and collage and more music and editorial abuse and POOK PEN PALS including Welsh lessons, (Wales being THE THING) and exam doodles and extreme ideas and anything except dull, boring, normal, flowers and stuff poems. Think Bukowsi. Think Celine. Think the best in the small press.

Addresses

Editorial:	The Vicarage, Pontllanfraith,Blackwood, Gwent, NP2 2DP, U.K.
Reviews:	As above
Subscriptions:	As above
Payment terms to contributors:	Free copies
Accept/Rejection approximate times:	As and when
Inserts accepted:	No
Price per 1000:	N\A
Circulation:	Thousands

AIREINGS

Frequency:	2 yearly
Subscription Cost:	£5.00 P.A inc postage
Single Issue:	£2.50
Back issue price:	£1.50
Cheques/PO Payable to:	AIREINGS PUBLICATION
Overseas subs:	£6.00 if in sterling, £12 if in Foreign
Payment Details:	Cheque or P.O to AIREINGS PUBLICATION

Description

Poetry magazine - 40 pages specialises in Womens Poetry but work from men welcome

Addresses

Editorial:	24 Brudenell Road, Leeds, LS6 1BD
Reviews:	As above
Subscriptions:	As above
Payment terms to contributors:	1 free copy/subscriber copy
Accept/Rejection approximate times:	Twice yearly, Spring/Autumn
Inserts accepted:	
Price per 1000:	
Circulation:	300

AMBIT

Frequency:	Quarterly
Subscription Cost:	UK £22 - £33 institution
Single Issue:	£6 - institution £9 - Overseas £8/$16 institution £11/$22
Back issue price:	£10 - institution £12 - Overseas £12/$24 institution £14/$28
Cheques/PO Payable to:	Ambit
Overseas subs:	£24 - $48 - £35/$70 institution
Payment Details:	Cheque/PO/Visa/Mastercard/American Express

Description

Ambit publishes a wide range of experimental new poetry, short fiction, fine art and illustration, plus a vigorous and stimulating reviews' section. Established writers appear alongside up-and-coming new talent and hitherto unpublished writers. Ambit, now funded by the Arts Council of England, was started in 1959 and has been published quarterly without interruption since. Meticulously edited by Martin Bax, Edwin Brock, Carol Ann Duffy, Henry Graham, J G Ballard, Geoff Nicholson and Mike Forman you can expect a consistently exciting and important selection of work in every issue.

Addresses

Editorial:	17 Priory Gardens, London, N6 5QY
Reviews:	As above
Subscriptions:	As above
Payment terms to contributors:	£5.00 per printed page
Accept/Rejection approximate times:	3 - 4 months
Inserts accepted:	Yes
Price per 1000:	£170
Circulation:	7000

AMMONITE

Frequency:	Occasional
Subscription Cost:	£3.50
Single Issue:	£1.75
Back issue price:	£1.50
Cheques/PO Payable to:	Ammonite publications
Overseas subs:	£5.00
Payment Details:	Cheque/IMO/PO/ Discount of 20% of total order value if 5 or more copies are ordered.

Description

Ammonite has become known for publishing the unexpected, the surprising, the unusual. Contributors stretch their imaginative boundaries when writing for Ammonite. A wealth of new writing Imagination beyond the straight rules of the speculative genre. Ammonite brings new dimensions to the thinking of all those who seek the challenge of ideas and images that stir the human mind and spirit to part veil of mundare, accepted views of reality. Ammonite is presented in A5 formal with 36 pages of poetry, fiction and ideas within a decorative art card cover.

Addresses

Editorial:	Ammonite Publications, 12 Priory Mead, Bruton, Somerset, BA10 0DZ
Reviews:	Same as above
Subscriptions:	Same as above
Payment terms to contributors:	2 free copies
Accept/Rejection approximate times:	8 weeks
Inserts accepted:	No
Price per 1000:	N\A
Circulation:	200

ANCHORS AWEIGH

Frequency:	Quarterly
Subscription Cost:	£6
Single Issue:	£1.50
Back issue price:	£1.50
Cheques/PO Payable to:	Forward Press
Overseas subs:	£6
Payment Details:	Visa/Cheque/P.O

Description
Anchors Aweigh is an informative chatty and friendly newsletter aimed at poets who enjoy simple accessible poetry. Packed with news and views on the poetry world, Anchors Aweigh offers poets the chance to communicate with each other.

Sections Include:
* Booklet Reviews
* Competition News
* Articles
* Get Together section

Addresses

Editorial:	1-2 Wainman Road, Woodston, Peterborough, Cambs, PE2 7BU
Reviews:	As above
Subscriptions:	As above
Payment terms to contributors:	Letters £2, Compass Points £5, Articles £10, Worms Eye View £5, Book Reviews £5
Accept/Rejection approximate times:	Six to eight weeks
Inserts accepted:	Yes
Price per 1000:	Free
Circulation:	2120

AND

Frequency:	Irregular
Subscription Cost:	No subscriptions taken
Single Issue:	£4
Back issue price:	£4
Cheques/PO Payable to:	New River Project
Overseas subs:	
Payment Details:	

Description

Specialised: concrete and visual poetry, linguistically innovative poetry, scores for performance, Etc.

Addresses

Editorial:	89a Petherton Road, London, N5 2QT
Reviews:	Same as above
Subscriptions:	N/A
Payment terms to contributors:	Two free copies plus any other at half price
Accept/Rejection approximate times:	Varies
Inserts accepted:	No
Price per 1000:	
Circulation:	500

ANGEL EXHAUST

Frequency:	Twice yearly
Subscription Cost:	£7
Single Issue:	£4
Back issue price:	Two for £7, one for £4
Cheques/PO Payable to:	ANGEL EXHAUST
Overseas subs:	£9 for a year
Payment Details:	

Description

The space, normally 128 pages, is divided equally between poetry and documentation on poetry. We are interested in the realm where formally innovative work overlaps with socially radical ideas, also in Gothic and New Age poetry. We do not publish work comfily snuggled inside the behavioural rules established before 1970. Ideal poets for this magazine would be Allen Fisher, Denise Riley, Maggie O'Sullivan, and J.H. Prynne. The prose arm aims at making visible the achievements of the British Poetry Revival as the history of the present, via interviews, survey articles, and in-depth reviews of new books. Special issues have been on the schools of Cambridge poetry, and London, an anthology of new poets, art and politics, the history of Cambridge poetry, and poetry and Socialist, Northern poetry. Special interests include Scottish informationism, the Socialism, poets of South Wales, the Gothic poetry of the Seventies, the Left, the critique of subjectivity, navigating in new information landscapes, the milieu of the text and peripheral or minority traditions, neoprimitivism, sociobiology, the periodization of the past 30 years of style history, and the Nincompoop school of poetry. An elite team of reviewers is dedicated to the unswathing of brilliance, the massacre of the insignificant, and the incomprehension of the incomprehensible.

Addresses

Editorial:	27 Sturton Street, Cambridge, CB1 2 QG, Cambs
Reviews:	Same as above
Subscriptions:	Same as above

Payment terms to contributors:	In offprints

Accept/Rejection
approximate times: 1 week
Inserts accepted: Yes
Price per 1000:
Circulation: 300

ANSIBLE

Frequency:	Monthly
Subscription Cost:	Free
Single Issue:	Send S.A.E.
Back issue price:	N/A (available on World Wide Web)
Cheques/PO Payable to:	N/A
Overseas subs:	N/A
Payment Details:	N/A

Description
Informal newsletter edited by David Langford, covering doings in the science fiction community, primarily in Britain. The first series ran from 1979 to 1987; the current incarnation (2pp A4 each issue) has appeared since 1991. Ansible received Hugo awards - the international SF 'Oscars' - in 1987, 1995 and 1996. Coverage includes events, meetings, gossip, award results, authors and publishers' misbehaviour, humourous items of related interest (e.g. examples of grotesquely badwriting from current SF/fantasy), and whatever else suits the editor's whim. Many noted SF authors have contributed. Ansible may be examined on the web at http:/www.dcs.gla.ac.uk/SF - Archives/Ansible....

Addresses

Editorial:	94 London Road, Reading, Berks, RGI 5AU; e-mail ansible @ cix.compulink.co.uk
Reviews:	N/A
Subscriptions:	SAEs to above address
Payment terms to contributors:	Free copies only
Accept/Rejection approximate times:	approximate times 1 month
Inserts accepted:	Flyers for non-commercial, non-profit SF events etc. only - by arrangement
Price per 1000:	Free
Circulation:	1200 + unknown on internet

APOSTROPHE

Frequency:	Twice yearly, March \ September
Subscription Cost:	£5.50 inc postage
Single Issue:	£2.25 inc postage
Back issue price:	£1.50
Cheques/PO Payable to:	MR PILLOWS PRESS
Overseas subs:	£6
Payment Details:	International money order or IRC

Description

Apostrophe is a bi-annual publication of poetry, both modern and in translation. The editorial policy is to emcompass the whole spectrum of human emotions and aspirations, not forgetting the importance of wit and humour. New poets are encouraged and there is always a balance between unknown and experienced contributors. There is an international readership. The editor welcomes well-crafted poetry on any topic and in any style. Short poems preferred.

Addresses

Editorial:	The Editor, Mr Pillows, 41 Canute Road, FAVERSHAM, Kent, ME13 8SH, England
Reviews:	As above
Subscriptions:	As above
Payment terms to contributors:	Complimentary copy
Accept/Rejection approximate times:	4-6 weeks Editors office closed for submissions during August and 16th December - 1st January
Inserts accepted:	Yes
Price per 1000:	£20 per 100
Circulation:	Circa 100

AQUARIUS

Frequency:	Yearly
Subscription Cost:	
Single Issue:	£5 plus post 70p
Back issue price:	
Cheques/PO Payable to:	AQUARIUS
Overseas subs:	$17 Dollars to cover postage and cost
Payment Details:	

Description

A serious poetry magazine brought by individuals and institutions world wide. Has featured work from George Barker to Fay Weldon. This magazine is one of the essential outlets for poetry. The editor likes writers who have bought and studied the style and form of the work published in the magazine.

Addresses

Editorial:	AQUARIUS - Flat 10, Room A, 116 Sutherland Avenue, Maida Vale, London W9,
Reviews:	As above
Subscriptions:	
Payment terms	
to contributors:	By agreement
Accept/Rejection	
approximate times:	
Inserts accepted:	Yes
Price per 1000:	£50
Circulation:	2,000

ARCADIAN THE

Frequency:	Bi-annual
Subscription Cost:	£3 p.a.
Single Issue:	£1.50
Back issue price:	£1.50
Cheques/PO Payable to:	Mike Boland
Overseas subs:	£5 p.a.
Payment Details:	IMO, cheque in sterling, postal order

Description

The Arcadian was founded in 1991, and includes editorial, reviews, news, readers letters as well as poems and essays. A regular feature is a chronological history of the Poets Laureate, with a different incumbent highlighted each issue. The editor has a blind spot concerning haiku, but otherwise all forms are considered. However most of the poems accepted tend to come out of a traditional/mainstream background. Poets published in previous issues include Sophie Hannah, William Oxley, Geoff Stevens and John Ward amongst many others, although submissions from new or unknown writers are particularly welcomed. No preference is given to subscribers, although it is strongly recommended that would-be contributors study the magazine before submission.

Addresses

Editorial:	11 Boxtree Lane, Harrow Weald, Middlesex HA3 6JU
Reviews:	As above
Subscriptions:	As above
Payment terms to contributors:	Free copy of magazine
Accept/Rejection approximate times:	Hopefully within 12 weeks
Inserts accepted:	Yes
Price per 1000:	£1
Circulation:	Healthy

ARTERY

Frequency:	Quarterly
Subscription Cost:	£50
Single Issue:	£15
Back issue price:	N/A
Cheques/PO Payable to:	Artery
Overseas subs:	£60
Payment Details:	International Ordering System (e.g. Whitakers)

Description

This is a limited edition magazine (100 copies) containing signed artworks, along with exclusive interviews. Each issue will focus on a particular artist and writer of international importance. Artery will contain literary essays, poems and a section on film (occasional interviews with film directors/producers). People are free to photocopy it as long as the material is always credited to Artery International. The title is set to suggest a bloody urgency of ideas.

Addresses

Editorial:	Patricia Scanlan 34 Waldemar Avenue, Fulham, London SW6 5NA
Reviews:	As above
Subscriptions:	£50
Payment terms to contributors:	Paid on date of publication
Accept/Rejection approximate times:	2 - 3 weeks
Inserts accepted:	Yes
Price per 1000:	
Circulation:	100 X 'x' by photocopier

ARTIST'S BOOK YEARBOOK 1996-97

Frequency:	Bi-annual
Subscription Cost:	£10 + p & p (£2)
Single Issue:	N/A
Back issue price:	£5 + p & p (£2)
Cheques/PO Payable to:	Magpie Press
Overseas subs:	N/A
Payment Details:	N/A

Description

Edited by T. Peixoto, John Bently, Stephanie Brown, ISBN 0 952 3880 6 5/ISBN 1355 - 0187Format 206 x 292 mm - 130 pp.No Arts council grant this year, but that won't stop us. So much has happened: Exhibitions, conferences, fairs, magazines, new courses. It's hard to keep up with it all. ABYB will focus on visual language in books, the page as a location, Russian contemporary artists' books, with interviews, articles and reviews by critics, art historians and practitioners. ABYB essential reading for all those interested in Book Arts.

Addresses

Editorial:	1 Hermitage Cottage, Clamp Hill,Stanmore, Middx. HA7 3JW
Reviews:	As above
Subscriptions:	As above
Payment terms to contributors:	None
Accept/Rejection approximate times:	6 - 10 weeks
Inserts accepted:	No
Price per 1000:	N/A
Circulation:	1000

ASWELLAS

Frequency:	Yearly
Subscription Cost:	£2.50 per copy
Single Issue:	Same
Back issue price:	£1.50
Cheques/PO Payable to:	West Essex Literary Society
Overseas subs:	£3.50 or £2.50 Back Issue
Payment Details:	Sterling cheque

Description

Aswellas now in its fourth year aims to give new writers (poetry and prose) a voice alongside the more well known, particularly writers who have an oblique and querky view of life. From Issue four we also feature drawings and B/W photographs.

Addresses

Editorial:	John Steer, 69 Orchard Croft, Harlow, Essex CM20 3BG
Reviews:	Not featured
Subscriptions:	As above
Payment terms to contributors:	Free copy of magazine
Accept/Rejection approximate times:	Approx. 3 - 4 weeks. Greater favour shown to those who subscribe
Inserts accepted:	No
Price per 1000:	N/A
Circulation:	Growing all the time

AUALLAUNIUS

Frequency:	2 per annum
Subscription Cost:	£15 (£18 overseas)
Single Issue:	£3.50
Back issue price:	£4.00
Cheques/PO Payable to:	The Arthur Machen Society
Overseas subs:	£18 US if appropriate
Payment Details:	

Description

The Journal is that of the society which offers the life and writing of Arthur Machen, the 1890s (mystery and imagination genre),Our president Barry Humphries Patron Julian Lloyd Webber

Addresses

Editorial:	Rita Tait, 19 Cross Street, Caerlean, Gwent, NP6 1AF
Reviews:	As above
Subscriptions:	As above
Payment terms	
to contributors:	None
Accept/Rejection	
approximate times:	N/A
Inserts accepted:	No
Price per 1000:	N/A
Circulation:	300

AXIOM

Frequency:
Subscription Cost: TBA
Single Issue: £1.25
Back issue price:
Cheques/PO Payable to:
Overseas subs:
Payment Details:

Description
Axiom requires quality material on Fiction, Sci - Fi, Fantasy, Horror, Poetry, Thoughts, nothing too sentimental. Contributors must enclose an SAE and a covering letter with work.

Addresses
Editorial: Michelle Oliver, 60 Greenfarm Road, Ely, Cardiff, CF5 4RH
Reviews:
Subscriptions: TBA
Payment terms
to contributors: £10.00 prize for best piece of published work
Accept/Rejection
approximate times:
Inserts accepted:
Price per 1000:
Circulation:

BACK BRAIN RECLUSE (BBR)

Frequency:	Annual
Subscription Cost:	UK: 4 issues £11
Single Issue:	UK £3.50
Back issue price:	UK £3.50
Cheques/PO Payable to:	Chris Reed
Overseas subs:	4 issues/£13.20, UK currency only
Payment Details:	Ireland/USA/Australia enquire with SAE for local agents

Description
BBR publishes some of the most startling and daring SF currently being written, and has developed a cult following around the world through a policy of emphasising the experimental and uncommercial end of the form. Recent contributors have included Richard Kadrey, Paul Di Filippo, Michael Moorcock, Misha, Don Webb and Mark Rich, as well as many exciting new names making their first professional appearance. "If you think you know what science fiction looks like, think again" - Covert Culture Sourcebook

Addresses

Editorial:	BBR, PO Box 625, Sheffield, S1 3GY, UK (for all correspondence)
Reviews:	
Subscriptions:	
Payment terms to contributors:	£10 ($15) per 1,000 words, on publication
Accept/Rejection approximate times:	1 Month
Inserts accepted:	No
Price per 1000:	
Circulation:	3,000

BARFLY

Frequency:	Quarterly
Subscription Cost:	£4.00
Single Issue:	£1.00
Back issue price:	£1.00
Cheques/PO Payable to:	J. Summers
Overseas subs:	$16/equivalent
Payment Details:	Cheque/Postal order/Cash

Description

Bukowski/beat influenced.... A magazine of real experiences/real thoughts/real emotions Poetry/prose accepted, but NO flowers, sunset meadows wanted: hard edged modern stuff.

Addresses

Editorial:	Jon Summers, 96 Brookside Way, West End, Southampton, SO30 3GZ
Reviews:	As above
Subscriptions:	As above
Payment terms to contributors:	Contributors copy only
Accept/Rejection approximate times:	1 Week
Inserts accepted:	No
Price per 1000:	
Circulation:	500 plus

BEAT SCENE

Frequency:	Quarterly
Subscription Cost:	£14 for 5 issues
Single Issue:	£3.50
Back issue price:	£3.50
Cheques/PO Payable to:	M. Ring
Overseas subs:	$35 payable to Mr D.HSU, PO Box 105, Cab
Payment Details:	

Description

This is a news type magazine about writers such as Jack Keroval, Burroveths, Bukowski, we include interviews, profiles, articles, even original material from the leading writers in the field, we are not a poetry magazine even though we are a magazine, we try and maintain standards as high as possible in presentation - 2 colour glossy covers - standard A4 magazine format. Our recent issue sports a Kerovac cover and an outgoing look at the Kerovac estate wrangle, Allen Ginsbergs records and more

Addresses

Editorial:	Kevin Ring, 27 Court Leet, Binley Woods, NR Coventry, CV3 2JQ
Reviews:	As above
Subscriptions:	£14 for 5 issues to above - payable to M. Ring
Payment terms to contributors:	None/Negotiated
Accept/Rejection approximate times:	1 Week
Inserts accepted:	
Price per 1000:	
Circulation:	

BIZZ THE

Frequency:	Twice a year
Subscription Cost:	N/A
Single Issue:	Free + 50p p & p
Back issue price:	N/A
Cheques/PO Payable to:	Lloyd Robson
Overseas subs:	N/A
Payment Details:	Cheque to 'Lloyd Robson'

Description
A drugs education - thro - entertainment - reduction magazine including new drug-related writing and editorial. Circulation varies (between 2,000 and 12,000).Subscription is not available Back issues are not available.

Addresses

Editorial:	c/o Black Hat, Top Flat, 18 Sapphire Street, Adamsdown, Cardiff, CF2 1PZ
Reviews:	As above
Subscriptions:	As above
Payment terms to contributors:	N/A
Accept/Rejection approximate times:	N/A
Inserts accepted:	No
Price per 1000:	N/A
Circulation:	2,000 - 12,000

BLACK CAT TALES OF 'THE UNEXPECTED'

Frequency:	2 - 3 a year
Subscription Cost:	N/A
Single Issue:	£2.25
Back issue price:	£2.25
Cheques/PO Payable to:	Millers Publications
Overseas subs:	$6 or $5 + IRCS
Payment Details:	Cheques or cash

Description

We publish new authors, as well as classic writers. Past publication include Bram Stokers 'The Squaw'. The format is A5 but will change shortly. No articles accepted.

Addresses

Editorial:	Mount Cottage, Grange Road, St. Michaels, Kent TN36 6EE
Reviews:	As above
Subscriptions:	As above
Payment terms to contributors:	Royalties on sales
Accept/Rejection approximate times:	2 - 6 weeks
Inserts accepted:	No
Price per 1000:	N/A
Circulation:	2500

BLADE

Frequency:	3 times yearly
Subscription Cost:	£9
Single Issue:	£3.50
Back issue price:	£3.50
Cheques/PO Payable to:	Blade Press
Overseas subs:	£15 Sterling Europe/America
Payment Details:	IMO, cheque in sterling, postal order

Description

Blade (founded November 1995) features poetry and reviews only, although the reviews give ' a sense of critical intelligence and purpose' Poets have included Brendan Kennelly, Maura Dooley, Geoff Hattersley, Brendan Cleary, Linda France, Mario Petrucci, George Szirtes, Janet Fisher and Geoffrey Holloway. The emphasis is on elegant, well-written poetry with a strong theme and clear voice. New poets welcomed.

Addresses

Editorial:	Jane Holland (Editor)'Maynrys,' Glen Chass, Port St Mary, Isle of Man, IM 9 5PN
Reviews:	As above
Subscriptions:	As above
Payment terms to contributors:	Free copy of magazine. Reviews£5 per 500 words on publication
Accept/Rejection approximate times:	2 weeks. Contributors should see the magazine before submitting.
Inserts accepted:	Yes
Price per 1000:	Negotiable
Circulation:	150 - 200

BORDERLINES

Frequency:	Twice yearly. May/June and December
Subscription Cost:	£3
Single Issue:	£1.50
Back issue price:	£1.50
Cheques/PO Payable to:	Anglo-Welsh Poetry Society
Overseas subs:	EU £4 Elsewhere £6
Payment Details:	IMO, cheque in sterling

Description

Magazine published by Anglo-Welsh Poetry Society, a poetry group founded to promote poetry in the Marches-border area. No axe to grind. The editors say 'We try not to have preconceived ideas about what poetry should be and try to be catholic in our choice of material - more instinctive than analytical. We are aware of needing to maintain a reasonable standard while providing encouragement where possible. We always seem to end up with a magazine with plenty of variety, a generally high standard and some first class material.'

Addresses

Editorial:	Nant y Brithyll, Llangynyw, Welshpool Powys, SY21 0JS
Reviews:	Do not do reviews
Subscriptions:	As above
Payment terms to contributors:	Complimentary copy of magazine
Accept/Rejection approximate times:	Up to 6 weeks
Inserts accepted:	Yes for reputable poetry promotion
Price per 1000:	Negotiable
Circulation:	200

BRAQUEMARD

Frequency:	Twice yearly
Subscription Cost:	£5 per 2 issues
Single Issue:	£2.90
Back issue price:	£2.90 (or any two for £5)
Cheques/PO Payable to:	David Allenby
Overseas subs:	£4 per issue, £7 for two
Payment Details:	Sterling cheques payable as above

Description

Like all magazines, BRAQUEMARD has its own distinctive flavour, and it is obviously best to see a copy before submitting. As a rough guideline, we tend to bad taste, black humour and the sick side of human nature. We avoid explicit religion, politics, ecology and PC attitudes. No style limitations - we have used sonnets, villanelles, haiku etc as well as free verse. Short story writers should note that we use only micro-fictions, 1000 words or less, and at most two per issue; we have had to return many excellent stories that were simply too long. Original black-and-white artwork is welcomed, but suitable work may be kept on file indefinitely, so please send only photocopies. BRAQUEMARD`s past contributors have included Fiona Pitt-Kethley, Sean O` Brian, Benjamin Zephaniah, Geoff Hattersley, Douglas Houston, Britan Patten, Joolz, Michael Daugherty, Ian MacMillan, Alison Chisholm, Margot K Juby and T.F Griffin as well as many lesser-known quality writers.

Addresses

Editorial:	David Allenby, 20 Terry Street, Hull HU3 1UD
Reviews:	No reviews carried
Subscriptions:	As above
Payment terms to contributors:	Copy of the magazine
Accept/Rejection approximate times:	Variable, up to 2 months
Inserts accepted:	Yes
Price per 1000:	Terms on application
Circulation:	

BREAKFAST ALL DAY

Frequency:	Quarterly
Subscription Cost:	£5
Single Issue:	£1.50
Back issue price:	£1.50
Cheques/PO Payable to:	B.A.D. Press
Overseas subs:	£7
Payment Details:	IMO cheque in sterling. Foreign currencies must allow for exchange

Description

Founded in 1995, a general interest magazine with cartoons, articles, photographs, short-stories and poems, free adverts of books and events.1 featured: London Wainwright III article, Suicide Notes. It's a Dogs life Cartoon, Poems by Eric Holmes. 2 featured: Metamorphosis in cartoon form, Fat is a feminist tissue by Philip Boxall and Poetry pages.3 featured: Small Creeps Day in cartoon form by Kevin Harrison and Poems by various contributor to B.A.D.

Addresses

Editorial:	43 Kingsdown House, Amburst Road, London E8 2AS
Reviews:	As above
Subscriptions:	As above
Payment terms to contributors:	None
Accept/Rejection approximate times:	2 months
Inserts accepted:	N/A
Price per 1000:	N/A
Circulation:	1000

BRITISH FANTASY SOCIETY NEWSLETTER THE

Frequency:	Bi-monthly
Subscription Cost:	Only available to members of the BFS. Annual subs
Single Issue:	N/A
Back issue price:	Write for details
Cheques/PO Payable to:	The BFS c/o 2 Harwood Street, Stockport SK4 1JJ
Overseas subs:	
Payment Details:	

Description

There is a group of people who know all the latest publishing news and gossip. They enjoy the very best in fiction from some of the hottest new talents around. They can read articles by and about their favourite British Fantasy Society.Foremost amongst the BFS's publications is the acclaimed Newsletter. Published on a bi-monthly schedule, it contains genre news, exclusives, publication information, interviews, features and other items of interest to members. The Newsletter also contains informed book reviews, and reviews of all other genre-related material including films, magazines, fanzines, small press magazines, television and radio productions, video and much more. There are regular celebrity columns, members' letters, artwork and lots more besides. Members also receive, magazines of fiction and comment as well as occasional 'specials.' These have included free BFS-published/funded paperback books. Members also receive discounted attendance to the BFS' FantasyCON event. The BFS is dedicated to genre works of all ages, so expect material on authors old and new, classic and forgotten, popular and unknown.The BFS has enjoyed the patronage of many established authors, artists and journalists. The BFS' own publications are regularly looked to by editors when selecting material for numerous 'Best Of' anthologies and numerous members have gone on to become published authors in their own right.FantasyCon is the convention organised by the BFS. Guests and attendees travel from around the world to take part, meet old friends and make new ones. Recent Guests of Honour have included Brian Lumley, Stephen Laws, Dan Simmons, Katherine Kurtz, Tom Holt, Christopher Fowler and Graham Joyce.

Addresses

Editorial:	2 Harwood Street, Stockport SK4 1JJ

Reviews: As above
Subscriptions: As above
Payment terms
to contributors: Complimentary copy of work
Accept/Rejection
approximate times: one month from receipt
Inserts accepted: Yes
Price per 1000:   £50 per mailing (plus pro rata postage if insert pushes rate
                      up).
Circulation: 500 and rising steadily

BURP

Frequency:	Once yearly
Subscription Cost:	£2.50 (all 3 issues)
Single Issue:	£1
Back issue price:	£1.50 (for issues 1 & 2 together)
Cheques/PO Payable to:	V. Pollard
Overseas subs:	£1 (+ IRC)
Payment Details:	Postage stamps/postal orders/cheques/well concealed cash (sterling only)

Description

Non-profit-making. Social issues (Rants), poetry, art (cartoons, doodles) music/literature reviews, quotes, ecology, etc.etc. (B/W, A5, 24 pages)Issue 1 includes: 'Panic of Age,' 'Pain of Existence' Short story, 'TV has lost the plot', etc.Issue 2 includes: 'Everything is a Conspiracy,' Anti-Neotie, Poems, 'Junk Mail,' Cartoons, 'Cyber-Surveillance,' etc.Issue 3 includes: 'Is script writing dead?' 'Geopathic stress,' 'You have to earn the right to moan,' Pets are naff!' plus: cartoon strips, artwork, poetry, *fake* adverts etc.

Addresses

Editorial:	5 Mount Caburn Crescent, Peacehaven, East Sussex BN10 8DW
Reviews:	As above
Subscriptions:	As above
Payment terms to contributors:	
Accept/Rejection approximate times:	As above
Inserts accepted:	No
Price per 1000:	N/A
Circulation:	100+

BUTTERFLY & BLOOMERS

Frequency:	Four per year
Subscription Cost:	£7
Single Issue:	£2
Back issue price:	N/A
Cheques/PO Payable to:	M. Allen
Overseas subs:	£7-50
Payment Details:	Cheque/postal order etc.

Description

Aimed at 'mature' writer. Stories/Articles/Poems or anything of interest to the older writer.Stories - general up to 1000 words Articles - Travel experiences/personal experiences, anything considered 800-1000 words.

Addresses

Editorial:	Crossgates, 12 Wetmoor Lane, Wath-upon-Dearne, Rotherham, S. Yorkshire S63 6DF
Reviews:	As above
Subscriptions:	As above
Payment terms to contributors:	* Star Story *Star Poem at present £2.50 (to be increased soon)
Accept/Rejection approximate times:	
Inserts accepted:	Yes
Price per 1000:	Free
Circulation:	Increasing with each issue (100-200 each quarter)

BYPASS

Frequency:	Twice yearly
Subscription Cost:	£5 for 3
Single Issue:	£2.20 inc. p & p
Back issue price:	£1.50 inc. p & p
Cheques/PO Payable to:	Bypass
Overseas subs:	$10
Payment Details:	Cash

Description

Bypass is a review magazine covering all forms of small press publishing with over 400 reviews in every issue alongside a few related articles and lots of contact addresses for useful resources. All lines received are reviewed by a varied panel of readers. A resource for publishers and goldmine for readers. Reviewers are needed, especially bilingual ones.

Addresses

Editorial:	P.O. Box 148, Hove BN3 3DQ
Reviews:	As above
Subscriptions:	As above
Payment terms to contributors:	Free copy of magazine
Accept/Rejection approximate times:	N/A
Inserts accepted:	No
Price per 1000:	N/A
Circulation:	2000

CADMIUM BLUE LITERARY JOURNAL THE

Frequency:	Bi-annual
Subscription Cost:	£10.00
Single Issue:	£5.00
Back issue price:	£5.00
Cheques/PO Payable to:	Precious Pearl Publications
Overseas subs:	£15.00
Payment Details:	British or foreign currency

Description

The journal of the Cadmium Blue Communion of romantic poets. Spearhead of the romantic renaissance movement. Poetry and articles aligned to the romantic school of poetry and to contemporary spirtiual romanticism. Traditional rhyme and rhythm favoured, and elegance and beauty of expression. Poems of reflection, heart and soul. Articles about the great romantics, spiritual philosophy, new age concerns. Elevated and inspirational poetry.

Addresses

Editorial:	Peter Geoffrey Paul Thompson, 71 Harrow Crescent, Romford, Essex, RM3 7BJ
Reviews:	As above
Subscriptions:	As above
Payment terms to contributors:	One complimentary copy
Accept/Rejection approximate times:	Usually within one month
Inserts accepted:	No
Price per 1000:	
Circulation:	500

CAMBRENSIS

Frequency:	Quarterly: Spring/Summer/Autumn/Winter
Subscription Cost:	£6 for year's 4 issues, post paid
Single Issue:	£1.50 post paid
Back issue price:	£1.50 (some available)
Cheques/PO Payable to:	'Cambrensis Magazine'
Overseas subs:	Via Blackwell's Periodicals, Oxford or Swets & Zeitlinger, Lisse, Holland.
Payment Details:	Sterling via these two companies

Description

A quarterly magazine, founded 1988, devoted solely to short stories by writers born or resident in Wales; no payment offered other than writers' 'copies;' short stories under 2500 words; only other material used - book reviews and features of Anglo-Welsh literary interest; art-work, mainly cartoon and line-drawings by Welsh artists; sae with submissions or IRC with overseas' inquiries; not more than one manuscript at one time; the magazine is supported by THE ARTS' COUNCIL OF WALES.

Addresses

Editorial:	41 Heol Fach, Cornelly, Bridgend, CF33 4LNTel: 01656-741-994
Reviews:	As above
Subscriptions:	As above
Payment terms to contributors:	'Copies' to writers
Accept/Rejection approximate times:	By return of post mainly
Inserts accepted:	Yes
Price per 1000:	Negotiable
Circulation:	Print-run: 350 copies per quarter

CANDELABRUM POETRY MAGAZINE

Frequency:	Twice yearly (April and October)
Subscription Cost:	£11.50 the volume
Single Issue:	£2
Back issue price:	£2
Cheques/PO Payable to:	The Red Candle Press
Overseas subs:	US $ 22
Payment Details:	

Description

A5 saddle - stitched 40pp. Established 1970 preference for traditionalist metrical and rhymed poetry, but free verse not excluded. English 5/7/5 haiku accepted. Any subject but NB no racialist or sexist matter S.A.E essential. Overseas poets IRC and self addressed envelope.

Addresses

Editorial:	9 Milner Road, Wisbech, Cambs, PE13 2LR
Reviews:	As above
Subscriptions:	As above
Payment terms	
to contributors:	ComplimenOtary copy
Accept/Rejection	
approximate times:	8 Weeks
Inserts accepted:	No
Price per 1000:	N/A
Circulation:	900

CASABLANCA

Frequency:
Subscription Cost: £12; Students £7; Institutions £20
Single Issue: £2.20
Back issue price: £1.50
Cheques/PO Payable to: CASABLANCA
Overseas subs: £16 (Europe airmail); £19.50 (worldwide
Payment Details: Cheque or credit cards, Credit card phoneline 0171
                          608 3784 FREE extra issue if student

Description
This magazine of politics, satire and the arts has been variously described as
devastating (private eye), peppery (The Guardian), spirited (Sunday Telegraph), clean,
true and fearless (The Face), a literary hand grenade (New Statesman & Society),
and unlimited cultural subversion (The Sunday Times). The select subscription list
includes film stars, MPs, novelists and a raft of investigative journalists who use
CASABLANCA to find out where their next story is coming from.

Addresses
Editorial: 31 Clerkenwell Close, London EC1R OAT, TEL: 0171 608 378,
                          FAX: 0170 608 3865
Reviews: As above
Subscriptions: As above
Payment terms
to contributors: Most contributions are voluntary
Accept/Rejection
approximate times: One month
Inserts accepted: Yes
Price per 1000:   £60
Circulation:

CASCANDO

Frequency:	Irregular - at least annually
Subscription Cost:	£13.50
Single Issue:	£4.50
Back issue price:	£3.00
Cheques/PO Payable to:	Cascando Press Ltd
Overseas subs:	$30 USA - £15.50 Europe
Payment Details:	Sterling/Cheque/PO/Bankers Draft/Foreign Currency (must allow for exchange comm)

Description

Cascando (founded 1991) features poems, stories, reviews, translations, drama, literary articles and interviews . . . all by students in Britain and around the world. Tomorrow's great writers are discovered and published here in their own forum, which is shaped by their particular concerns. Interviews with writers of all persuasions have been included, Tom Paulin, Eleain Ni Chuilleanain, Colm Toibin, Dermot Bolger (all in the recent Irish issue 1996), and Tom Morrison, Tony Harrison, Benjamin Zephaniah, Ranjit Bolt, John Hegley and Jung Chang. Young student writers we published include Sinéad Morrissey (youngest ever winner of the Patrick Kavanagh Poetry Award), David Wheatley and Tobias Hill.

Cascando includes magazine listings and a literary diary. Copies of all six issues are available (limited stock).

Addresses

Editorial:	Cascando Press Ltd, PO Box 1499, London SW10 9TZ
Reviews:	As above
Subscriptions:	As above
Payment terms to contributors:	Free copies of relevant magazine
Accept/Rejection approximate times:	4 months
Inserts accepted:	Yes
Price per 1000:	£65
Circulation:	3000

CELTIC HISTORY REVIEW

Frequency:	Quarterly
Subscription Cost:	£7.00 (stg & Ir)
Single Issue:	£1.50
Back issue price:	£1.50
Cheques/PO Payable to:	An Clochan
Overseas subs:	$US 15.00, FF 70
Payment Details:	Cheques/cash/postal orders

Description
Celtic History Review aims to explore the histories of the 6 Celtic nations Ireland, Scotland, Isle of Man, Wales, Brittany and Cornwall from their own perspectives plus inter Celtic, and not as peripheral areas to British and French history.

Addresses

Editorial:	Micheal O Siochrie Rye Bothar, Na Eaglaise, Mulloch Ide, Co Athachatt, Eire
Reviews:	As above
Subscriptions:	Manland Europe Dalchamp, Sory B.P 251, 56102, Lorient-Ceder, Brittany,
Payment terms to contributors:	
Accept/Rejection approximate times:	Two weeks
Inserts accepted:	Yes
Price per 1000:	£40.00
Circulation:	c £400

CELTIC PEN THE

Frequency:	Quarterly
Subscription Cost:	£5.00 (stg plus Ir)
Single Issue:	£1.00 (plus 25p p & p)
Back issue price:	£1.00
Cheques/PO Payable to:	The Celtic Pen
Overseas subs:	US $15.00 FF 40
Payment Details:	Cheque/cash/postal order

Description

The Celtic Pen started in 1993, is primarily in English but deals with literature written in the 6 Celtic languages (Lush, Scots, Gaelic, Manx, Welsh, Breton and Cornish) for example, features on writers or genres. It also carries inter-Celtic and English-Celtic translations of poetry etc, and a book review section. All periods of literature are covered.

Addresses

Editorial:	36 Fruithill Park, Belfast, BT11 8GE
Reviews:	As above
Subscriptions:	As above
Payment terms to contributors:	
Accept/Rejection approximate times:	Two weeks
Inserts accepted:	Yes
Price per 1000:	£55.00
Circulation:	c 800

CENCRASTUS

Frequency:	Quarterly
Subscription Cost:	£12 individual, £15 institutions
Single Issue:	£2.25
Back issue price:	£2.50
Cheques/PO Payable to:	Cencrastus
Overseas subs:	£15 individual, £17 institutions
Payment Details:	In advance of subscription

Description
Scottish and international literature, Arts and Affairs Submission of articles, short stories, poetry and reviews welcomed speculatively, payment by negotiation. Editors: Raymond Ross and Ruth Bradley.

Addresses
Editorial:	Ruth Bradley, Cencrastus magazine, Unit 1 Abbeymouth, Techbase, 2 Easter Road, Edinburgh, ED8 8EJ
Reviews:	As above
Subscriptions:	As above
Payment terms to contributors:	Negotiable
Accept/Rejection approximate times:	6 Weeks
Inserts accepted:	No
Price per 1000:	N/A
Circulation:	Approx 3,000

CHAPMAN

Frequency:	Quarterly
Subscription Cost:	£14.00
Single Issue:	£3.50
Back issue price:	£3.50 (inc p&p)
Cheques/PO Payable to:	CHAPMAN
Overseas subs:	£19.00
Payment Details:	By cheque, PO or IMO

Description

Chapman is Scotland's leading literary magazine, controversial, influential, outspoken and intelligent. Founded in 1970, it has become a dynamic force in Scottish culture, covering theatre, politics, language, and the arts. Our highly-respected forum for poetry, fiction, criticism, review and debate is essential reading for anyone interested in contemporary Scotland.Chapman publishes the best in Scottish writing - new work by well-known Scottish writers in the context of lucid critical discussion. With our strong commitment to the future, we energetically promote new writers, new ideas and approaches. Several issues have been landmarks in their field, in Scots language, women's writing, cultural politics in Scotland, and we have published extensive features on important writers: Hugh MacDiarmid, Tom Scott, Iain Crichton Smith, Ian Hamilton Finley, Alasdair Gray, Naomi Mitchison, Hamish Henderson, Jessie Kesson, to name but a few. We also publish poetry and short fiction by up-and -coming writers, as well as critical articles, book reviews and items of general cultural interest. Our coverage includes theatre, music, visual arts, language, and other matters from time to time. Each issue includes Scots and Gaelic, as well as English although most of the work is in English. Although the focus is on Scotland, Chapman has a long history of publishing international literature, both in English by non-Scots and in translation from other languages.Chapman will interest anyone researching British and Scottish literature. It has a natural outlet in universities and institutions of secondary education. With its emphasis on new creative writing, it is of interest to anyone with a love of literature.We also publish poetry collections and plays under the heading of Chapman Publishing. Our New Writing Series is dedicated to giving first publications to promising young writers. The Theatre Series brings the best of Scottish theatre before a wider audience.

Addresses

Editorial:	4 Broughton Place, Edinburgh, EH1 3RX
Reviews:	As above
Subscriptions:	As above
Payment terms to contributors:	Token Fix
Accept/Rejection approximate times:	1-3 months
Inserts accepted:	Yes
Price per 1000:	£50
Circulation:	2,000

CITY WRITERS

Frequency:	2/year
Subscription Cost:	£2 plus 72p postage
Single Issue:	£1 plus 36p postage
Back issue price:	£1 plus 36p postage - when available
Cheques/PO Payable to:	City Writers
Overseas subs:	£2 sterling, $5 U.S or $6 Canada plus 2
Payment Details:	Cheque, postal order, stamps, cash (at sender's risk) all acceptable.

Description

CITY WRITERS MAGAZINE, whose production team is currently led by editor Megan Miranda, is the magazine of CITY WRITERS, the Southampton-based literary organisation. CITY WRITERS brings poets and novelists of national acclaim to our readings at the Gantry Arts Centre. CITY WRITERS MAGAZINE supports these activities by publishing a wide range of poetry, short prose writers, events, publications, we encourage submission from all corners of Britain and beyond. In our last issue we published work from as far as Ireland and America.Our editorial tastes are eclectic in style and content, but we particularly favour writing that engages with the larger community and current debates in contemporary writing. We are pleased to receive experimental submissions on controversial topics. Located in Southampton, we also strive to link the realms of the university with that of the southern writing community as a whole, and we are constantly broadening our interests as we expand our readership and submission pool. We are a non-profit, community-based group and thus try to keep the price of the magazine one of the lowest around to maximise its accessibility.Submissions should come from writers willing to view their own work critically in the context of contemporary prose and poetry. Reading CITY WRITERS first is helpful but not compulsory. Submissions should be addressed to the Editor; we will consider up to six poems and/or 2,500 words of prose at a time, preferably typed. All submissions should be accompanied by sufficient return postage, and obviously we accept no responsibility for work lost in the post so please do not send originals. All submissions eventually receive a personal reply from the editor, so please be patient. We look forward to hearing from you and reading your work.Megan Miranda

Addresses

Editorial:	Megan Miranda, Editor, City Writers Magazine, c/o The Gantry Arts Centre, Off Blechynden Terrace, Southampton, SO15 16W
Reviews:	
Subscriptions:	
Payment terms to contributors:	No payment as non-profit status.
Accept/Rejection approximate times:	February for March issue, August for September issue - but submissions considered at all times.
Inserts accepted:	Yes
Price per 1000:	N/A
Circulation:	150

CIVIL SERVICE AUTHOR

Frequency:
Subscription Cost:
Single Issue:
Back issue price:
Cheques/PO Payable to:
Overseas subs:
Payment Details:

Description
They have to be members of the Civil Service first. They are then sent the appropriate information.

Addresses
Editorial: Iain R Mcintyre, 8 Bantree Close, Sutton, Surrey, SM2 5LQ
Reviews:
Subscriptions:
Payment terms
to contributors:
Accept/Rejection
approximate times:
Inserts accepted:
Price per 1000:
Circulation:

COMMUNITY OF POETS

Frequency:	Quarterly
Subscription Cost:	UK £6 p.a. (incl p & p) Non UK £10 p.a (incl p & p
Single Issue:	£1.50 incl. p & p
Back issue price:	£1.50 incl. p & p
Cheques/PO Payable to:	Community of Poets Press
Overseas subs:	£10 p.a. (incl p & p)
Payment Details:	Cheque perferred

Description

Community of Poets is an independent not-for-profit poetry publication founded by Philip Bennetta in 1994. Its simple aim is to encourage those writers, especially first voices, interested in focusing on their communities - be these local, regional, global, temporary or company based. It seeks to publish work concerned with the inseparable nature of individual and organisational potential and work of any genre is welcome. It is advisable to see a recent issue prior to submitting work for publication.

Addresses

Editorial:	Hatfield Cottage, Chilham, Kent CT4 8TP
Reviews:	As above
Subscriptions:	As above
Payment terms to contributors:	Free copy of magazine to non-subscribers
Accept/Rejection approximate times:	1 month
Inserts accepted:	No
Price per 1000:	N/A
Circulation:	Increasing

COTTAGE GUIDE TO WRITERS' POSTAL WORKSHOPS THE

Frequency:	On request
Subscription Cost:	N/A
Single Issue:	£2 post free
Back issue price:	N/A
Cheques/PO Payable to:	Catherine Gill
Overseas subs:	N/A
Payment Details:	N/A

Description
The guide is a pocket-sized directory of postal workshops/ foliod giving 16 names and addresses of 16 editors and a brief description of 16 types of workshop, viz miscellaneous, poetry, short stories etc. The directory is desktop published so that it can be upgraded as soon as new information is received.

Addresses
Editorial:	Croftspun Publications, Drakemyre Croft, Cairnorrie, Methlick, Ellon, Aberdeenshire AB41 7JN
Reviews:	As above
Subscriptions:	As above
Payment terms to contributors:	None
Accept/Rejection approximate times:	N/A
Inserts accepted:	No
Price per 1000:	N/A
Circulation:	N/A

CRITICAL WAVE

Frequency:	5 issues/year
Subscription Cost:	£11.50
Single Issue:	£2.45
Back issue price:	£2.45
Cheques/PO Payable to:	Critical Wave Publications
Overseas subs:	Send reply-paid envelope for Rates
Payment Details:	As above

Description
Founded in 1987, now established as the leading independent European journal of Science fiction, fantasy and horror news/criticism. Contributors have included Michael Moorcock (who called it the 'most consistently interesting and intelligent' magazine of its kind), Clive Barker, Andrew Darlington, Terry Pratchett, Steve Sneyd, Graham Joyce, Storm Constantine and Joel Lane. Also features regular art portfolios (those featured include Jim Porter, Dave Carson, Jim Pitts, Harry Turner and Alan Hunter) and the most extensive convention listing available in print. Placed in the SFX 'Top Ten' Readers' Poll 1996. Does not carry poetry, but reviews genre poetry collections and carries historical analysis of the field (including Sneyd's landmark essays on SF poetry)

Addresses

Editorial:	Steve Green, 33 Scott Road, Ulton, Solihull B92 7LQ
Reviews:	Critical Wave, c/o 33 Scott Road, Olton, Solihull B92 7LQ
Subscriptions:	Martin Tudor, 24 Ravensbourne Grove, Off Clarkes Lane, Willenhall WV13 1HX
Payment terms to contributors:	Complimentary copy of issue
Accept/Rejection approximate times:	Six weeks (enclose reply-paid envelope)
Inserts accepted:	No
Price per 1000:	By negotiation
Circulation:	800-1000

CURRENT ACCOUNTS

Frequency:	2 Per year
Subscription Cost:	£3 annually
Single Issue:	£1.50
Back issue price:	£1.50
Cheques/PO Payable to:	Bank Street Writers
Overseas subs:	£5 per year
Payment Details:	Sterling cheque, P.O. or cash only

Description
Mainly features poetry and prose by members of Bank Street writers, but high-quality submissions from non-members are welcome. No restriction on subject matter apart form usual considerations of taste and decency. Previous contributors include M.R. Peacocke, Pat Winslow & Gerald England

Addresses

Editorial:	167 Brownlow Road, Horwich, Bolton BL6 7EP
Reviews:	As above
Subscriptions:	As above
Payment terms to contributors:	Free copy of magazine
Accept/Rejection approximate times:	One month
Inserts accepted:	Yes
Price per 1000:	Free
Circulation:	30+

CYPHERS

Frequency:	2 - 3 yearly
Subscription Cost:	£6
Single Issue:	£2
Back issue price:	£1.50
Cheques/PO Payable to:	Cyphers
Overseas subs:	$20
Payment Details:	Cheque

Description
Poetry, prose, cirticism, translations.

Editors: Leland Bardwell
Pearse Hutchinson
Eiléan Ní Chuilleanáin
Macdara Woods

Addresses

Editorial:	3 Selskar Terrace, Dublin 6
Reviews:	As above
Subscriptions:	As above
Payment terms to contributors:	£10 a page
Accept/Rejection approximate times:	3 - 6 months
Inserts accepted:	No
Price per 1000:	
Circulation:	350

DAM (Disability Arts Magazine)

Frequency:	Quarterly (March, June, September, December)
Subscription Cost:	£12 (four issues) £6 concession for unwaged indivi
Single Issue:	£2
Back issue price:	£2
Cheques/PO Payable to:	DAM
Overseas subs:	£20 (outside E.E.C)
Payment Details:	Cheques in pounds sterling through UK bank.

Description

DAM is a quarterly magazine which promotes the arts activities of disabled people and promotes access to the arts for disabled people. The magazine is run, staffed and controlled entirely by disabled people, through DAM Publishing Ltd. a registered charity. All art forms are regularly featured and reviewed: visual arts: paintings and sculpture; creative writing: fiction and poetry; performance arts: theatre, cinema and television etc. Venues visited by reviewers are assessed for accessibility for other disabled people. As the original full name Disability Arts Magazine suggests DAM focuses on Disability Arts, where the subject matter of a piece of artwork draws on the experience of the disabled artist as disabled people.This magazine should be of interest to anyone who has an interest in art. The art disabled people produce and access issues disabled people have.

Addresses

Editorial:	DAM, 11A Cleveland Avenue, Lupset Park, Wakefield, WF2 8LE
Reviews:	As above
Subscriptions:	As above
Payment terms to contributors:	DAM only pays for work by disabled persons
Accept/Rejection approximate times:	Variable
Inserts accepted:	
Price per 1000:	
Circulation:	1500 plus copies printed.

DANDELION ARTS MAGAZINE

Frequency:	Bi-annual
Subscription Cost:	£7 UK
Single Issue:	Half of the cost of subscription
Back issue price:	The cost of the subscription
Cheques/PO Payable to:	J Gonzalez-Marina
Overseas subs:	£12 Europe £18 USA £28 Australia & NZ
Payment Details:	In sterling by cheque, bankers draft or postal order

Description

Dandelion Arts Magazine is an international non-profit making publication created and founded in 1978 in London by Jacqueline Gonzalez-Marina who has been the publisher ever since. Its aims have always been to provide an outlet for poets, journalists and illustrators world-wide. Contributions are welcome but subscription is a must if seeking publication. All submissions should be accompanied by a sae. Personal advice will be gladly given on an individual basis.

Addresses

Editorial:	Fern Publications - Casa Alba, 24 Frosty Hollow, East Hunsbury, Northants NN4 0SY
Reviews:	Dandelion Magazine c/o The Editor at above address
Subscriptions:	The Publisher, Dandelion Magazine at above address
Payment terms to contributors:	No payment given, just the publicity and advice
Accept/Rejection approximate times:	
Inserts accepted:	Yes
Price per 1000:	£8
Circulation:	1000

DARK HORIZONS

Frequency:	2/3 yearly
Subscription Cost:	£17 UK. BFS Membership
Single Issue:	£3.50
Back issue price:	£3
Cheques/PO Payable to:	British Fantasy Society
Overseas subs:	£20 Europe, $75 USA, £25 Elsewhere
Payment Details:	US Dollars & Sterling only - cheques, IMO

Description

Founded in 1971 at the beginning of the Society. Dark Horizons features articles on all genre-related topics, as well as occasional fiction. Recently combined with two other BFS Annuals - Mystique (Fantasy Fiction) & Chills (Dark Fantasy) - Dark Horizons will be re-launched in 1997. Fiction and factual material will be given equal weight.

Addresses

Editorial:	46 Oxford Road, Acocks Green, Birmingham B276DT (Fiction)8 Milton Close, Shrewsbury, Shropshire SY1 2UE (Art & Articles)
Reviews:	As above
Subscriptions:	As above
Payment terms to contributors:	In copies
Accept/Rejection approximate times:	4 - 6 weeks
Inserts accepted:	No
Price per 1000:	N/A
Circulation:	500 and increasing

DASKHAT

Frequency:
Subscription Cost:
Single Issue:
Back issue price:
Cheques/PO Payable to:
Overseas subs:
Payment Details:

Description
Production of the third issue is currently suspended although it is believed to be almost ready for publication. It is uncertain at present whether or not it will be possible to publish the third edition but any further issues are unlikely.

Addresses
Editorial: 90 Dunstable Road, Luton, Beds, LU1 1EH
Reviews:
Subscriptions:
Payment terms
to contributors:
Accept/Rejection
approximate times:
Inserts accepted:
Price per 1000:
Circulation:

DATA DUMP

Frequency:	6 Monthly (approx)
Subscription Cost:	See payment details
Single Issue:	70p. incl. post
Back issue price:	Available only as photostat reprints, by arrangement, as all prior issues o.o.p (i.e.S 1-14 at time of writing) Cost of full set £7 incl. p. & p.
Cheques/PO Payable to:	S Sheyd (Not Data Dump or Hilltop Press, the imprint.
Overseas subs:	Indiv. copies $2 cash (US currency) or small denominations (50¢ or less) US stamps to that amount.
Payment Details:	I do not take advance subscriptions as price/format may vary, but those wanting to be sure of getting each copy as produced can place a 'till cancelled' order and pay for each issue when received.

Description

This is a publication which gathers and disseminates information on genre poetry - science fiction poetry as a priority, but also fantasy and horror. Topics covered include new collections/anthologies, articles on the field, early work, novels incorporating poetry, poetry in fantasies, humorous S.F. poetry, and picturesque/human-data, SF poetry in unusual settings (media, film, opera, radio). The intention is to give an ongoing update on the field, plus a backfill of its past, with apreponderance of attention to the UK but some coverage of USA, Australia, Europe etc. Original poetry is not sought.

Addresses

Editorial:	S Sneyd, 4 Nowell Place, Almondbury, Huddersfield, West Yorks. HD5 8PB. See* Otherwise No unsolicited MSS.
Reviews:	Mentions/V. occasional, V. brief reviews of Genry poetry (S/F F/H) Related poetry collections/anthologies only, as edit address
Subscriptions:	As edit address
Payment terms to contributors:	None

Accept/Rejection approximate times:	* Not relevant. Information of relevance welcomed, and, as and when included, source acknowledged.
Inserts accepted:	Yes
Price per 1000:	Do not charge - will distribute flyers on an exchange basis by prior arrangement
Circulation:	100

DAY BY DAY

Frequency:	Monthly
Subscription Cost:	£9.25 UK
Single Issue:	75p
Back issue price:	75p
Cheques/PO Payable to:	Day By Day
Overseas subs:	Europe £11. USA, Australia, S.Africa $24
Payment Details:	UK cheque or postal order. Euro cheque, Sterling cheque or IMO

Description
Founded 1963, it is a news commentary, digest of national and international affairs and review of the arts, independent of all major political parties, with an emphasis on non-violence and social justice. Anti-war and anti-racialist, it is concerned about conservation, pollution, cruelty to animals, arms trade, poverty, unemployment, homelessness and moral and civilised values. It publishes short poems, reports cricket, reviews exhibitions, films, plays, opera and musicals. It very rarely publishes short stories. No illustrations. Reviews books on art, cricket and other sport, current affairs, economics, education, films, conservation, music, history, politics, religion, peace, non-violence, literature, war etc. Unsolicited manuscripts must be accompanied by a sae. It is worth studying an issue or two first, since we like outside contributions to harmonise with the spirit of our editorials.

Addresses

Editorial:	Woolacombe House, 141 Woolacombe Road, Blackheath, London SE3 8QP
Reviews:	As above
Subscriptions:	As above
Payment terms to contributors:	By arrangement
Accept/Rejection approximate times:	10 days provided accompanied by sae
Inserts accepted:	No. But will accept exchange of advertisement
Price per 1000:	N/A
Circulation:	20,000

DAYDREAMS, NIGHTMARES AND...

Frequency:	Biannual
Subscription Cost:	£1.50 two copies
Single Issue:	£1 Europe, £1.50 Row
Back issue price:	Negotiable
Cheques/PO Payable to:	Tony Eaton
Overseas subs:	£2.00
Payment Details:	

Description

Centralised around Art, Music and Fiction. Content: art, articles on bands and labels, contact list, reviews. Any black and white artwork welcome, No larger than A4 but magazine is A5. Anything factual is wanted as well as Science Fiction and horror but no poetry, work no longer than 2 A4 pages. Please enclose SAE for return of unused work.

Addresses

Editorial:	Tony, PO Box 471, Peckham, London, SE15 2JX
Reviews:	As above
Subscriptions:	As above
Payment terms to contributors:	Complimentary copy
Accept/Rejection approximate times:	As soon as decided
Inserts accepted:	No
Price per 1000:	N/A
Circulation:	750

DOORS - INTO AND OUT OF DORSET

Frequency:	January, May, September
Subscription Cost:	£4.65 for three issues, £1.70 for one copy
Single Issue:	£1.70
Back issue price:	£1.70
Cheques/PO Payable to:	Wanda Publications
Overseas subs:	£4.65 plus postage and packing
Payment Details:	Sterling

Description

First published in 1979 Doors aims to bring poets and readers from Dorset into contact with poets and readers elsewhere. Each issue has a different editor - someone who's either from Dorset or has a story link with the county. About one third of the contents come from within Dorset. Doors appears in January, May and September contributions should reach, Wanda Publications by the last day of these months for possible publication in the next issue. Send no more than 6 poems with name and address and SAE. We also welcome material for review.

Addresses

Editorial:	Wanda Publications, (Doors magazine), 61 Westborough, Wimbourne, BH21 1LX
Reviews:	As above
Subscriptions:	As above
Payment terms to contributors:	6, 1st class stamps for each poem published
Accept/Rejection approximate times:	4-6 months
Inserts accepted:	No
Price per 1000:	
Circulation:	

DRAGON CHRONICLE THE

Frequency:	4 times a year
Subscription Cost:	£5
Single Issue:	£1.50
Back issue price:	£1.50
Cheques/PO Payable to:	Dragons Head Press
Overseas subs:	$12/$4 Single Issue
Payment Details:	Cash only $ Bills or Sterling

Description

The Dragon Chronicle (Founded 1993) Ed. Ade Dimmick. Published by Dragon's Head Press. Special interest journal dedicated entirely to dragons in all their forms and aspects. Features dragon-related and dragon-inspired myth, magic, paganism, astrology, folklore, fantasy, spirituality and tradition. Plus artwork and poetry. A draco phibs delight! Dragon's Head Press (formerly Dragon Trust Publications) is an independent small press publishing project specialising in dragon-interest. Publishes The Dragon Chronicle as well as publishing and distributing books about dragons. Mail order book service.

Addresses

Editorial:	PO Box 3369, London SW6 6JN
Reviews:	As above
Subscriptions:	As above
Payment terms to contributors:	Free subscription
Accept/Rejection approximate times:	Generally accept anything in keeping with editorial policy.
Inserts accepted:	Yes
Price per 1000:	Free to dragon-orientated flyers from subscribers/supporters
Circulation:	1000

DRAGONS BREATH

Frequency:	Monthly
Subscription Cost:	£2.50
Single Issue:	Free for stamped addressed envelope
Back issue price:	Not available
Cheques/PO Payable to:	Tony Lee
Overseas subs:	Send I.R.C and SAE for free sample
Payment Details:	

Description
The International small press review and independent monthly newsletter.

Addresses

Editorial:	Zine Kat, c/o Pigasus Press, 13 Hazely Combe, Arrezton, Isle Of Wight, PO30 3AJ, England
Reviews:	As above
Subscriptions:	Tony Lee, Pigasus Press, (address as above)
Payment terms to contributors:	None
Accept/Rejection approximate times:	N/A
Inserts accepted:	Yes
Price per 1000:	Free
Circulation:	Unknown

DREAMBERRY WINE

Frequency:	Bimonthly (approx)
Subscription Cost:	£5
Single Issue:	£1
Back issue price:	N/A
Cheques/PO Payable to:	Dreamberry Wine
Overseas subs:	£10
Payment Details:	IMO/Sterling cheque/UK postal order

Description
Dreamberry Wine is primarily a mail order catalogue, specialising in science-fiction, fantasy and related areas of books and magazines. However, DW also carries an increase of 2-3 pages of book reviews, occasional author interviews, news from the SF field; even, rarely, short fiction - very short fiction.

Addresses

Editorial:	233 Maine Road, Manchester M14 7W9
Reviews:	As above
Subscriptions:	As above
Payment terms to contributors:	None
Accept/Rejection approximate times:	Variable
Inserts accepted:	No
Price per 1000:	N/A
Circulation:	430 copies approx.

EASTERN RAINBOW

Frequency:	Twice yearly
Subscription Cost:	£6 for 4 issues
Single Issue:	£1.50
Back issue price:	£1
Cheques/PO Payable to:	Peace & Freedom
Overseas subs:	$13
Payment Details:	UK by cheque or Postal order. Overseas by IMO or Banknotes.

Description
Eastern Rainbow is a magazine which focuses on 20th century culture via poetry, prose & art. We also run poetry competitions and forms are available for an SAE/IRC. Full guidelines for contributions are available for an SAE/IRC

Addresses

Editorial:	17 Farrow Road, Whaplode Drove, Spalding, Lincs. PE12 OTS
Reviews:	Address as above
Subscriptions:	Address as above
Payment terms to contributors:	Free issue of magazine when work is published
Accept/Rejection approximate times:	Less than 3 months
Inserts accepted:	Yes
Price per 1000:	£20/$50
Circulation:	300

ECHO ROOM YEARBOOK THE

Frequency:	Yearly
Subscription Cost:	£10 for two years
Single Issue:	£5.95 + postage 55p
Back issue price:	As above
Cheques/PO Payable to:	The ECHO Room
Overseas subs:	N/A
Payment Details:	Free copies

Description

Founded in 1985 The ECHO Room published 'Poetry That Matters.' It was highly influential within the small-press publishing scene of the 1980s and early 90s. After a period just publishing pamphlets Editor Brendan Cleary has now decided to restart the magazine on an annual basis publishing poetry, short stories, articles. The first yearbook is due in 1997 (Jan) featuring new writing from the North-East and other items of interest.

Addresses

Editorial:	45 Bewick Court, Princess Square, Newcastle upon Tyne, NE1 8EG, Tyne and Wear
Reviews:	As above
Subscriptions:	As above
Payment terms to contributors:	Free copies
Accept/Rejection approximate times:	2-3 weeks
Inserts accepted:	Yes
Price per 1000:	By exchange
Circulation:	500-600

EDGE THE

Frequency:	5 times per year
Subscription Cost:	£7 (four issues) post free
Single Issue:	£1.95 post free
Back issue price:	£2 post free
Cheques/PO Payable to:	The Edge
Overseas subs:	$20
Payment Details:	US cheques or US dollars cash. Or IMO at UK prices

Description

SF/modern horror/imaginative fantasy up to 8000 words. Fiction by John Shirley, Christopher Fowler, Michael Mormock, Paul Di Filippo, Gary Kaworth, Keith Brookes, Eric Brown plus completely new writers. Previously unpublished writers welcome! (But standards are high). Includes interviews. Film & book reviews, comment columns. The Edge does not publish poetry! All overseas correspondence/orders sent air mail. Reply within one month.

Addresses

Editorial:	1 Nichols Court, Belle Vue, Chelmsford, Essex CM2 0BJ
Reviews:	As above
Subscriptions:	As above
Payment terms to contributors:	£5/1000 words/negotiable
Accept/Rejection approximate times:	N/A
Inserts accepted:	Yes
Price per 1000:	£100
Circulation:	Well into four figures; over 100 outlets plus subscribers.

EDINBURGH REVIEW

Frequency:	Twice a year
Subscription Cost:	Individual: £15 / institution: £30
Single Issue:	£7.95
Back issue price:	£7.95
Cheques/PO Payable to:	Edinburgh University Press
Overseas subs:	Individual: £16.95 / institution £33
Payment Details:	

Description
This acclaimed literary and cultural review publishes a wide range of original and topical material with a new emphasis on the literary by both new and established writers. Lively, controversial and electric, `Edinburgh Review` is the only forum which positively asserts the rich diversity of Scottish arts and culture while attending to International literary and cultural events.

Addresses

Editorial:	Edinburgh University Press, 22 George Square, Edinburgh, EH8 9LF
Reviews:	As above
Subscriptions:	As above
Payment terms to contributors:	By negotiation
Accept/Rejection approximate times:	Two months
Inserts accepted:	Yes
Price per 1000:	£135
Circulation:	800

ENVOI

Frequency:	3 issues per annum
Subscription Cost:	£12 per annum
Single Issue:	£4
Back issue price:	£4, sample £3
Cheques/PO Payable to:	Envoi
Overseas subs:	£15 or $30 p.a. current copy £4 or $8
Payment Details:	Preferably in USA dollar bills if sterling not available

Description

Current editor Roger Elkin. SUBSCRIPTION BRINGS YOU 176 pages each issue. Groups of poems (up to 8) by any one writer. Long(er) poems , over 40 lines of most magazine. Sequences, or extracts from longer sequences. Poems in collaboration. Poems in translation. First Publication feature for new writers. Articles on poetry, creativity and style. Competition and Adjudicator's Report each issue. Comparative reviews of current poetry publications. Letters and Comment. Free critical comment (3 poems per year) on request. And oodles of poems

Addresses

Editorial:	44 Rudyard Road, Biddulph Moor, Stoke-on Trent, ST8 7JN
Reviews:	As above
Subscriptions:	As above
Payment terms to contributors:	2 complimentary copies
Accept/Rejection approximate times:	6-8 weeks
Inserts accepted:	Yes
Price per 1000:	£50
Circulation:	800-1000

ESSENCE OF BEING

Frequency: Irregular
Subscription Cost:
Single Issue: 50p each plus SAE
Back issue price:
Cheques/PO Payable to:
Overseas subs:
Payment Details:

Description
This is a collection of thoughts by Andoon Hinley Dink and Faene Nuff, other people's work may be included.

Addresses
Editorial: Andoon & Steph, c/o 13 Spencer Drive, Sutton Height Telford, Shropshire, TF7 4JY

Reviews:
Subscriptions:
Payment terms
to contributors:
Accept/Rejection
approximate times:
Inserts accepted:
Price per 1000:
Circulation:

EXILE

Frequency:	Quarterly
Subscription Cost:	£8 inc p&p
Single Issue:	£2
Back issue price:	£2
Cheques/PO Payable to:	Exile
Overseas subs:	
Payment Details:	

Description
A5 20pp poetry magazine. New poetry in English, up to 30 lines always welcome, Poetry books reviewed.

Addresses

Editorial:	8 Snow Hill, Clare, Suffolk, CO10 8QF
Reviews:	
Subscriptions:	
Payment terms to contributors:	No fee
Accept/Rejection approximate times:	3 months
Inserts accepted:	No
Price per 1000:	
Circulation:	

FAIRACRES CHRONICLE

Frequency:	3 times yearly
Subscription Cost:	£4.50
Single Issue:	£1 + 50p p. & p.
Back issue price:	£1 + p.& p.
Cheques/PO Payable to:	S.L.G. Press
Overseas subs:	Europe £5 Other Surface £4.75 or $9 USA
Payment Details:	Sterling or US Dollars only

Description

The journal of the Anglican contemplative religious community, The Sisters of the Love of God. A mix of community news and articles on prayer and spirituality with a bias towards contemplative prayer. Current books on Christian spirituality/prayer are reviewed. Poetry not accepted for publication.

Addresses

Editorial:	The Sister in Charge, S.L.G. Press, Convent of the Incarnation, Fairacres, Oxford OX4 1TB
Reviews:	As above
Subscriptions:	As above
Payment terms to contributors:	Major articles 5 free copies of magazine. Reviewers 2 free copies
Accept/Rejection approximate times:	Within two weeks of receiving manuscript.
Inserts accepted:	No
Price per 1000:	N/A
Circulation:	1000 copies worldwide

FIRST IMPRESSION

Frequency:	Monthly
Subscription Cost:	N/A
Single Issue:	£2.50
Back issue price:	£2.50
Cheques/PO Payable to:	First Impression
Overseas subs:	N/A
Payment Details:	

Description

First Impression is a unique combination of poetry competition and self-publication. First poem can be entered free of charge. Subsequent poems are entered for £7.50. All poems are published and all participating poets vote for monthly winning poem and runner up. Prize money £20 + £10. Please send sae for details. Poems to be no longer than 40 lines (approx) and not to contain unsuitable language.

Addresses

Editorial:	First Impression, P.O. Box 111, Scarborough YO13 9YX
Reviews:	As above
Subscriptions:	As above
Payment terms to contributors:	Copy of magazine plus chance of winning competition
Accept/Rejection approximate times:	All poems conforming to Editor's rules are published *
Inserts accepted:	No
Price per 1000:	N/A
Circulation:	Increasing. Poems to be no longer than 40 lines (approx) and not to contain unsuitable language.

FIRST OFFENSE

Frequency:	1 or 2 yearly
Subscription Cost:	£2.75
Single Issue:	£2.75
Back issue price:	£2.50
Cheques/PO Payable to:	Tim Fletcher
Overseas subs:	£2.75
Payment Details:	Cheque

Description
The magazine is for contemporary poetry and is not traditional, but is received by most ground-breaking poets.

Addresses

Editorial:	Tim Fletcher 'Syringh,' Stodmarsh, Canterbury, Kent CT3 4BA
Reviews:	As above
Subscriptions:	As above
Payment terms to contributors:	N/A
Accept/Rejection approximate times:	N/A
Inserts accepted:	No
Price per 1000:	N/A
Circulation:	300

FIRST TIME

Frequency:	Bi-Annual
Subscription Cost:	£6.00 per annum plus £1.00 postage
Single Issue:	£2.50 plus p&p
Back issue price:	£1,25 plus p&p
Cheques/PO Payable to:	
Overseas subs:	US $13.00 per annum inc surface mail
Payment Details:	

Description
A well established magazine / too large to be called little. I publish work of all kinds and welcome work from disabled people who are in institutions. A bi-annual magazine designed to encourage First Time poets.

Addresses
Editorial:	Burdett Cottage, 4 Burdett Place, George Street, Hastings, E. Sussex, TN34 3ED
Reviews:	N/A at the moment
Subscriptions:	As above
Payment terms to contributors:	Free copy of the magazine in which they appear
Accept/Rejection approximate times:	1 month
Inserts accepted:	Yes
Price per 1000:	£20
Circulation:	1000

FLAIR NEWSLETTER

Frequency:	Alternative months
Subscription Cost:	£7.50 (includes membership of Flair Network)
Single Issue:	On request with A5 sae
Back issue price:	£1
Cheques/PO Payable to:	Cass and Janie Jackson
Overseas subs:	Europe £10.50 Elsewhere £13.50
Payment Details:	Cheque/Postal Order. Overseas payment in £ sterling on an English bank.

Description

Established in 1988. Flair Newsletter is the journal of Flair Network, a writers' support system which includes a free Advisory Service and Specialist Register. Also offered: handbooks and Yellow Pages on all aspects of writing: two mini-courses: audio cassettes: criticism and assessment service. Members qualify for 10% discount on all prices. Newsletter devoted entirely to writing topics, but with strong emphasis on positive thought. Contributions from members only.

Addresses

Editorial:	5 Delavall Walk, Eastbourne BN23 6ER
Reviews:	As above
Subscriptions:	As above
Payment terms to contributors:	No payment
Accept/Rejection approximate times:	N/A
Inserts accepted:	Yes
Price per 1000:	No charge
Circulation:	500 and rising

FLAMING ARROWS

Frequency:	Annual
Subscription Cost:	£5.80
Single Issue:	£5.00
Back issue price:	£5.00, Issues 2 and 3, £2.50 Issue 4, £3.95 Issue 1
Cheques/PO Payable to:	Co Sligo VEC
Overseas subs:	
Payment Details:	Cost plus p&p, 80p postage and packing

Description

Literary journal, contemporary styles of fiction and poetry. New writers sought with distinctive style; polished prose, coherent, lucid, direct and strong poetry. Contemplative metaphysical, mystical, spiritual themes are sought which are well grounded. Also interested in close relationship with landscape/environment of character in narrative or personal poetry. Where is the sacred incomtemporary life, how is it identified and sustained? Also seek original graphic and photography for black and white repro.

Addresses

Editorial:	Leo Regan, Co Sligo VEC Riverside, Sligo, Ireland
Reviews:	Not accepted
Subscriptions:	As above
Payment terms to contributors:	Complimentary copy
Accept/Rejection approximate times:	3 months
Inserts accepted:	No
Price per 1000:	N/A
Circulation:	500

FOCUS

Frequency:	bi-annual
Subscription Cost:	Included in B.S.F.A. Membership £18 UK
Single Issue:	£1 + p & p
Back issue price:	Some back issues available at 50p + p & p
Cheques/PO Payable to:	In UK BSFA Ltd. In US. Cy Chauvin (BSFA)
Overseas subs:	Contact Membership secretary for details
Payment Details:	UK Sterling cheque, British postal order, IMO

Description

Focus is the writers' magazine of the British Science Fiction Association. It specialises in articles on the creative processes of SF from the original spark of ideas to publication, and publishes material by both aspiring and published writers. We feature a forum where a particular issue is discussed by several writers. Focus also publishes fiction, poetry and artwork - also 'drabbles' (stories of exactly 100 words).
Contributors have included John Brunner, Gwyneth Jones, Diana Wynne Jones, Dave Langford, Steve Sneyd and Sue Thomas, also a regular column by author and critic Colin Greenland. Submissions should be up to 5000 words for fiction and articles, a maximum of 50 lines for poetry; forum pieces should be of 600-800 words (contact the editors for details of the current forum. Previous subjects have included Characters, Worldbuilding, Aliens and Other Animals and Writers' Workshops). Artists should ideally send photocopied examples/submissions in the first instance (sorry, no colour). We are open to submissions from members and non-members.

Addresses

Editorial:	Julia Venner, 42 Walgrave Street, Newland Avenue, Hull HU5 2LT Carol Ann Green, Flat 3, 141 Princes Avenue, Hull HU5 3EL
Reviews:	As above
Subscriptions:	Membership secretary: Paul Billinger, 82 Kelvin Road, New Cubbington, Leamington Spa, Warwickshire CV32 7TA
Payment terms to contributors:	Contributor's copy
Accept/Rejection approximate times:	8-12 weeks. Receipt is acknowledged

Inserts accepted:	By negotiation with the BSFA
Price per 1000:	As above
Circulation:	900* The BSFA is the British Science Fiction Associaton. Members receive Vector (the critical journal); Mabrix (the news magazine) and Focus (the writers' magazine).

FORUM

Frequency:	13 annually
Subscription Cost:	£35
Single Issue:	£3.20
Back issue price:	£3.20 + £1 p & p
Cheques/PO Payable to:	Northern & Shell
Overseas subs:	£50 Europe. £60 Rest of World
Payment Details:	

Description

Forum (Founded 1967) is the international journal of human relationships, dealing with all aspects of sex and sexuality. It features serious medical and relationship-based articles, interviews, erotic fiction by leading names in the genre and newcomers. Expert advice to readers' problems and a world-famous letters page. A regular feature offers budding poets the chance to see their work in print.

Addresses

Editorial:	Northern & Shell Tower, P.O. Box 381, City Harbour, London E14 9GL
Reviews:	As above
Subscriptions:	43 Mill Harbour, London E14 9TR
Payment terms to contributors:	£10 per poem. £125 per short story
Accept/Rejection approximate times:	2-3 months
Inserts accepted:	Yes
Price per 1000:	£15
Circulation:	30,000

FROGMORE PAPERS THE

Frequency:	Bi-annual (March / September)
Subscription Cost:	£6.00
Single Issue:	£3.30 (inc P&p)
Back issue price:	£1.00
Cheques/PO Payable to:	The Frogmore Press
Overseas subs:	U.S $12.00, Europe £8.00
Payment Details:	U.S subs in bills only no U.S cheques

Description
The Frogmore Papers publish poetry and prose by new and established writers. Founded in 1983, the magazine has featured work by a wide variety of poets from Linda France, John Mole and Sophie Hannah to Elizabeth Garrett, Pauline Stainer and Katherine Pierpoint. The annual Frogmore poetry prize founded in 1987 was won by Tobias Hill in 1995, previous winners include Joan Latham and Caroline Price.

Addresses
Editorial:	6 Vernon Road, London N8 0QD,
Reviews:	127 Horton Road, Manchester, M14 7QD
Subscriptions:	The Frogmore Press, 42 Morehill Avenue, Folkestone, Kent, CT19 4EF
Payment terms to contributors:	Complimentary copy
Accept/Rejection approximate times:	1-3 months
Inserts accepted:	No
Price per 1000:	
Circulation:	300

FRONTAL LOBE

Frequency:	Quarterly
Subscription Cost:	£5.00 for 4 issues
Single Issue:	£1.25 inc p&p
Back issue price:	
Cheques/PO Payable to:	
Overseas subs:	
Payment Details:	

Description

Prose, Poetry, Articles, Music, Cartoon, Artwork, Short Stories, max 4000 words, poems, articles - 1000 words, all must be typed. Please enclose SAE for return of work. Also a short review.

Addresses

Editorial:	18 Stile Common, Primrose Hill, Newsome, Huddersfield, W. Yorks., HD4 GDY
Reviews:	As above
Subscriptions:	As above
Payment terms to contributors:	A free copy of the magazine
Accept/Rejection approximate times:	
Inserts accepted:	
Price per 1000:	
Circulation:	

GAIRM

Frequency:	Quarterly
Subscription Cost:	£10 overseas and Ireland, £8 U.K
Single Issue:	£1.60
Back issue price:	Variable; pack of 50 back issues £28
Cheques/PO Payable to:	Gairm Publications
Overseas subs:	£10.00
Payment Details:	Cheque to Gairm Publications

Description

A quarterly publication, in Scottish Gaelic, encompassing fiction, poetry, current affairs, articles on technical topics, folklore, song, reviews with some pictorial features. The periodical was founded in 1951-52, and has now reached issue number 175. Gairm Publications also publish a wide range of books: dictionaries, grammars, novels, short stories, poetry, children's books, Gaelic music books etc. Only Scottish Gaelic contributions accepted.

Addresses

Editorial:	29 Waterloo Street, Glasgow, G2 6BZ
Reviews:	As above
Subscriptions:	As above
Payment terms to contributors:	Approx. £10 per page
Accept/Rejection approximate times:	2-3 weeks
Inserts accepted:	Yes
Price per 1000:	£30
Circulation:	2000

GHOSTS & SCHOLARS

Frequency:	Twice a year
Subscription Cost:	£14 (overseas £15 / $25)
Single Issue:	£4 (overseas £4-30 / $7)
Back issue price:	£4 (overseas £4-30 / $7)
Cheques/PO Payable to:	Rosemary Pardoe
Overseas subs:	(See above)
Payment Details:	No foreign cheques (but U.S $ cash okay)

Description

Ghosts & Scholars publishes new ghost stories in the M.R. James Tradition (no other kind of ghost story will be considered). The M.R. James Tradition is not the same as Traditional Prospective contributions should be familiar with M.R. James` work. Mss up to 8000 words Non-fiction on MRJand other writers in the James Tradition also welcome (up to 8000 words)

Addresses

Editorial:	Rosemary Pardoe, Flat One, 36 Hamilton Street. Hoole, Chester, CH2 3JQ
Reviews:	As above
Subscriptions:	As above
Payment terms to contributors:	Contributors copies only (3)
Accept/Rejection approximate times:	Two weeks maximum
Inserts accepted:	No
Price per 1000:	
Circulation:	400

GLOBAL TAPESTRY JOURNAL

Frequency:	Irregular
Subscription Cost:	£7.50 4 postal issues
Single Issue:	£2 single postal copy
Back issue price:	Usually out of print
Cheques/PO Payable to:	B.B. Books
Overseas subs:	£8 in sterling
Payment Details:	Sterling cheques. USA currency

Description

A manifestation of exciting creativity. Innovative prose writing and novel extracts. Contains PM NEWSLETTER - reviewing small alternative networks and large publishing house releases. Bohemian, post-Beat and counter-culture orientation.

Addresses

Editorial:	Spring Bank, Longsight Road, Copster Green, Blackburn, Lancs. BB1 9EU
Reviews:	As above
Subscriptions:	As above
Payment terms to contributors:	issue of magazine only
Accept/Rejection approximate times:	One month
Inserts accepted:	Yes
Price per 1000:	£10
Circulation:	1300 to 1500

GOOD SOCIETY REVIEW THE

Frequency:	Bi-annual
Subscription Cost:	£10.00
Single Issue:	£4.95
Back issue price:	
Cheques/PO Payable to:	
Overseas subs:	$20
Payment Details:	

Description

We are now publishing THE GOOD SOCIETY REVIEW on a bi-annual basis, each issue round a particular theme. The annual subscription is £10 or twenty USA dollars. (Copies £4.95 in the shops.) Please note we have also moved the publisher's address to the one below. These details over-ride the information given in the Writers' and Artists' Yearbook.

Publishing twice a year does mean we have to hold contributions a long time before making any decisions on them. Contributors are of course free to offer their work elsewhere in the meantime, but we would like them to tell us if anything they have sent us is to be published elsewhere. We would not want to publish work which has already been accepted by another journal.

There has been a further delay in publication this year while we are waiting the outcome of an application for revenue funding. This would make a big difference to our ability to plan ahead. We hope our subscribers and contributors will bear with us over this delay.

Addresses

Editorial:	Holman's Press, Elm Lodge, Union Place, Anstrultner, Fife KY10 3HQ
Reviews:	As above
Subscriptions:	As above
Payment terms to contributors:	
Accept/Rejection approximate times:	See above
Inserts accepted:	

Price per 1000:
Circulation:

GOOD STORIES

Frequency:	Quarterly
Subscription Cost:	£10.00 post free
Single Issue:	£2.95 plus 45p postage
Back issue price:	£1.50 post free
Cheques/PO Payable to:	Oakwood Publications
Overseas subs:	£16.00
Payment Details:	Sterling only

Description

A magazine of all kinds of short stories, mainly aimed at a family readership. Our aim is to encourage new writers, and the magazine is non-profit making, so that all surplus income can be used to pay contributors.

Addresses

Editorial:	Oakwood Publications, 23 Mill Crescent, Kingsbury, Warwickshire, B78 2LX
Reviews:	As above
Subscriptions:	As above
Payment terms to contributors:	Amount can vary but usually about £35 per 1000 words
Accept/Rejection approximate times:	Two weeks
Inserts accepted:	Yes
Price per 1000:	£15.00
Circulation:	3000

HANDSHAKE

Frequency:	Irregular
Subscription Cost:	SAE/IRC/Stamps?Trade
Single Issue:	Same
Back issue price:	Same - very few ever available
Cheques/PO Payable to:	IRC/Stamps/Trade
Overseas subs:	
Payment Details:	Contributor's copy only

Description

Handshake is a very specialised magazine, consisting of a single sheeet of A4 devoted entirely to SF poetry. One side of the magazine consists of news and information about genre poetry - information submitted should be typed, single-spaced, ready for photocopying. Adverts are OK if Small. Side two has now evolved into a 'poetry magazine' - but being only one side of a single sheet means I can take no epics! Short poems preferred, and as I always have more poems than information I prefer the latter. You are advised to see a copy before submitting. All rights revert to author on publication. All submissions must be accompanied by an sae, and have not been published elsewhere.

Addresses

Editorial:	J.F. Haines, 5 Cross Farm, Station Road, Padgate, Warrington WA2 0QG
Reviews:	As above
Subscriptions:	As above
Payment terms to contributors:	copy of newsletter
Accept/Rejection approximate times:	Soon as I can and within a month if possible, though if you're close to an issue being printed it could be longer
Inserts accepted:	Yes. About 60 copies - genre poetry related only
Price per 1000:	N/A (no more than about 60 - trade?)
Circulation:	60+

HEADLOCK

Frequency:	Twice yearly
Subscription Cost:	£6 UK
Single Issue:	£3.50 UK only
Back issue price:	£2.50
Cheques/PO Payable to:	Headlock Press
Overseas subs:	£7 EC/£8 worldwide
Payment Details:	All payments in sterling

Description

Wall-to-wall poetry, occasional prose essay on the state of poetry. Famous biographies. Some illustration (B/W only). No reviews. Submissions always welcome, must be accompanied by sae. Overseas submitters, send disposable copies and IRC. Editor's tastes are eclectic - experimental/provocative work elbows with good traditional writing. South-West contributors encouraged, but not given special preference.

Addresses

Editorial:	Tony Charles, Old Zion Chapel, The Triangle, Somerton, Somerset TA11 6QP
Reviews:	N/A
Subscriptions:	As above
Payment terms to contributors:	Free copy
Accept/Rejection approximate times:	Usually one month
Inserts accepted:	Yes
Price per 1000:	£10
Circulation:	150

HEADPRESS

Frequency:	Three yearly
Subscription Cost:	£14
Single Issue:	£4.95
Back issue price:	£3.75
Cheques/PO Payable to:	Headpress
Overseas subs:	£16 Europe £20 USA/Rest of world
Payment Details:	UK Bankable cheque or giro

Description

Headpress is the journal of sex religion death. For almost five years has enjoyed considerable cult status at the forefront of 'transgressive' writing. Incisive and cutting-edge essays on films and filmmakers, religious manias, fanaticism, weird crime cases, sex queens, curious music, feticism, art, pornography, trash and sleaze. As of Headpress 13, the magazine goes book format!

Addresses

Editorial:	Headpress, 40 Rossall Avenue, Radcliffe, Manchester M26 1JD
Reviews:	As above
Subscriptions:	As above
Payment terms to contributors:	Complimentary copy of Headpress
Accept/Rejection approximate times:	3 to 4 weeks
Inserts accepted:	No
Price per 1000:	N/A
Circulation:	2500

HELICON POETRY MAGAZINE

Frequency:	Quarterly
Subscription Cost:	£9
Single Issue:	£2.50
Back issue price:	£2
Cheques/PO Payable to:	Cherrybite Publications
Overseas subs:	£11 or £3 per single issue
Payment Details:	Sterling or travellers cheque

Description
A high quality poetry magazine of no particular genre. We reject a lot so its advisable to study the magazine before submitting work. A5 format, card cover, 44 pages.

Addresses

Editorial:	Linden Cottage, 45 Burton Road, Little Neston, South Wirral L64 4AE
Reviews:	As above
Subscriptions:	As above
Payment terms to contributors:	£2 per poem + free copy
Accept/Rejection approximate times:	1 month
Inserts accepted:	Yes
Price per 1000:	Reciprocal
Circulation:	250

HJOKFINNIES SANGLINES

Frequency:	Quarterly
Subscription Cost:	N/A
Single Issue:	No. 4 £2.50
Back issue price:	Nos. 3 & 4 £3
Cheques/PO Payable to:	Jim Inglis
Overseas subs:	
Payment Details:	

Description

Hjokfinnies Sanglines is a Broadsheet for poems, music, polemics, Broadsheet advantages:combines the arts of writer, artist and printer,maximum impact for a modest outlay,a good format for poetry HJFS intends a creative interaction of English, Gaelic and Scots languages from its base in Easter Ross. AYONT THE NOVEL (Editor's poem) ... I'm nae concerned wi writin stories/ Whit I wark at are/specific syntropic realisations - demonstraitin/the technological requirements o Freedom: /structural dynamics an metabolic energy efficiency: /hoo the multifarious vital regenerativ pooer o Nature/can be maintained, an whaur dwinin revived,/ on theis large geodesic-spheric three-quarter water girt walrd:/ti alloo, aawhere, economic democracy/an metaphysical evolution/ for aa wimmen an men.

Addresses

Editorial:	8 Knockbain Road, Dingwall, Ross-Shire, Scotland, IV15 9NR
Reviews:	As above
Subscriptions:	As above
Payment terms	
to contributors:	Usually in broadsheets
Accept/Rejection	
approximate times:	varies - please send photocopy
Inserts accepted:	No
Price per 1000:	N/A
Circulation:	500 print run

HOLLYWOOD MUSICALS SOCIETY

Frequency:	3 / Year (4 / Year 1989 - 1994)
Subscription Cost:	£5
Single Issue:	£2
Back issue price:	£2
Cheques/PO Payable to:	P Gent
Overseas subs:	$20 cash only or £15
Payment Details:	UK cheques or US $ bills

Description

Founded in 1989 featuring articles, photos and drawings of stars, directors, etc., of Hollywood musicals and related genres. Members in every continent. Free small ads to subscribers. Free service to find photos, videos etc., autographed photos received from stars e.g. Doris Day, Jane Powell, Deborah Kerr, Deanna Durbin, Debbie Reynolds, Howard Keel, Ricardo Mentalsan etc.

Sister magazine: Deneuve Centre dedicated to Catherine Deneuve

Addresses

Editorial:	1 Pond Meadow, Milford Haven, Pembs, Wales, UK
Reviews:	As above
Subscriptions:	As above
Payment terms to contributors:	Free copy
Accept/Rejection approximate times:	Few rejections
Inserts accepted:	Yes
Price per 1000:	Free
Circulation:	300

HOLOGRAM TALES

Frequency:	Monthly
Subscription Cost:	Free
Single Issue:	Free
Back issue price:	Free
Cheques/PO Payable to:	N/A
Overseas subs:	N/A
Payment Details:	N/A

Description

Hologram Tales is the leading on-line science fiction & fantasy magazine, found on the internet of http://www.sf-fantasy.com. It is available to access free of charge and acts as a platform for new writers and authors, publishing fiction, book and film reviews, author interviews, articles and debate. It has become one of the most popular magazines on the worldwide web. Hologram Tale's house style is light-hearted and accessible.

Addresses

Editorial:	12 Shannon Court, 1 Tavistock Croydon, Surrey CRO 2AL
Reviews:	As above
Subscriptions:	As above
Payment terms to contributors:	No payment
Accept/Rejection approximate times:	One month
Inserts accepted:	No
Price per 1000:	N/A
Circulation:	668,000 people a month visit the site.

HQ; THE HAIKU QUARTERLY POETRY MAGAZINE

Frequency:	Quarterly
Subscription Cost:	£9 UK
Single Issue:	£2.60
Back issue price:	£2.60
Cheques/PO Payable to:	The Haiku Quarterly
Overseas subs:	£12
Payment Details:	Cheques and postal orders in UK. Cash/sterling cheques non UK.

Description

HQ (founded in 1990) is an international poetry magazine that publishes a broad range of work - from the highly experimental to the very traditional. The emphasis is on quality and originality. About one third of the magazine's space is given over to haiku and haikuesque/poetry; the rest to mainstream poetry and reviews/articles. HQ encourages the publication of new work by established writers (Kirkup, Redgrove, Brownjohn, Middleton, Clemp, Gross, Stryk, Lydiard etc. in previous issues) and developmental/experimental work by new poets (Hogan, Rollinson, Savage, Marks, Mcmahon, etc.) It should be noted that Howard Sargeant and Roland John at 'Outposts' and Mike Shields at 'Orbis' have been a strong influence on HQ's editor, and this is reflected in the magazine's style.

Addresses

Editorial:	39 Exmouth Street, Swindon, Wiltshire SN1 3PU
Reviews:	As above
Subscriptions:	As above
Payment terms to contributors:	Free copy(s) of magazine - some financial assistance to contributors in need
Accept/Rejection approximate times:	Up to 6 months depending upon workload
Inserts accepted:	Yes
Price per 1000:	By arrangement
Circulation:	500 (Readership via libraries etc. 1000+)

HRAFNHOH

Frequency:	Irregular
Subscription Cost:	£5.25 for next three issues (US $13 / $16 inc Air
Single Issue:	£2 (US $6 inc Airmail)
Back issue price:	Usually Gratis
Cheques/PO Payable to:	Joseph Biddulph
Overseas subs:	As above but about £1.75 for postage
Payment Details:	Almost any currency accepted as banknotes if willing to risk in post, or exchange.

Description
Probably different from every other little magazine mostly but not exclusively in English, interested in Family History, Surnames, Heraldry, Philosophy, Theology, Nonconformist History and metrical poetry, Languages and Dialect, across a very miscellaneous field, giving special encouragement to Pro-life writing, and now with a non - populationist Africana / African Diaspora section 'Black Eagle' combining eyewitness accounts, religious, social and political issues with snippets of African linguistics. Extremely editor-dominated with specific themes.

Addresses
Editorial:	32 Stryd Ebeneser, Pontypridd, CF37 5PB, Cymru / Wales
Reviews:	As above
Subscriptions:	As above
Payment terms to contributors:	None
Accept/Rejection approximate times:	From return of post up to about 2 months.
Inserts accepted:	Yes if compatible with contents
Price per 1000:	Free
Circulation:	Nowhere near enough, up to 200

HU (formerly THE HONEST ULSTERMAN)

Frequency:	2/3 times a year
Subscription Cost:	UK - £10 for 4 issues inc p&p
Single Issue:	£2.50
Back issue price:	Varies
Cheques/PO Payable to:	HU Publications
Overseas subs:	£14
Payment Details:	Institutions - different rate - please write

Description

The North of Irelands longest running and most respected literary magazine. Our focus is Ireland - especially The North - but our only criterion is quality, and we welcome contributions from anywhere.While we are primarily a poetry magazine, we also publish book reviews, general criticism and articles, short stories, interviews, etc, etc. Every second issue comes with a free poetry pamphlet.

Addresses

Editorial:	49 Main Street, Greyabbey, County Down, BT22 2NF
Reviews:	As above
Subscriptions:	As above
Payment terms to contributors:	Nominal fee & 2 copies
Accept/Rejection approximate times:	2/3 months
Inserts accepted:	Yes
Price per 1000:	£35
Circulation:	1,000

HYBRID

Frequency:	Twice yearly (From 1997)
Subscription Cost:	£4 annually
Single Issue:	£2
Back issue price:	£2
Cheques/PO Payable to:	Kevin Cadwallender
Overseas subs:	$8 America £6 Europe
Payment Details:	IMO, cheque in sterling, postal order. Foreign currencies must allow for exchange.

Description
Hybrid (Founded in 1990) is probably the most accessible magazine in the world. New writers are found alongside established writers and those established writers have included Lawrence Ferlinghotti, Linda France, Barry Graham plus a host of writers from all over the planet. Occasional reviews are accepted but the magazine is devoted to poetry, poetry of all kinds. The Editor has an open mind and likes to read good poetry of whatever ilk.

Addresses
Editorial:	42 Christchurch Place, Peterlee, Co. Durham SR8 2NR
Reviews:	As above
Subscriptions:	As above
Payment terms to contributors:	Free copy of magazine
Accept/Rejection approximate times:	N/A
Inserts accepted:	Yes
Price per 1000:	
Circulation:	Increasing

IMPACTE MACABRE

Frequency:	Irregular
Subscription Cost:	N/A
Single Issue:	£2
Back issue price:	£2
Cheques/PO Payable to:	T.Gay
Overseas subs:	N/A
Payment Details:	cheques/postal orders

Description
Thoughtful thought provoking fiction in SF/horror/fantasy genre. Whimsical, metaphysical and profound with simple and surreal illustrations. Simple presentation.

Addresses

Editorial:	8 Chamberlain Street, Crawcrook,Tyne & Wear NE40 4TZ
Reviews:	As above
Subscriptions:	As above
Payment terms to contributors:	Free copy of magazine
Accept/Rejection approximate times:	Varies wildly depending on circumstances between several days and several weeks.
Inserts accepted:	Yes
Price per 1000:	Generally by exchange
Circulation:	Small but national

INTERPRETER'S HOUSE THE

Frequency: 3 times yearly
Subscription Cost: £9 (under review)
Single Issue: £2.50
Back issue price: £2.50
Cheques/PO Payable to: The Interpreter's House
Overseas subs:
Payment Details:

Description
We obtained a grant from Eastern Arts to start this magazine, because we felt it was important to encourage writers in Bedfordshire and the neighbouring counties, where there isn't much cultural life. Our title comes from Pilgrims Progress. We publish poems and short stories (up to 2000 words). Writers from the region get preference, but anyone may submit, and I am anxious to publish the best work I can get. When I say in the leaflet that work should be 'understandable' I do not mean initially simple, but I do want to avoid work which is meaningless to the common reader, and I do not want it to be dominated by cliques. I have got ambitions to make it one of the best literacy magazines around.

Addresses
Editorial: Merryn Williams, 10 Farrell Road, Wootton, Bedfordshire
                               MK43 9DU
Reviews: N/A
Subscriptions: 24 Bower Street, Bedford MK40 3RE
Payment terms
to contributors: 1 free copy
Accept/Rejection
approximate times: Normally within one week
Inserts accepted: Yes
Price per 1000:   N/A
Circulation: We print 200 copies

INTERZONE

Frequency:	Monthly
Subscription Cost:	£30
Single Issue:	£2.75
Back issue price:	£2.75
Cheques/PO Payable to:	Interzone
Overseas subs:	£36
Payment Details:	International money order, Eurocheque, or by credit card

Description
Interzone publishes science-fiction and fantasy short stories, plus reviews, interviews, etc. It does not publish verse, and therefore is not a 'poetry-related magazine.'

Addresses

Editorial:	217 Preston Drove, Brighton BN1 6FL
Reviews:	As above
Subscriptions:	As above
Payment terms to contributors:	£30 per 1000 words
Accept/Rejection approximate times:	2 months
Inserts accepted:	No
Price per 1000:	N/A
Circulation:	8000

INTIMACY

Frequency:	Irregular
Subscription Cost:	Varying dependent on issue size
Single Issue:	As subscription costs
Back issue price:	Issues 1 - 4 £15.00 inc
Cheques/PO Payable to:	Adam Mckeown
Overseas subs:	
Payment Details:	In sterling only

Description

INTIMACY is an irregularly produced journal seeking to gather together differing response to a common theme, or themes, collating diverse topologies, dialogue, contradiction, openings, closures, etc, and the play of text/images which exist both in their own right, and as sites that feed off, and into each other. The journal devotes itself to innovative writers and artists, and has developed a tendency to couple archival material (Artaud, Bataille, Bellmer, Krafft-Ebing, etc) with a contemporary arena, Influences are multiple, although, if a magazine has to be cited as a reference point, Paul Buck's seminal Curtains must rank as an indication of editorial policy. Subjects of interest: Art, Writing, Literature (particularly French), Philosophy, Psychology, Crime and Criminology, Sexuality, Poetry, Music, Film. A specialism would be in the area of how a writer constitutes his, or her, identity in the act of writing (from and earlier editorial statement). The journal does not operate as a catch-all forum for writers and compulsive submitters, and thus, some knowledge of the journal's concerns is recommended prior to sending material. All feedback is very welcome.

Addresses

Editorial:	Apt. C. Ramney House, 1 Charles Street, Maidstone, Kent ME16 8EU
Reviews:	As above - only if of relevance
Subscriptions:	As above
Payment terms to contributors:	What planet are you on
Accept/Rejection approximate times:	

Inserts accepted: Yes but only for journals of interest
Price per 1000:
Circulation: 200

IOTA

Frequency:	Quarterly
Subscription Cost:	£6 a year
Single Issue:	£1.50
Back issue price:	£1
Cheques/PO Payable to:	Iota or David Holliday
Overseas subs:	$US 10 or equivalent
Payment Details:	Cash, cheque or money order, but if non-UK cheque, add $10 to cover charge

Description

Poetry, and reviews of poetry publications (both books and magazines). The editor claims neither facilities nor expertise for concrete verse; but apart from that, anything goes. For obvious reasons, shorter poems are at an advantage. Looking for well-crafted verse with something to say.

Addresses

Editorial:	67 Hady Crescent, Chesterfield, Derbyshire,S41 OEB
Reviews:	As above
Subscriptions:	As above
Payment terms to contributors:	Two complimentary copies
Accept/Rejection approximate times:	First reaction, a couple of weeks (except when the next issue is in preparation) but final acceptance/rejection may take up to a year.
Inserts accepted:	Yes
Price per 1000:	So far, no charge has been made (though that could alter)
Circulation:	400

IRON

Frequency:	Three time a year
Subscription Cost:	£14.00 (four editions) post-free
Single Issue:	£4.00
Back issue price:	£3.50
Cheques/PO Payable to:	IRON Press
Overseas subs:	$40
Payment Details:	Dollar cheques allowable. Transfer money orders can be made in sterling for £14.

Description

IRON vigorously promotes new writing, and has done since 1973. Early 1997 will see the 81st edition. We respond quickly and with comment to all the work sent in as long as authors stick to our guidelines which is no more than five poems or two stories per submission (max. no. of words on prose is 6000). We feature approx. two dozen poets and fiction writers each addition as well as having a books review section, Poetry Live (a review of live poetry events), letters, and the work of many graphic artists. IRON encourages new writers and reputations count for nothing with us. But we do urge authors if possible to see the magazine first. Much of the work is totally unsuitable, many writers are submitting to IRON too soon (we take only about two per cent of work sent in). Also, writers should ask themselves are they ready to submit. To be able to answer no is often part of the necessary process. We pay around £10 per page. Energy and creative originality are important to us; well-crafted formula work is unlikely to be taken.

Addresses

Editorial:	95 Queens Road, Whittley Bay, Northumberland NE26 3AT
Reviews:	As above, c/o reviews editor, Valerie Laws
Subscriptions:	As above
Payment terms to contributors:	£10 per page of work
Accept/Rejection approximate times:	Maximum two weeks
Inserts accepted:	Yes

Price per 1000:   Negotiable
Circulation: 900

ISSUE ONE/THE BRIDGE

Frequency:	Twice in each subscription
Subscription Cost:	£3 plus 2 A5 SAE
Single Issue:	Free
Back issue price:	Not available
Cheques/PO Payable to:	Ian Brocklebank
Overseas subs:	$6 US plus 2 International reply coupons
Payment Details:	

Description

Issue One accepts work from new and established writers and welcomes submissions from overseas writers, there are no restrictions on the style or subject or length of pieces with the exceptions of racism and sexism, prose submissions are not appropriate to this title. The Bridge presents work on single subjects by groups or individuals the subjects are nominated by the editors, the title will also include information relevant to the subject.

Addresses

Editorial:	2 Tewkesbury Drive, Grimsby South, Humberside, DW34 4TL
Reviews:	As above
Subscriptions:	As above
Payment terms to contributors:	No payment except in copies review of policy due in 1996 dependent on new funding.
Accept/Rejection approximate times:	One month for both titles
Inserts accepted:	Yes
Price per 1000:	No current charges paid by sender
Circulation:	Combined 750

JOURNAL OF CONTEMPORARY ANGLO - SCANDINAVIAN POETRY

Frequency:	Biannual
Subscription Cost:	£7
Single Issue:	£4
Back issue price:	£2
Cheques/PO Payable to:	Sam Smith
Overseas subs:	£9 (USA £11)
Payment Details:	No cheques from outside UK banking system IRCs as cash accepted

Description
The aim of the magazine is to be a showcase for contemporary Scandinavian poetry in translation alongside contemporary poetry written in English. Anything interesting, new, modern considered... poetry that wants to say something, not just be poetry. No. I don't want to prejudge any work, to deter the submission that could change my mind. If you think your work deserves publication, try me. Better still - try a sample copy first.

Addresses

Editorial:	Sam Smith, 11 Heatherton Park, Bradford on Tone, Taunton, Somerset, TA4 1EU
Reviews:	
Subscriptions:	As above
Payment terms to contributors:	1 complimentary copy
Accept/Rejection approximate times:	Within 4 weeks
Inserts accepted:	No
Price per 1000:	
Circulation:	150

KIMOTA

Frequency:	Twice yearly
Subscription Cost:	£9 for 4 (free p & p)
Single Issue:	£2.50
Back issue price:	£2.50
Cheques/PO Payable to:	G. Hurry
Overseas subs:	International money order (UK prices) please.
Payment Details:	Cheque or postal order

Description

Illustrated small press magazine concentrating on S.F. fantasy and horror as well as genre reviews' and articles.

Addresses

Editorial:	52 Cadley Causeway, Fulwood, Preston, Lancs, PR2 3RX
Reviews:	As above
Subscriptions:	As above
Payment terms to contributors:	£2 per 1000 words
Accept/Rejection approximate times:	1 month
Inserts accepted:	Yes
Price per 1000:	£1.50
Circulation:	Increasing slowly

KRAX

Frequency:	Nine monthly approx.
Subscription Cost:	£7.50 for 3 subsequent issues
Single Issue:	£2
Back issue price:	On request
Cheques/PO Payable to:	A. Robson
Overseas subs:	$15 (cash only)
Payment Details:	

Description
Light-hearted poetry magazine, witty and quirky, with one fiction piece per nine monthly edition. Usually an interview with writer or artist of interest plus a sizeable review section of books, magazines and tapes of related topics, Photos and graphics included on whimsy. A high percentage of American writing contributions.

Addresses

Editorial:	A Robson, c/o 63 Dixon Lane, Leeds,LS12 4RR, Yorkshire, UK
Reviews:	As above
Subscriptions:	As above
Payment terms to contributors:	Single copy of magazine unless otherwise agreed - payment for cover art on publication.
Accept/Rejection approximate times:	Up to ten weeks overseas
Inserts accepted:	No
Price per 1000:	
Circulation:	60% U.K, 40% USA

KYLE'S KLUB U.K

Frequency:	Twice a year
Subscription Cost:	N/A
Single Issue:	£1.50
Back issue price:	£1.00
Cheques/PO Payable to:	M. Coleman
Overseas subs:	3 IRC`S per single copy
Payment Details:	Cheque or P.O payable to M. Coleman Secured cash accepted Trades welcomed

Description
Three magazines have been published since August 1993 under the banner of KYLE'S KLUB U.K. These magazines were freedom rock and love : I stand infected, freedom rock and exciting and controversial look at the darker side of modern writing spawned two issues both of which are now completely sold out with no plans for reprints love: I stand infected was first printed in February 1995 and consists of short stories, articles and poetry with love as the main theme. The magazine was updated and reprinted in October 1995 and this version is currently available priced £1.

Addresses

Editorial:	18 Sunningdale Avenue, Sale, Cheshire,M33 2PH U.K
Reviews:	As above
Subscriptions:	N/A
Payment terms to contributors:	Payment in copy
Accept/Rejection approximate times:	Three - four weeks
Inserts accepted:	Yes
Price per 1000:	N/A
Circulation:	150 - 200

LATERAL MOVES

Frequency:	6 p.a./bi-monthly
Subscription Cost:	£12 includes free p. & p.
Single Issue:	£2 + 35p. p & p
Back issue price:	£1.50 + 35p/ £2 + 35p. depending on issue
Cheques/PO Payable to:	Aural Images
Overseas subs:	£15 Europe £18 rest of world
Payment Details:	Sterling cheques, postal orders, bank drafts, IMO.Beer or interesting pictures.

Description

Lateral Moves (Founded 1993) is the arts/literary magazine with extra tusk. Honest and forthright (we hope), the magazine features poetry, stories and miniatures (of around 250 words), articles on writing, philosophy, psychology, an open letters page. A watchdog column, a futurism and computing section, reviews and news, and regular humour columns; Art examined with wit and a gruff (Northern?) sense of mischief. Described by Geoff Lowe (Psycholoemca) as 'a really great little mag,packed with smart stuff and little quirky surprises in odd corners. The only magazine I know that, even without contributors' material, would still be worth reading and enjoying. Thanks for enjoying what you do. It shows!' Lateral Moves is a magazine which subscribers and contributors may help to direct and certainly enrich. We welcome contributions of all kinds - however, potential contributors may like to view a copy first, as much of the accepted work is quite dark in nature. Lateral Moves eats curries! Come on, brighten our sad lives...

Addresses

Editorial:	Alan White & Nick Britton, 5 Hamilton Street, Astley Bridge, Bolton BL1 6RJ (01204) 596369 http://basil,acs.bolton-ac.uk/-pla1.
Reviews:	As above
Subscriptions:	As above
Payment terms to contributors:	Free copy of magazine
Accept/Rejection approximate times:	3 months - may vary depending upon type of material

Inserts accepted:	YesPrice per 500: Free to partners/subscribers/exchange publicity
Price per 1000:	N/A
Circulation:	500

LONDON MAGAZINE

Frequency:	Bi-monthly
Subscription Cost:	£28-50
Single Issue:	£5.99
Back issue price:	£3.50
Cheques/PO Payable to:	London Magazine
Overseas subs:	£33.50
Payment Details:	

Description
Poems, stories, memoirs, art, photography, theatre, architecture plus 40 pages of reviews.

Addresses

Editorial:	30 Thurloe Place, London SW7
Reviews:	As above
Subscriptions:	As above
Payment terms to contributors:	Variable Poems £20 - £50, Stories £20 - £75, Reviews £25 - £35
Accept/Rejection approximate times:	1 week
Inserts accepted:	Yes
Price per 1000:	£70
Circulation:	3500 plus

LONDON REVIEW OF BOOKS

Frequency:	Fortnightly
Subscription Cost:	£54 (24 issues)
Single Issue:	£2.25
Back issue price:	£3
Cheques/PO Payable to:	LRB LTD.
Overseas subs:	Varies country to country.
Payment Details:	Sterling cheque, International Girobank, Mastercard, DinersClub, Visa, Access

Description
In-depth reviews of current books on politics, literature, history, the arts

Addresses

Editorial:	28-30 Little Russell Street, London WC1A 2HN
Reviews:	As above
Subscriptions:	As above
Payment terms to contributors:	Not for disclosure
Accept/Rejection approximate times:	As above
Inserts accepted:	Yes
Price per 1000:	£73
Circulation:	23,504 (ABC)

LONG POEM GROUP NEWSLETTER THE

Frequency:	Occasional
Subscription Cost:	Free - For sae of 26p. A5 or larger envelope
Single Issue:	As above
Back issue price:	As above
Cheques/PO Payable to:	N/A
Overseas subs:	N/A
Payment Details:	N/A

Description
A4pp well-printed newsletter devoted to debating the long poem in our time, and publishing: The transactions of the Long Poem Group; a checklist of long poems published in the last 30 years; and one or two reviews of newly-published long poems.(Internet No. d.g.d. clark @ bath.ac.uk WWW pages at Lttp://www.bath.ac.uk/-exxdgdc at bath univ).

Addresses

Editorial:	William Oxley & Sebastian Barker, Editors, 6 The Mount, Furzeham, Brixham, S. Devon TQ5 8QY
Reviews:	As above
Subscriptions:	Free
Payment terms to contributors:	None
Accept/Rejection approximate times:	N/A
Inserts accepted:	No
Price per 1000:	N/A
Circulation:	250

LOVELY JOBLY

Frequency:	Quarterly, now ceased
Subscription Cost:	N/A
Single Issue:	N/A
Back issue price:	£20
Cheques/PO Payable to:	Super real
Overseas subs:	N/A
Payment Details:	Cheque

Description
1990 - 1992, contemporary arts, mostly visual arts- issue focus on Samuel Beckett- American art - yoko and Allen Ginsberg. International Arts.

Addresses

Editorial:	Patricia Hope Scan Lan
Reviews:	As above
Subscriptions:	
Payment terms to contributors:	One - to - one arrangement
Accept/Rejection approximate times:	2 weeks
Inserts accepted:	Not applicable
Price per 1000:	
Circulation:	

LOW LIFE

Frequency:	Bimonthly
Subscription Cost:	
Single Issue:	£1.50
Back issue price:	
Cheques/PO Payable to:	J. Tuiker
Overseas subs:	
Payment Details:	

Description

Low Life features SF/Horror/Weird fiction, Gothic, Ghost stories, and also non - fiction in the form of Gothic band reviews, articles and photos. Work can have been published before but please state where, work must be A4 double spaced and no longer than 4 pages. The standard of work is high, horror is very welcome but include a good plot. Low Life is a music based magazine with Fiction and comedy.

Addresses

Editorial:	59 Burclett Road, London, E3 4TN
Reviews:	As above
Subscriptions:	
Payment terms	
to contributors:	
Accept/Rejection	
approximate times:	One week - please include SAE or IRC for return of work
Inserts accepted:	
Price per 1000:	
Circulation:	International readership

MAD COW

Frequency:	1 per annum
Subscription Cost:	£7.00
Single Issue:	£7.00
Back issue price:	None left - signed copies £60
Cheques/PO Payable to:	J Whittington
Overseas subs:	£10
Payment Details:	Cheque (dollars or sterling)

Description

100 pages of college cartridge and coloured sugar paper cut to A5, spiral bound with stiff board covers on which the title is letterpress embossed and packaged in a slipcase. Previous contributors include Thomas A Clark, Simon Cutts, Stuart Mills, Harry Gilonis, Colin Sackett, Robert Lax, Jonathan Williams, Cid Corman, Iliassa Seguin, Dick Higgins, Brendan McMahon, Rob Mackenzie. 'Beautifully presented new work by great poets' - Marie Claire.

Addresses

Editorial:	Jon T Whittington, 33 Kingsley Place, Highgate, London N6 5EA
Reviews:	No
Subscriptions:	No
Payment terms to contributors:	No
Accept/Rejection approximate times:	One poet, Brendan McMahon, was accepted after sending in material
Inserts accepted:	
Price per 1000:	
Circulation:	500

MADAM X

Frequency:	Twice yearly
Subscription Cost:	N/A
Single Issue:	£5
Back issue price:	£5
Cheques/PO Payable to:	Colophon Press
Overseas subs:	N/A
Payment Details:	Cheque, cash, credit card

Description

Magazine of new writing by new and extablished writers. Emphasis on short stories, but also poetry, interviews, criticism.

Addresses

Editorial:	18A Prentis Road, London SW18 1QD
Reviews:	As above
Subscriptions:	As above
Payment terms to contributors:	Free copies, otherwise please apply
Accept/Rejection approximate times:	Reasonably fast, but variable
Inserts accepted:	Yes
Price per 1000:	Please apply
Circulation:	1000

MAELSTROM

Frequency:	Twice yearly
Subscription Cost:	2/£3.50, 4/£6.50
Single Issue:	£1.80
Back issue price:	Nos. 1 - 5 £1, Nos. 6&7 £1.80
Cheques/PO Payable to:	Sol Publications
Overseas subs:	US 2/$10, 4/$20
Payment Details:	Equivalent in cash - no foreign cheques

Description

MAELSTROM is a genre fiction magazine, publishing short stories up to 10,000 words in length. We publish mainly science fiction, fantasy, horror and mystery stories, plus a few poems of a similar nature. We also publish a few book reviews and letters, as well as artwork illustrating the stories.

Addresses

Editorial:	24 Fowler Close, Southchurch, Southend - on - Sea, Essex, SS1 2RD
Reviews:	As above
Subscriptions:	As above
Payment terms to contributors:	£4 per 1000 words, £5 per 1000 words if supplied on disc
Accept/Rejection approximate times:	3 months
Inserts accepted:	Yes
Price per 1000:	35p per 100g
Circulation:	250

MAGAZINE THE

Frequency:	Twice yearly
Subscription Cost:	N/A
Single Issue:	£3 + postage
Back issue price:	£5
Cheques/PO Payable to:	Sally Russell, Editor
Overseas subs:	N/A
Payment Details:	Sterling cheques

Description

A publication of the Creative Writing Programme of Open Studies, Warwick University. Poems and short stories. Poems up to 40 lines. Stories up to 1200 words. Subjects eclectic, tasteful.

Addresses

Editorial:	Sally Russell, c/o Warwick Open Studies Dept. of Continuing Ed, University of Warwick, Coventry CV4 7AL
Reviews:	As above
Subscriptions:	None - available in local bookstores
Payment terms to contributors:	One free copy
Accept/Rejection approximate times:	3-4 months - send sae for all replies.
Inserts accepted:	No
Price per 1000:	Too much
Circulation:	Mysterious

MAGMA

Frequency:	3 times yearly
Subscription Cost:	£8
Single Issue:	£2.50
Back issue price:	£2
Cheques/PO Payable to:	Magma
Overseas subs:	£11
Payment Details:	IMO, sterling cheque

Description

Founded in 1994 and published by the Stukeley Press. Each issue is edited by a different member of the press within a common editorial approach. Poems in the mainstream - modernist range. Increasing interest in experimental work. Recent interviews with Carol Ann Duffy and Matthew Sweeney. Contacts with writing groups being sought. Occasional reviews/articles. Images (B/W) also welcome, whether accompanying poems or freestanding.

Addresses

Editorial:	The City Lit. Stukeley Street, London WC2B 5LJ
Reviews:	As above
Subscriptions:	As above
Payment terms to contributors:	Free copy of magazine
Accept/Rejection approximate times:	Usually within 2 months, except for work submitted in July/August when City Lit is closed.
Inserts accepted:	Yes
Price per 1000:	£10
Circulation:	300

MAIN STREET JOURNAL

Frequency:	Quarterly
Subscription Cost:	£16
Single Issue:	£4
Back issue price:	N/A
Cheques/PO Payable to:	'The Main Objective Ltd.'
Overseas subs:	N/A
Payment Details:	-

Description

An attempt to re-energise literary magazines by taking literature to its root-narrative. Publishing, within poetry, fiction, music and essays, a vast range of material; specialising in urban performance poetry and fast, A-B-C-E fiction as well as music anecdotes/focuses and polemical cultural pieces. Loads of fun and you ought to have it. No journalism!

Addresses

Editorial:	PO Box 2168 London W1A 1TG
Reviews:	Don't Run them
Subscriptions:	29 Princes Road, Ashford, Middlesex TW15 2LT
Payment terms to contributors:	Apply first to our Bank Manager (address on request as well as phial of iodine)
Accept/Rejection approximate times:	2 weeks max.
Inserts accepted:	Yes
Price per 1000:	£1
Circulation:	500

MALFUNCTION PRESS

Frequency:	Not fixed
Subscription Cost:	1st class S.A.E only
Single Issue:	Same
Back issue price:	Same
Cheques/PO Payable to:	P.E Presford
Overseas subs:	
Payment Details:	

Description
Poetry must have a S.Fiction or fantasy slant.Works with an Italian connection regarded with interest.Castle & Fortification Studies also considered for Postern Magazine.

Addresses
Editorial:	Malfunction Press, (P.E Presford), Rose Cottage, 3 Tram Lane, Flintshire, Wales,CH7 3JB
Reviews:	
Subscriptions:	Postern only £1.25 per issue
Payment terms to contributors:	
Accept/Rejection approximate times:	
Inserts accepted:	No
Price per 1000:	
Circulation:	To demand

METROPOLITAN

Frequency:	2 x a year
Subscription Cost:	£7.00 a year
Single Issue:	£3.50
Back issue price:	£4.00 inc. postage
Cheques/PO Payable to:	Metropolitan Magazine
Overseas subs:	£8.00 Europe/Ireland £10 rest of world
Payment Details:	Sterling (cheques and PO`s) or other currencies + £3

Description
A4 magazine of short stories and b/w photos challenging and contemporary ethos. No restriction on Genre or Style - but originality and high standard are main requirements, ESSENTIAL TO VIEW MAG BEFORE SUBMITTING TO SEE WHAT IS REQUIRED.Length - No restriction but format makes it difficult to include stories over 6000 words - therefore stories over this stand less chance. (2000 - 3000 ideal) we publish one piece of commentary or author interview per issue but these are usually in-house or commissioned - open to ideas though: send idea/proposal with note of experience and sample of previous work (relevant).SAE ESSENTIAL WITH ALL COMMUNICATIONS. Unsolicited stories welcome please type, double spaced on one side of A4 paper. DO NOT place in plastic folders. Number and staple pages, DO NOT send multiple submissions - if 3 or 4 stories are suitable for Metropolitan why waste 2 or 3 of them (since we can only accept 1 at a time) If not, it is not our job, but yours to decide which one is - we don't have the time.

Addresses
Editorial:	19 Victoria Avenue, Didsbury, Manchester,M20 2GY
Reviews:	
Subscriptions:	As above
Payment terms	
to contributors:	Negotiable on publication
Accept/Rejection	
approximate times:	1-3 months - have to be passed from 1st to 2nd editor - they read everything
Inserts accepted:	No

Price per 1000:
Circulation: 1500 copies (clearly readership is larger)

MICROPRESS MIDLANDS POETRY

Frequency: 10 per year
Subscription Cost: £10 p.a. £5 for 5 issues
Single Issue: N/A
Back issue price: N/A
Cheques/PO Payable to: G Stevens
Overseas subs: N/A
Payment Details:

Description

Small A5 magazine devoted to poetry. Will include supplement of near-miss/beginner's poetry called 'Rejection Slip. 'First issue December 1996

Addresses

Editorial: 111 Mill lane, Northfield, Birmingham, B31 2RP
Reviews: None
Subscriptions: As above
Payment terms
to contributors: None
Accept/Rejection
approximate times: 1 month max.
Inserts accepted: Yes
Price per 1000:   Negotiable
Circulation: Not Known

MIDNIGHT IN HELL

Frequency:	Quarterly
Subscription Cost:	-
Single Issue:	£3 ($7)
Back issue price:	-
Cheques/PO Payable to:	G.N. Houston
Overseas subs:	-
Payment Details:	Pounds Sterling or U.S. Dollars

Description
It is a cult media journal. Midnight in Hell is an A4 magazine containing poetry, articles and fiction with graphics to back them up.

Addresses

Editorial:	'Grave Orc,' The Cottage, Smithy Brae, Kilmacolm, Renfrewshire, PA13 4EN, Scotland
Reviews:	As above
Subscriptions:	None
Payment terms to contributors:	Contributor's copy
Accept/Rejection approximate times:	2 weeks prior to publication
Inserts accepted:	No
Price per 1000:	N/A
Circulation:	300

MODERN DANCE

Frequency:	2 -3 - 4 months
Subscription Cost:	Free with SAEs
Single Issue:	Free with SAE
Back issue price:	No back issues
Cheques/PO Payable to:	N/A although donations welcome D. Hughes
Overseas subs:	Not available
Payment Details:	

Description

Music review magazine that reviews all types of music - mainly CDs, (albums), occasional music related videos and books. Pop, rock, jazz, classical, metal, blues and opera - indeed, everything!

Addresses

Editorial:	12 Blailestones Road, Slaithwaite, Huddersfield,HD4 5UQ
Reviews:	As above
Subscriptions:	Donations to above
Payment terms to contributors:	N/A
Accept/Rejection approximate times:	N/A
Inserts accepted:	Yes
Price per 1000:	£10
Circulation:	4000

MODERN POETRY IN TRANSLATION

Frequency: Twice yearly
Subscription Cost: £19 annually for individuals. £30 for institutions.
Single Issue: £9.50 post free
Back issue price: £8.50 post free (our issues are never 'out of date')
Cheques/PO Payable to: King's College London
Overseas subs: £24 or $36 (U.S. dollars) for individual
Payment Details: Send to Editorial address (below)Sterling preferred:
                            IMO or American Express mon

Description

MPT, an international journal founded by Daniel Weissbort and Ted Hughes in the
60s, has been relaunched by King's College, London under Daniel Weissbort's
editorship. Published twice a year, the journal is dedicated to new translations into
English of poems from all over the world, with no restrictions on period and no
ideological bias. MPT also publishes articles on translation (with the emphasis on
practice rather than theory), reviews of new translations and occasional features on
individual translators. There is generally a substantial 'themed' section: issues 1 to 8
have featured Yves Bonnefoy, Franz Baermann Steiner (a bi-lingual edition with
previously unpublished poems and Michael Hamburger's translations), Anna
Kamienska and other Polish and East European poets, the Jerusalem International
Poetry Festival, Galician-Portuguese troubadours, Brazil, Wales and France; No 9 has
a section on Filipino poetry and poems from the Pacific Rim. Most issues of the New
Series have run to 200-248 pages; MPT is effectively a well-designed paperback
book. The Autumn 1996 issue (No 10) will be devoted to Russian poetry.

Addresses

Editorial: Professor Norma Rinsler, MPT, School of Humanities, King's
                            College, London, Strand, London WC2R 2LS
Reviews: As above
Subscriptions: As above
Payment terms
to contributors: £10 per poem or £12 per page as appropriate
Accept/Rejection
approximate times: 6 weeks, generally sooner

Inserts accepted: Not at present
Price per 1000:   N/A at present
Circulation: 300+ and growing - many library subscriptions

MONAS HIEROGLYPHICA

Frequency:	Twice yearly
Subscription Cost:	£2.40
Single Issue:	£1.20
Back issue price:	£1.50
Cheques/PO Payable to:	Jamie Spracklen
Overseas subs:	£1.50 (single issue) £2.70 (Subscription
Payment Details:	IMO, sterling cheque

Description

Monas Hieroglyphica concerns itself with both the Gothic music scene and subjects of interest in this area. Fiction, art and poetry feature strongly in it's pages, the exotic and strange being generally accepted. Each issue tries to feature a writer or bond of interest to the Gothic culture, plus contains a large review section as well. Also each issue contains articles about Alchemy and the Hotomist Dr John Dee, whose book 'Monas Hieroglyphica' gave the magazine it's name.

Addresses

Editorial:	58 Seymour Road, Hadleigh, Benfleet, Essex SS7 2HL
Reviews:	As above
Subscriptions:	As above
Payment terms to contributors:	Free copy of the magazine
Accept/Rejection approximate times:	Varies
Inserts accepted:	Yes
Price per 1000:	Varies
Circulation:	100+

MOONSTONE

Frequency:	Quarterly at the Festivals
Subscription Cost:	£6 p.a.
Single Issue:	£1.60
Back issue price:	£2
Cheques/PO Payable to:	Talitha Clare
Overseas subs:	$20 p.a. US/Canada/Australia/Europe
Payment Details:	Notes/bills only. No cheques except in sterling

Description

Moonstone was founded in 1979 'to keep the flag of pagan poetry flying in Abion.' The magazine features pagan poetry and short prose items of all descriptions. Regular contributors include Steve Sneyd, Patricia Prime and Kenneth C. Steven. Notes on contributors, short reviews and exchange listings for other pagan magazines are included.Occasionally black and white as artwork is accepted. Opinions given by contributors are not necessarily those of the Editors. Previously unpublished work, clearly typed with sae should be sent to the address below

Addresses

Editorial:	Talitha Clare, 'Moonstone' S.O.S., The Old Station Yard, Settle, N. Yorks, BD24 9RP
Reviews:	As above
Subscriptions:	As above
Payment terms to contributors:	Free copy of magazine - contributors retain their copyright, by request
Accept/Rejection approximate times:	All contributions of a pagan nature considered within six weeks, - eight. sae essential. Study of magazine advised
Inserts accepted:	Yes
Price per 1000:	£1
Circulation:	Increasing

NARROW PATH THE

Frequency:	Yearly
Subscription Cost:	N/A
Single Issue:	£2
Back issue price:	£2
Cheques/PO Payable to:	FCW c/o Mrs Janice Fixter
Overseas subs:	£2.50
Payment Details:	Sterling cheque, postal order, IMO

Description

The Narrow Path is a collection of winning and selected entries from the Fellowship of Christian Writers annual competition. Details are announced in the FCW's own magazine each year. The competitions are open to non-members. Poetry/fiction (as appropriate) need not be explicitly Christian, but please bear in mind this is a Christian organisation. More information about the FCW and competition entry forms are available from address below. First issue due out in March 1997, closing date of current competition is December 20th 1996.

Addresses

Editorial:	13 Queenhill Road, Selsdon, South Croydon, Surrey CR2 8DU
Reviews:	N/A
Subscriptions:	As above
Payment terms to contributors:	None
Accept/Rejection approximate times:	N/A
Inserts accepted:	No
Price per 1000:	N/A
Circulation:	Lots! - I hope!

NEVER BURY POETRY

Frequency:	Quarterly
Subscription Cost:	7.50 inc. p&p (annual)
Single Issue:	£1.50 or £2.00 post free
Back issue price:	£1 post free
Cheques/PO Payable to:	Never Bury Poetry
Overseas subs:	£1.50 per year, sample copy £1.50 post paid.
Payment Details:	Payment in sterling or cash dollars US or Australian.

Description

A4 format quality paper one poem to a page max. 40 lines. Each issue to a theme to be interpreted creatively. Bury Live Lines magazine Never Bury Poetry, is published quarterly. We are in our 9th year and have a small but thriving subscription list, including members from outside the British Isles. We publish in Spring, Summer, Autumn and Winter. We have cut-off dates for contributions which are always mentioned in the current magazine, ready for the next issue. We also publish the theme of the next issue, which should be interpreted creatively to give a wide scope of the subject matter. Poems may be sent in on spec.. and if she considers them publishable, the editor will ask permission to hold them over until a compatible theme arrives.

Addresses

Editorial:	Eileen Holroyd, 12a Kirkstall Gardens, Radcliffe, Manchester, M26 0QS, UK
Reviews:	
Subscriptions:	Bettina Jones, 30 Beryl Avenue, Tottington Bliky, Lancs, BL8 3NF
Payment terms to contributors:	We are non-profit making so cannot pay, only the printer is paid, we make enough
Accept/Rejection approximate times:	Approx. 1 month
Inserts accepted:	No
Price per 1000:	N/A
Circulation:	150 Worldwide

NEW DAWN FADES

Frequency:	Irregular
Subscription Cost:	£10 / 4 issues and Newsletters
Single Issue:	£2.00
Back issue price:	£2.00
Cheques/PO Payable to:	New Dawn Fades
Overseas subs:	
Payment Details:	Cheques or postal orders

Description
A magazine of SF, Fantasy, Horror, Fiction, Reviews, Art. Fiction must be under 10,000 words and non-fiction 2000 words plus shorter items considered for the review section. Illustrations for stories are commissioned, cartoons and comic stripes are also published.

Addresses

Editorial:	44 Clermiston Road North, Edinburgh,EH4 7BN, Scotland
Reviews:	As above
Subscriptions:	As above
Payment terms	
to contributors:	Free copy of relevant issue
Accept/Rejection	
approximate times:	4 weeks
Inserts accepted:	No
Price per 1000:	
Circulation:	100

NEW HOPE INTERNATIONAL

Frequency:	Irregular-up to 6 issues p.a. 2 or 3 issues often published
Subscription Cost:	£15 for 6 issues
Single Issue:	£3
Back issue price:	(NHI Writing £2: NHI Review £1)
Cheques/PO Payable to:	G. England
Overseas subs:	£20
Payment Details:	Non-sterling cheques under $100 not accepted. Preferred International Giro

Description

Issues may be NHI Writing, NHI Review or Special Edition Chapbooks. NHI Writing is an eclectic collection of poetry and short prose, from the traditional to the avant-garde, haiku to long poems, including translations. A collage of writing that consistently surprises. NHI Review covers books, magazines, cassettes, CDs, PC-software, videos. A unique guide to items you probably won't find in your local shop. Reviews run from three to thirty lines or more and reviewers are afraid neither to praise nor to damn. Though its first love is poetry, it covers world and local affairs, literature, music, art, history, religion, science, computers, health and much more. Essential reading for writers, librarians and all lovers of words. Most review issues also include short poetry. Chapbooks are single author collections or special issues such as The Art of Haiku a guide to the genre, or Briggflatts Visited a tribute to Basil Bunting. Poetry submissions are considered principlally for NHI Writing but may be used in NHI Review. Unsolicited reviews are not published, but would-be reviewers may inquire. Enquiries about Chapbooks should only be made by writers who already have a body of work published in magazines (not necessarily in NHI). Poetry may be any length but prose should be a maximum of 2000 words. A disc-based mag for PCs is planned - write for details.

Addresses

Editorial:	30 Werneth Avenue, Gee Cross, Hyde, Cheshire SK14 5NL
Reviews:	As above
Subscriptions:	As above

Payment terms
to contributors: Contributor's copy; discount on extra copies
Accept/Rejection
approximate times: Usually speedily, but can be up to 3 months at very busy
                        periods
Inserts accepted: Up to 50 (with exchange service)
Price per 1000:   Free; otherwise £30 for 600; 10% discount for members of
                        ALP
Circulation: 600+

NEW SCOTTISH EPOCH

Frequency:	Depending on funds (usually twice yearly minimum)
Subscription Cost:	£5 for 5 issues
Single Issue:	£1
Back issue price:	Sample copy of early editions on request
Cheques/PO Payable to:	The Corbie Press
Overseas subs:	£10 Europe/America
Payment Details:	IMO. Sterling cheque, postal order, foreign currencies must allow for exchange charge.

Description

Epoch (founded 1991) features Scottish material in the context of European and World literature & art. Epoch is open to politics, philosophy, poetry. Leading article is usually on a major figure in Scottish literature (e.g. R.B. Cunninghame Grahame) plus articles on European artists (e.g. Goya) and writers (e.g. Victor Serge). Liberal/socialist ethos but not dogmatic - have carried articles on Nietszche in the past!

Addresses

Editorial:	57 Murray Street, Montrose, Angus, Scotland, DD10 8JZ
Reviews:	As above
Subscriptions:	As above
Payment terms to contributors:	Two free copies
Accept/Rejection approximate times:	About one in ten acceptances, usually over-subscribed with poetry! Decision time about 6-10 weeks
Inserts accepted:	Yes
Price per 1000:	Free if reciprocated
Circulation:	Increasing

NEW WELSH REVIEW

Frequency:	Quarterly
Subscription Cost:	£28 for two years
Single Issue:	£3.60 + p&p
Back issue price:	£3.00
Cheques/PO Payable to:	New Welsh Review Ltd
Overseas subs:	Sub cost + £2 surface £6 airmail
Payment Details:	Sterling P.O./cheque/visa

Description
A literary magazine publishing literary articles, previously unpublished new short stories and poems and reviews of books with a Welsh connection.

Addresses

Editorial:	Chapter Arts Centre, Marret Road, Canton, Cardiff, Wales, CF5 1QE
Reviews:	As above
Subscriptions:	As above
Payment terms to contributors:	Articles £20 per 1000 words, Short stories £50
Accept/Rejection approximate times:	3 months
Inserts accepted:	Yes
Price per 1000:	£100
Circulation:	900

NEW WRITER THE

Frequency: 10 per annum
Subscription Cost: £29.50
Single Issue: £2.95
Back issue price: £2.95
Cheques/PO Payable to: The New Writer
Overseas subs:
Payment Details: Sterling

Description

The New Writer is a contemporary writing magazine which publishes the best in fact, fiction and poetry. It is for anyone who wants to read the best in contemporary writing. The New Writer incorporates the old Quartos and Acclaim magazines.

Addresses

Editorial: P.O. Box 60, Cranbrook, Kent, TN17 2ZR
Reviews: As above
Subscriptions: As above
Payment terms
to contributors: £20 per 1000 words non-fiction£10 per story - £3 per poem
Accept/Rejection
approximate times: 1 month
Inserts accepted: Yes
Price per 1000:   £50
Circulation: 2000

NIGHT DREAMS

Frequency:	Quarterly
Subscription Cost:	£10.50
Single Issue:	£2.80
Back issue price:	£2.50
Cheques/PO Payable to:	Kirk S King
Overseas subs:	£12.50
Payment Details:	IMO, cheque, postal order

Description
Night Dreams (Founded 1994) features poetry, short stories and articles concerning the weird, the frightening and the gruesome. It follows the style of the pulp magazines of the '30s and '40s. Each issue approximately 48 A4 pages.

Addresses

Editorial:	52 Denman Lane, Huncote, Leicester LE9 3BS
Reviews:	As above
Subscriptions:	47 Stephens Road, Walmley, Sutton Coldfield, West Midlands B76 2TS
Payment terms to contributors:	£3 per 1000 + free copy
Accept/Rejection approximate times:	
Inserts accepted:	Yes
Price per 1000:	£10
Circulation:	300 (increasing weekly)

NINETIES POETRY

Frequency: Quarterly
Subscription Cost:
Single Issue: £4.95 + 38p postage
Back issue price: £4.95 + 38p postage
Cheques/PO Payable to: G. Ackroyd
Overseas subs: N/A
Payment Details: N/A

Description
Perfect bound A5 booklet. Containing poems from a variety of writers.

Addresses
Editorial: 33 Lansdowne Press, Hove BN3 1HF
Reviews:
Subscriptions:
Payment terms
to contributors: When I have money
Accept/Rejection
approximate times: N/A
Inserts accepted: No
Price per 1000:   N/A
Circulation: 200

NORTH THE

Frequency:	Twice a year
Subscription Cost:	£10 for 2 issues post free
Single Issue:	£5.50 plus £1 p&p
Back issue price:	£2
Cheques/PO Payable to:	The Poetry Business Ltd
Overseas subs:	£16 for 2 issues
Payment Details:	Cheque, P.O, Cash in sterling

Description
The North magazine offers the best of contemporary poetry by new and established writers, as well as critical articles, reviews, Submissions are welcome (up to 6 poems; please enclose SAE).

Addresses
Editorial:	The North, The Studio, Byram Arcade, Westgate, Huddersfield, HD1 1ND
Reviews:	As above
Subscriptions:	As above
Payment terms to contributors:	By arrangement
Accept/Rejection approximate times:	1 month
Inserts accepted:	Yes
Price per 1000:	Minimum charge £10
Circulation:	500

NORTHWORDS

Frequency:	3 per year
Subscription Cost:	7.50 per 3 issues
Single Issue:	2.50
Back issue price:	2.50
Cheques/PO Payable to:	NORTHWORDS
Overseas subs:	£10.00 per 3 issues
Payment Details:	Prefer sterling / cheque

Description

Fiction, poetry, reviews in English, Gaelic, Scots (all varieties) Submissions: SAE up to 5 poems, 3 stories, fiction: prefer not over 3000 words. It is ESSENTIAL to read the magazine before submitting - no bonnie purple heather poems please.

Addresses

Editorial:	Tom Bryan, Editor, 68 Straithkanaird, Ullarpool, Wester Ross, Scotland, IV26 2TU
Reviews:	As above
Subscriptions:	As above
Payment terms to contributors:	Complimentary copies only
Accept/Rejection approximate times:	6 - 8 weeks, needs change - study magazine we get a surplus of poetry
Inserts accepted:	
Price per 1000:	
Circulation:	500 plus

OASIS

Frequency:	6 times a year (currently mailed in batches of 2 , 3 times a year.
Subscription Cost:	£5.00
Single Issue:	£1.50
Back issue price:	
Cheques/PO Payable to:	Oasis Books
Overseas subs:	$15.00 or sterling equivalent
Payment Details:	

Description

OASIS aims to present a wide range of excellent writing, concentrating on originality of thought, expression and imagination. In doing this , it tends to veer towards the non-traditional, the experimental, in both poetry and prose. Translations are a strong feature of the magazine. Those intending to submit work should, ideally , purchase a copy or two first to discover the nature of the magazine. Only about 1% of submissions are accepted.

Addresses

Editorial:	12 Stevenage Road, London, SW6 6ES
Reviews:	As above
Subscriptions:	As above
Payment terms to contributors:	Copies
Accept/Rejection approximate times:	1 month
Inserts accepted:	
Price per 1000:	
Circulation:	Circulated only to subscribers, (c.350) no bookshop sales.

OBJECT PERMANENCE

Frequency:	3 issues yearly
Subscription Cost:	£7.50 (inc. p & p)
Single Issue:	£2.50
Back issue price:	£2.50
Cheques/PO Payable to:	Object Permanence
Overseas subs:	£9 surface mail £12 airmail
Payment Details:	UK Cheque/postal order. Overseas Sterling IMO if possible

Description

Open to most kinds of short stories. Has a definite bias towards experimental/modernist work. Each issue contains texts from exemplars of the aberrant traditions of the U.S. and the U.K. plus a substantial reviews section and as much information as will fit. Featured writers have included Clark Coolidge, Barry Macsweeney, Fiona Templeton and Drew Milne.

Addresses

Editorial:	Robin Purves, 121 Menock Road, Kingspark, Glasgow G44 5SD
Reviews:	As above
Subscriptions:	As above
Payment terms to contributors:	No payment. Contributors get free copies
Accept/Rejection approximate times:	1 month
Inserts accepted:	No
Price per 1000:	
Circulation:	International

OCULAR

Frequency:	Frequency Quarterly
Subscription Cost:	£8
Single Issue:	£2.25
Back issue price:	£2
Cheques/PO Payable to:	Lesley E Wilkinson
Overseas subs:	£1 extra
Payment Details:	Cheque, postal order, cash - cash overseas

Description

Ocular has sections on: articles, artwork, short stories, cartoons, poems, news and letters. All written work sent for consideration should be typed or legibly handwritten.

Addresses

Editorial:	Rosewood Cottage, Langtoft, East Yorks YO25 OTQ
Reviews:	As above
Subscriptions:	As above
Payment terms to contributors:	Free magazine
Accept/Rejection approximate times:	1 month
Inserts accepted:	Yes
Price per 1000:	£1
Circulation:	Growing

ODYSSEY

Frequency:	3 times a year
Subscription Cost:	£8.00 (3 issues)
Single Issue:	£3.00
Back issue price:	£2.50
Cheques/PO Payable to:	Odyssey Poets
Overseas subs:	Europe £10.00 / £3.50: USA £15.00 / £5.0
Payment Details:	Sterling only

Description

A spine bound magazine publishing new poetry and prose relevant to the present time frequently features special issues:# 18. Poetry and Place# 20. Poetry of the City (guest editor Elisabeth Bletsoe)# 21. 21st Anniversary issue (double issue)

Addresses

Editorial:	Coleridge Cottage, Nether Stowey, Somerset, TA5 1NQ
Reviews:	As above
Subscriptions:	As above
Payment terms to contributors:	Free copy
Accept/Rejection approximate times:	4 - 8 weeks
Inserts accepted:	Yes
Price per 1000:	Usually on exchange basis
Circulation:	c 300

ONE

Frequency:	Quarterly
Subscription Cost:	£4 p.a.
Single Issue:	£1.20
Back issue price:	70p
Cheques/PO Payable to:	One
Overseas subs:	3 x IRCs per magazine, Annual subs quote
Payment Details:	Send to the editor

Description

One is a gentle Christian correspondence magazine. It features articles, stories, letters, poetry, a book review, record reviews, Astronomy and Bible studies. There is a literary competition in each edition. There is also a Befriender service, a cassette and paperback postal library. An information service, a penfriend club, a blanket bank where readers knit for charity, and a free birthday card on request (UK only). Anyone may contribute to the One magazine.

Addresses

Editorial:	Mrs. Wendy K. Caroy, 48 South Street, Colchester, Essex CO2 7BJ
Reviews:	As above
Subscriptions:	As above
Payment terms to contributors:	One free copy if work is published
Accept/Rejection approximate times:	3 weeks
Inserts accepted:	Yes
Price per 1000:	Free
Circulation:	200

ORBIS

Frequency:	Quarterly
Subscription Cost:	£15
Single Issue:	£4
Back issue price:	£2
Cheques/PO Payable to:	Orbis magazine
Overseas subs:	U.S $28
Payment Details:	£5 per acceptance, £50 per issue in prizes

Description

This is from No 94 (Autumn 94): primarily a poetry magazine and though we do publish prose titles occasionally, we do not use much in a year. (max:1000 words, not formula fiction) We use virtually every kind of poetry, except the more extreme experimental type or poetry in which the message occludes the language. Likely to accept work from new writers, but accept only about 2% of what we receive.

Addresses

Editorial:	199 The Long Shoot, Nuneaton, Warks,CV11 6JO
Reviews:	As above
Subscriptions:	As above
Payment terms to contributors:	£5 per acceptance
Accept/Rejection approximate times:	Return post
Inserts accepted:	Yes
Price per 1000:	£50
Circulation:	1000

OTHER POETRY

Frequency:	3 issues p.a.
Subscription Cost:	£9
Single Issue:	£3
Back issue price:	£1.50
Cheques/PO Payable to:	Other Poetry
Overseas subs:	£9.50 surface mail £10 airmail
Payment Details:	In sterling

Description

Other Poetry was published in Leicester from 1979 to 1989, and was revived in Newcastle in 1994. It consists of poetry and reviews. The poetry is judged by a panel of four editors, and is considered on no other grounds than merit.

Addresses

Editorial:	Evangeline Paterson, 8 Oakhurst Terrace, Benton, Newcastle upon Tyne NE12 9NY Tel. 0191 266 2311
Reviews:	Michael Standen, 29 Western Hill, Durham DH1 4RL
Subscriptions:	As Editorial
Payment terms to contributors:	£5 per poem
Accept/Rejection approximate times:	4-6 weeks
Inserts accepted:	Yes
Price per 1000:	£20
Circulation:	130-150

OUTPOSTS POETRY QUARTERLY

Frequency:	Quarterly
Subscription Cost:	£12 for 4. £22 for 8 UK rate
Single Issue:	Varies on average £4.00
Back issue price:	£3.00 except specials
Cheques/PO Payable to:	Hippopotamus Press
Overseas subs:	£16 for 4, £26 for 8
Payment Details:	Visa / Access / Master Card.

Description

For more than fifty years OUTPOSTS has published new poetry both by the established and the yet to be recognised. The magazine has never supported a dogma, nor a coterie: it has been our policy to publish the best from the unsolicited material we receive.Two issues each year are general issues of new poetry plus reviews, one of which will usually include an essay on some aspect of poetry such as Peter Dale's informed essay on modern rhyme techniques in issue 168. One issue a year will look at the work of a living poet, such as our issues on Edward Lowbury, Sylvia Kantaris and Derek Walcott and the fourth is a larger anthology issue with a section for translations. OUTPOSTS is one of the few magazines open to new translations.It has been said that OUTPOSTS is the place to find tomorrow's poets today. Our policy of printing the unrecognised alongside the established is probably the reason for the magazine's survival for more than fifty years. The magazine is part of the HIPPOPOTAMUS PRESS and it is not surprising that some who had their first poems printed in OUTPOSTS have gone on to have full collections published by HIPPOPOTAMUS PRESS. Recent issues have included new poetry by Alan Brownjohn, Elizabeth Bartlett, Peter Dale, John Heath-Stubbs, Elizabeth Jennings, James Kirkup, Lotte Kramer, Edward Lowbury, Peter Regrove, Peter Russell, C.H. Sisson, Vernon Scannell, Penelope Shuttle and prose from Peter Dale, Anna Martin, Brian Merrikin Hill, Shaun McCarthy, William Oxley.

Addresses

Editorial:	Hippopotamus Press, 22 Whitewell Road, Frome, Somerset, BA11 4EL
Reviews:	As above

Subscriptions:	As above
Payment terms to contributors:	Small, £5 a page, more for commisioned articles
Accept/Rejection approximate times:	One week
Inserts accepted:	Yes
Price per 1000:	£90
Circulation:	1200

OUTREACH MAGAZINE

Frequency:	Quarterly
Subscription Cost:	Free to housebound elderly, disabled
Single Issue:	N/A
Back issue price:	N/A
Cheques/PO Payable to:	N/A
Overseas subs:	N/A
Payment Details:	N/A

Description
Outreach Founded 1964 as a magazine solely for housebound elderly and disabled. Accepts articles: short stories, poetry, comic articals and illustrations, gardening, cookery and other interesting topics. The idea of magazine is to produce a lively magazine to bring a bit of life interest to people who are shut away at home between four walls 24 hours a day, 365 days a year.

Addresses

Editorial:	7 Grayson Close, Stocksbridge, Sheffield, S.Yorks S30 5BJ
Reviews:	-
Subscriptions:	As above
Payment terms to contributors:	Nil
Accept/Rejection approximate times:	-
Inserts accepted:	Yes
Price per 1000:	£1.50
Circulation:	Circulation 700/800

OXFORD POETRY

Frequency:	3 times per year (irregular)
Subscription Cost:	£7.50
Single Issue:	£2.40 plus p&p
Back issue price:	£1 plus p&p
Cheques/PO Payable to:	Oxford Poetry
Overseas subs:	
Payment Details:	Overseas payments by IMO

Description
Since its arrival in 1983 Oxford Poetry has attached a sound leadership and many favourable reviews. Tom Paulishars called it one of the best magazines in the country The main purpose of the magazine is to be a forum for new poets work (and we have a talent for spotting poets early!), but each issue also includes reviews, interviews, features, a translation competition and work by famous writers. In 1990 Seamus Heaney established the Richard Ellman prize for the best poem in each volume of the magazine.

Addresses

Editorial:	Sinead Garrigan, Oxford Poetry, Magdalen College, Oxford, OX1 4AU
Reviews:	As above
Subscriptions:	As above
Payment terms to contributors:	No payment
Accept/Rejection approximate times:	6 months max.
Inserts accepted:	No
Price per 1000:	N/A
Circulation:	500

OXFORD QUARTERLY REVIEW

Frequency:	Quarterly
Subscription Cost:	Institutional - £20, Individual - £16
Single Issue:	£5
Back issue price:	£3.50
Cheques/PO Payable to:	Oxford Quarterly Review
Overseas subs:	USA $25 or $30 institutional
Payment Details:	

Description
The Oxford Quarterly Review is a high-quality literary journal devoted to publishing the finest in contemporary poetry and fiction. Issue one featured new poetry by Les Murray and an essay on film-montage by David Marnet. The second issue featured poetry by eight Pulitzer prize-winning authors, as well as Edwin Morgan, Miles Chapman and first-time translations of top Rumanian and Polish poets. The third issue: new poetry by Adrienne Rich, James Dickey, Donald Justice, Philip Levine, Michael Middleton and Louise Glück. Unsolicited poems, fiction welcome as are reviews of contemporary writing.

Addresses
Editorial:	Editor, St Catherine's College, Oxford, OX1 3VS
Reviews:	As above
Subscriptions:	As above
Payment terms to contributors:	Copy
Accept/Rejection approximate times:	2 weeks, unless held for consideration
Inserts accepted:	Yes
Price per 1000:	£100
Circulation:	500

P.N. REVIEW

Frequency:	6 times a year
Subscription Cost:	£24.50 1 year US $49 1 year £46.50 2 years US $93
Single Issue:	£4.50
Back issue price:	£4.50
Cheques/PO Payable to:	P.N Review
Overseas subs:	US $49 1 year US $93 2 years
Payment Details:	Sterling cheque/Access/Visa

Description

Six times a year. Reports, articles, poems, translations and reviews compete for space in Britain's most independent literary magazine. Committed to the traditional and the expermental in poetry. P.N. Review has remained above contemporary trends in theory and criticism. The emphasis is always on poems before poets, content over personality. From its pugnacious beginning in the early seventies, to its present distinction as a place of disvoery and appraisal, P.N. Review has been at the cutting edge of intellectual debate. Well away from the London-Oxbridge axis, P.N. Review has carved out a unique niche in the precarious world of literary magazines. In an age of post-modern relativism and uncertainty, it has taken its bearings from Modernism in the crucial foundation of the twentieth century canon. Contriutors include: Eavan Boland, C.H. Sisson,Mark Doty, John Ashbery, David Constantine & Sujata Bhatt.

Addresses

Editorial:	402-406 Corn Exchange, Manchester M4 3BY
Reviews:	As above
Subscriptions:	As above
Payment terms to contributors:	Dependent on length of article
Accept/Rejection approximate times:	4/6 weeks to hear - fluctuates
Inserts accepted:	Yes
Price per 1000:	£380 for all subscribers
Circulation:	1500

PAGES

Frequency:	Irregular - several a year
Subscription Cost:	£12 for 12 issues (post free)
Single Issue:	£3
Back issue price:	£3
Cheques/PO Payable to:	Robert Sheppard
Overseas subs:	£24 in sterling equivalent
Payment Details:	

Description

PAGES, in the current second series (the 12 issues), is subtitled resources for the linguistic innovative poetries. It features a selected writer, with 10pp of her or his work , a page essay, a 2 page response to the texts in the issue and a bibography. The attempt is to raise awareness of a particular question of writers. I am not looking for contributions to this series (but I don't know what a third series might bring). The poets are : Adrian Clarke, Ulli Freer, John Wilkinson, Hazel Smith, Alan Halsey, Rod Menghan. Virginia Firuberg, Ken Edwards, Maggie O` Sullivan, Cris Cheek, Peter Middleton, and Gilbert Adair.

Addresses

Editorial:	15 Oakapple Road, Southwick, Sussex BN42 4YL
Reviews:	As above
Subscriptions:	As above
Payment terms to contributors:	Free copies
Accept/Rejection approximate times:	
Inserts accepted:	No
Price per 1000:	
Circulation:	100 plus

PALADIN

Frequency:	Annually at present
Subscription Cost:	£1.50 a copy
Single Issue:	As above
Back issue price:	£1
Cheques/PO Payable to:	Ken Morgan
Overseas subs:	£2 a copy
Payment Details:	

Description
Publishes stories, poems, articles on a literary topic, puzzles and jokes accepted too.
28 - 36 pages. We hope to publish twice a year, if possible.

Addresses

Editorial:	Ken Morgan, 66 Heywood Court, Tenby, Dyfed, SA70 8BS
Reviews:	As above
Subscriptions:	As above
Payment terms to contributors:	Copies of magazines occasionally free booklets and pamphlets.
Accept/Rejection approximate times:	As soon as possible usually within a month.
Inserts accepted:	Yes
Price per 1000:	Free if smaller than A5 page
Circulation:	50 - 100

PALPI (poetry and little press information)

Frequency: 2 per year
Subscription Cost: £4.50 (for 3 issues)
Single Issue: £1.50
Back issue price: £1.50
Cheques/PO Payable to: Association of Little Presses (ALP)
Overseas subs:
Payment Details:

Description
PALPI is a bibliographical listing magazine of books of all kinds published by smaller, independent publishers two others.** It is possible to subscribe to PALPI without being a member of ALP.

Addresses
Editorial: 12 Stevenage Road, London SW6 6ES
Reviews: N/A
Subscriptions: To: ALP
Payment terms
to contributors: N/A
Accept/Rejection
approximate times: N/A
Inserts accepted: No
Price per 1000:
Circulation: To members of ALP and other subscribers (c500)

PARATAXIS: Modernism + Modern Writing

Frequency:	Twice a year
Subscription Cost:	£6.00 / £10 institutions
Single Issue:	£3.00 / £5 institutions
Back issue price:	£3.00 / £5 institutions
Cheques/PO Payable to:	Drew Milne
Overseas subs:	
Payment Details:	In sterling

Description

Parataxis is devoted to the critical re-thinking of modernism and to the publication and discussion of contemporary writing. It seeks to provide a forum for discussing critical theory and critical issues, in relation to avant-garde literary traditions of various kinds. Parataxis does not publish unsolicited poetry. The journal will publish occasional issues devoted to particular topics and writers. Anyone thinking of writing for Parataxis is advised to discuss it with the editor first.

Addresses

Editorial:	Drew Milne, School of English and American Studies, University of Sussex, Falmer, Brighton, BN1 9QN
Reviews:	As above
Subscriptions:	As above
Payment terms to contributors:	None - 2 copies of issue in which work appears
Accept/Rejection approximate times:	
Inserts accepted:	Yes
Price per 1000:	Free to non-profit organisations
Circulation:	250 copies sold per issue

PASSION

Frequency:	Quarterly
Subscription Cost:	£10, £15 institutions
Single Issue:	£2.50
Back issue price:	£2.50
Cheques/PO Payable to:	Crescent Moon
Overseas subs:	$22.00 Individuals, $30 Institutions
Payment Details:	In US dollars to J Robinson or in sterling

Description

Poetry, Fiction, Arts, Criticism, Culture.* Each year Crescent Moon is publishing four collections of poetry, fiction, reviews, and essays on fine art, cinema, music, politics, philosophy, the media, feminism and many kinds of criticism drawn from the UK, Europe, Canada and North America.* Many writers are being published for the first time here, while others are established writers who are featured in publications throughout the world.* Well-known poets and artists such as Andrea Dworkin, Richard Long, V.S Naipaul, Peter Redgrove, D.J. Enright, Penelope Shuttle, Colin Wilson, Ronald Blythe, Edwin Mullins, Geoffrey Ashe, Alan Bold and Jeremy Reed featured in the first issues.* The work ranges from the passionate, erotic and spiritual, to the humorous, polemical and incisive but it is always entertaining.

Addresses

Editorial:	PO Box 393, Maidstone, Kent ME14 5XY
Reviews:	As above
Subscriptions:	As above
Payment terms to contributors:	Negotiable
Accept/Rejection approximate times:	4 months
Inserts accepted:	Yes
Price per 1000:	£30.00
Circulation:	200

PAUSE

Frequency: bi-annual
Subscription Cost: £5
Single Issue: £2.50
Back issue price: £2.50
Cheques/PO Payable to: National Poetry Foundation
Overseas subs: £8 p.a.
Payment Details: Sterling money order only

Description
Perfectly bound magazine now in its 23rd year. Usually 51 pages, work of NPF subscribers and general information.

Addresses
Editorial: 27 Mill Road, Fareham, Hants PO16 0TH Editor: Helen
                         Robinson
Reviews: Only NPF Subscribers
Subscriptions: As above
Payment terms
to contributors: NPF subscribers only
Accept/Rejection
approximate times: by return of post
Inserts accepted: We carry flyers of things of value to poetry and poets free. If
                         we do not feel the item is of value we will not carry it for any
                         money!
Price per 1000:   Free
Circulation: 1204 at present

PEACE & FREEDOM

Frequency:	Twice yearly
Subscription Cost:	£6 for 4 issues
Single Issue:	£1.50
Back issue price:	£1
Cheques/PO Payable to:	Peace & Freedom
Overseas subs:	$13
Payment Details:	UK by cheque or postal order. Overseas by IMO or bank notes.

Description

Peace & Freedom is a magazine of poetry, prose and art which focuses on humanitarian/environmental issues mainly, but not solely. We also run poetry competitions and forms are available for an SAE/IRC. Peace & Freedom was established in 1985 and has issued a number of booklets and books under the Peace & Freedom Press banner. For full details of Peace & Freedom Press please send an SAE/IRC.

Addresses

Editorial:	17 Farrow Road, Whaplode Drove, Spalding, Lincs PE12 0TS
Reviews:	As above
Subscriptions:	As above
Payment terms to contributors:	Free issue when work is published
Accept/Rejection approximate times:	Less than 3 months
Inserts accepted:	Yes
Price per 1000:	£20/$50
Circulation:	500

PEEPING TOM

Frequency:	Quarterly
Subscription Cost:	£8
Single Issue:	£2.25
Back issue price:	£1.50 (3 or more back issues £1 each)
Cheques/PO Payable to:	Peeping Tom Magazine
Overseas subs:	Europe £9.75 USA $22
Payment Details:	

Description

Small press magazine (52 x A5 pages) of short stories in the horror genre (Psychological/Supernatural/Dark Fantasy). Illustrated (5 full page b/w illos per issue). Twice winner of the British Fantasy Society Award for 'best small press.' Includes 'big names' and newcomers. No poetry, no articles, no reviews. Strictly fiction only. Stories should be 100-3000 words, the longer stories used if exceptional.

Addresses

Editorial:	Stuart Hughes, 4 Pottery Close, Belper, Derbyshire DE56 0HU
Reviews:	-
Subscriptions:	David Bell, Yew Tree House, 15 Nottingham Road, Ashby-de-la-Zouch, Leics LE65 1DJ
Payment terms to contributors:	£2.50 per thousand words + complimentary copy
Accept/Rejection approximate times:	3 weeks
Inserts accepted:	No (but adverts accepted £10 per A5 page £5 per half page)
Price per 1000:	N/A
Circulation:	350

PENDRAGON

Frequency:	3 yearly
Subscription Cost:	£6
Single Issue:	£2
Back issue price:	£2
Cheques/PO Payable to:	Pendragon
Overseas subs:	Write for info. enclose IRCs (2)
Payment Details:	IMO Sterling cheque

Description

Pendragon is an Arthurian interest magazine produced by the membership of the Pendragon Society since 1959. It has a wide readership in this Country and around the World. News, reviews, articles, letters, some poetry. All aspects of Arthurian and related interests: archaelogy, history, folklore, legend, literature, the arts and the media. Membership of the society is extended to annual subscribers who are given half price advertising rates and priority contribution acceptance.

Addresses

Editorial:	9 Earls Lea, Flint, Clwyd CH6 5BT
Reviews:	As above
Subscriptions:	Smithy House, Newton-by-Frodsham, Cheshire WA6 6SX
Payment terms to contributors:	Free copy
Accept/Rejection approximate times:	2 weeks
Inserts accepted:	Yes
Price per 1000:	£12
Circulation:	600 subscribers, increasing rapidly

PENINSULAR

Frequency:	Quarterly
Subscription Cost:	£10.50 per 4 issues
Single Issue:	£3.00
Back issue price:	£2.50
Cheques/PO Payable to:	Cherrybite Publications
Overseas subs:	£12 or £4.50 single issue
Payment Details:	Sterling or travellers cheques

Description
A literary magazine featuring well written stories and short articles, designed to inform and entertain. Essential to study magazine or send for guide lines before submitting. A5 format, card cover, 48 pages.

Addresses

Editorial:	Cherrybite Publications, Linden Cottage, 45 Burton Road, Little Weston, S-Wirral, L64 4AE
Reviews:	As above
Subscriptions:	As above
Payment terms to contributors:	£5 per 1000 words, plus free copy
Accept/Rejection approximate times:	Hopefully within a month MUST enclose S.A.E.
Inserts accepted:	Yes
Price per 1000:	Reciprocal
Circulation:	200

PENNILESS PRESS THE

Frequency:	Quarterly
Subscription Cost:	£8.50
Single Issue:	£2.50
Back issue price:	£2.50
Cheques/PO Payable to:	Penniless Press
Overseas subs:	£8.50
Payment Details:	Cheque/postal order

Description

Founded in 1995 by Alan Dent, Penniless Press publishes poems, stories, philosophy, criticism and reviews. Prose writers should try to limit their articles/stories to 3000 words approx.The magazine seeks to embrace a wide range of intellectual and artistic interests and to be international in outlook. It has published articles on American literature, jazz, modern Greek poetry, French philosophy, working-class fiction, Freud, the state of contemporary Britain, translations of contemporary Latin American poets, poems by established and previously unpublished writers, and short fiction as well as reviews of poetry, philosophy, prose and new drama. Its eclectic nature gives it appeal to readers who are prepared to stray beyond the normal boundaries of little magazines. In prose, the editor admires the clarity of George Orwell and Irving Howe. In poetry, the openness of Whitman and the simplicity of Neruda.Forthcoming issues will include work on Abstract Expressionism, Bebop, Odysseus Elytis, the idea of Progress, Elizabeth Bishop, Dwight Macdonald, Delmore Schwartz drama (including essays on Howard Korder, Kevin Elyd, Conar McPhersan, David Mamet). New short fiction with a story each issue from Tom Wood and poems by Fred Voss, Joan Jobe Smith, Steven Blyth, David Caddy, Nicholas Guillen, Mario Montalbetti, Jose Cerna, Jose Watanabe and others.

Addresses

Editorial:	100 Waterloo Road, Ashton, Preston PR2 1EP
Reviews:	As above
Subscriptions:	As above
Payment terms to contributors:	None
Accept/Rejection	

approximate times: 2 weeks
Inserts accepted: Yes
Price per 1000:   Will exchange inserts
Circulation: 200

PENNINE INK

Frequency:	Yearly
Subscription Cost:	£2.10 (including postage per issue)
Single Issue:	£1.85
Back issue price:	£1.50
Cheques/PO Payable to:	Pennine Ink Writers Workshop
Overseas subs:	N/A Cost per magazine + suitable postage
Payment Details:	Cash, cheque, postal order, IMO

Description

Pennine Ink, founded in the 1980s by Pennine Ink Writers workshop, is a yearly magazine featuring poetry, prose and illustrations. It accepts a wide variety of poems (no more than 40 lines), and prose (short stories and articles 1200 words maximum). Illustrations should be suitable for an A5 format. Given that Pennine Ink is published only once a year, it is happy to accept Small Press magazines for review. Work from overseas as well as from the UK is welcomed. Contributions can only be returned if sae with sufficient postage is included. 38p or equivalent to cover cost of sending magazine to successful contributors would be appreciated. Publication of Pennine Ink No 18 is due June 1997.

Addresses

Editorial:	Christine Potter c/o Mid Pennine Arts, Yorke Street, Burnley, Lancs BB11 1HD
Reviews:	As above
Subscriptions:	Joan McEvoy c/o Mid Pennine Arts at above address
Payment terms to contributors:	Free copy of magazine
Accept/Rejection approximate times:	Up to 12 months
Inserts accepted:	Yes
Price per 1000:	N/A
Circulation:	300+ increasing

PENNINE PLATFORM

Frequency:	3 per year
Subscription Cost:	£8.50 for three
Single Issue:	£2.50 plus 30p post
Back issue price:	£2.50 plus 30p post
Cheques/PO Payable to:	Pennine Platform
Overseas subs:	£12.00 in sterling or £17 in currency
Payment Details:	

Description

A magazine whose policy is independent, avoiding all establishments and sects. All contributions welcome but preference for form (not aimless free verse with no ordering) and for poems of awareness, personal, socio-political and religious, but avoiding propaganda and the conventional. Translations welcome. Submit no more than six poems at once, with name and address on every sheet, and S.A.E. Editorial comments on submissions are rare. Contains reviews, usually by editor or commissioned.

Addresses

Editorial:	Ingmanthorpe Hall Farm Cottage, Wetherby, LS22 5EQ
Reviews:	As above
Subscriptions:	As above
Payment terms to contributors:	None, Two copies
Accept/Rejection approximate times:	Three months
Inserts accepted:	Yes
Price per 1000:	£15, £5 for each issue
Circulation:	300

PEOPLES POETRY THE

Frequency:	Quarterly
Subscription Cost:	£5.00
Single Issue:	£1.50
Back issue price:	£1.50
Cheques/PO Payable to:	The Peoples Poetry
Overseas subs:	£5.00 and sufficient IRCs
Payment Details:	British or Foreign currency

Description
A magazine of allessible poetry on any theme but specialises in lyrical poetry and poetry of the romantic school, particularly sympathetic to traditional rhyme and rhythm and traditional poetic forms. A high romantic and spiritual emphasis, poems containing slang and swear words are unlikely to be accepted, poems of the heart rather than the head are favoured.

Addresses

Editorial:	Peter Geoffrey Paul Thompson, 71 Harrow Crescent, Romford, Essex, RM3 7BJ
Reviews:	As above
Subscriptions:	As above
Payment terms to contributors:	One complimentary copy
Accept/Rejection approximate times:	Normally within four weeks
Inserts accepted:	No
Price per 1000:	
Circulation:	500

PERSPECTIVE

Frequency:	Irregular soon to be monthly. Also internet pages
Subscription Cost:	Distributed to Guild Members
Single Issue:	
Back issue price:	
Cheques/PO Payable to:	
Overseas subs:	
Payment Details:	

Description

It is often very difficult for new writers to their work published: as the platform for short fiction has traditionally been limited. Even the magazines aimed at new writers. offer few opportunities, being in the main full of helpful articles by established authors. Our magazine provides an opportunity for new writers to see their work in print and to receive feedback. Perspective is a mixture of articles and the work of new writers. It presents new talent to a broad audience. Copies are sent to agents and publishing houses as well as to selected libraries. Material is selected by means of our annual open competition. Readers are given the opportunities to air their views and provide feedback for fellow writers. Our aim is to produce a magazine containing useful information about competitions, forthcoming events and getting work published, as well as continuing our present policy of giving general advice and promoting writing workshops. We have expanded our range by publishing a limited number of longer works. Copyright remains with the author. Extracts on internet at http://ourworld CompuServe. com / homepages / authors

Addresses

Editorial:	PO Box 1352. Glasgow G45 ODS and C15 100127.2304 or 100127.2304@ compuServe.com
Reviews:	As above
Subscriptions:	

Payment terms to contributors:	Variable, No fee for competition entries but prizes and bursaries awarded.

Accept/Rejection
approximate times: Variable
Inserts accepted: Yes
Price per 1000:   Variable - free to £50
Circulation:

PHOENIX

Frequency:	Bimonthly
Subscription Cost:	£14 a year
Single Issue:	£2.50
Back issue price:	£2.50
Cheques/PO Payable to:	Alan Baker
Overseas subs:	$30 USA ($5 for single issue)
Payment Details:	IMO, sterling cheque, postal order, foreign currency.

Description

Phoenix (Founded 1996) deals with all aspects of the paranormal/unexplained, including UFOs, hauntings, crytozoology, ESP, strange science, etc. Articles are welcomed on all of the above, together with unusual newsclippings (dated and sourced). Book reviews are also invited (items reviewed must be on relevant subjects).

Addresses

Editorial:	60 The Upper Drive, Hove, East Sussex BN3 6NE
Reviews:	As above
Subscriptions:	As above
Payment terms to contributors:	Free copy of magazine
Accept/Rejection approximate times:	1 to 2 weeks (allowing for transit in mail)
Inserts accepted:	No
Price per 1000:	N/A
Circulation:	Increasing

PLANET - The Welsh Internationalist

Frequency:	Bi-monthly
Subscription Cost:	£12.00 (UK)
Single Issue:	£2.50 (61p p&p)
Back issue price:	Varies
Cheques/PO Payable to:	Planet
Overseas subs:	£13 surface mail/airmail rates on appl.
Payment Details:	Overseas subscription preferably by bank draft in £/sterling

Description
PLANET is a bi-monthly magazine of the arts and current affairs centred on Wales but in a broader context of European culture. Articles range across subject areas such as the media, the environment, politics, theatre, visual arts, science and literature. Most of this material is commissioned. We also publish 1 short story and about 8 poems per issue, most of which are drawn from submitted material.

Addresses

Editorial:	Planet, PO Box 44, Aberystwyth, Ceredigion SY23 3ZZ
Reviews:	As above
Subscriptions:	As above
Payment terms to contributors:	£40.00 per 1000 words for prose; minimum of £25.00 per poem. Payment on publication.
Accept/Rejection approximate times:	4 Weeks
Inserts accepted:	Yes
Price per 1000:	£25.00
Circulation:	c. 1400

POETIC HOURS

Frequency:	Bi-annually
Subscription Cost:	£5 p.a.
Single Issue:	£2.50
Back issue price:	£2.50 + p & p
Cheques/PO Payable to:	Erran Publishing
Overseas subs:	£7 p.a. sterling only
Payment Details:	By standing order (UK only) sterling cheque

Description

Poetic Hours (Founded 1993) is the newsletter of the Dreamlands Poetry Group whose subscribers write much of the poetry and features within it - although outside contributors are welcomed. The magazine consists of a mixture of articles on famous poetry/poets and readers poetry. Poets are not paid but all the profits of the magazine are donated to major charities with each issue carrying reports of how money has been spent. This policy generates a positive attitude within the contributors which results in a wide range of diverse material from writers with a real enthusiasm for all aspects of poetry. Poetic Hours welcomes all types of work and subscribers are talented 'amateurs' of all ages from the UK and beyond. The magazine tends to reflect the interests poets have in reading the work of others like themselves, so regular features like 'My Xanadu' - where a subscriber examines his favourite poem and 'featured poet' allow people to read about the lives and influences of others. Poetic Hours is not for anyone who takes themselves too seriously, but should be of interest to all those who love poetry and are keen to learn and write their own.

Addresses

Editorial:	8 Dale Road, Carlton, Notts NG4 1GT (Editor Nick Clark)
Reviews:	As above
Subscriptions:	As above
Payment terms to contributors:	None
Accept/Rejection approximate times:	-

Inserts accepted:	No, unless relating to non-profit making organisations
Price per 1000:	N/A
Circulation:	Increasing

POETRY AND AUDIENCE

Frequency:	2 times/year
Subscription Cost:	£4 per annum
Single Issue:	£2.00
Back issue price:	£1.50
Cheques/PO Payable to:	The University of Leeds
Overseas subs:	£6
Payment Details:	Cheque / P/O payable as above

Description

We do not discriminate against any form of poetry but our own interests bend towards, on the one hand, a more lyrical style, and on the other, language - based experimentation. Having said this, we publish purely on the basis of merit, and obscurity is welcomed. Previous contributors include Carol Ann Duffy, Geoffrey Hill and Tony Harrison, part of an established tradition which provides a forum for unpublished poets to see their work alongside the better known practitioners.

Addresses

Editorial:	C/O School of English, University of Leeds LS2 9JT
Reviews:	As above
Subscriptions:	As above
Payment terms to contributors:	Free copy of issue
Accept/Rejection approximate times:	1 month (occasionally backlog means response takes 2 months).
Inserts accepted:	No
Price per 1000:	
Circulation:	200

POETRY IRELAND REVIEW

Frequency:	Quarterly
Subscription Cost:	Ir. £20 p.a Ireland & UK
Single Issue:	£5.00
Back issue price:	£5.00
Cheques/PO Payable to:	Poetry Ireland Ltd
Overseas subs:	£28.00 surface, £40.00 Airmail
Payment Details:	By cheque/postal order/credit card

Description

The DEFACTO journal of record in contemporary Irish poetry. We publish the best of contemporary poetry from Ireland & overseas. We review every collection of poems published in Ireland each year. The editor is appointed for 4 issues (1 year) with occasional special issues. Recent contributors: Seamus Heaney, Derek Mahon, and Paula Meehan.

Addresses

Editorial:	Poetry Ireland Review, Birmingham Tower, Dublin Castle, Dublin 2
Reviews:	As above
Subscriptions:	As above
Payment terms to contributors:	£10 per contribution or 1 years sub for poems, reviews, and articles by arrangement.
Accept/Rejection approximate times:	3 - 4 months
Inserts accepted:	Yes
Price per 1000:	£100
Circulation:	1600

POETRY LIFE

Frequency: 3 times a year
Subscription Cost: £6 per year
Single Issue: £2
Back issue price: £2
Cheques/PO Payable to: Poetry Life
Overseas subs:
Payment Details:

Description

Poetry Life was launched on the 15th April 1994 and is now fairly established as one of the UKs leading poetry magazines. The founding principle behind the magazine is to explore the booming and rich poetry scene in the UK and worldwide. To publish real interviews with poets both famous and great, produce quality articles on poetry publishers, getting work published, festivals, performance poetry, style, reviews and the politics of poetry. In the first six issues POETRY LIFE has had interviews with CAROL ANN DUFFY, JOOLZ, MICHAEL DONAGHY, LES MURRAY, JOHN COOPER CLARKE, BENJAMIN ZEPHANIAH, JAMES FENTON, WILLIAM SIEGHART, MICHAEL LONGLEY, BRIAN PATTEN and KAMAU BRATHWAITE. We have published quality articles by RICHARD TYRRELL, PAUL HYLAND, PETER FINCH, and A.A. GILL. plus articles on poetry in Zimbabwe, Performance poets in Liverpool, The R.A.B. Assessment Services, Poems on the Underground - The Poetry success story, Swansea-The UK Year of Literature, The European Association for the Promotion of Poetry, The Nuyoricans, The Sarajevo Poetry Festival, Poets of the Machine, Poetry on the Internet and 'Fifteen Years in Jail for a Poem', the true story of the poet Ali Idrissi Kaitouni by Amnesty International. All this and THE POETRY LIFE OPEN POETRY COMPETITIONS, now established as one of the premier national competitions, bringing talented poets to wider public attention.

Addresses

Editorial: Poetry Life, 14 Pennington Oval, Lymington, Hampshire, SO41 8BQ
Reviews: As above

Subscriptions: As above
Payment terms
to contributors: Payment on negotiation
Accept/Rejection
approximate times: Three months
Inserts accepted: Yes
Price per 1000:   £100
Circulation: 1300

POETRY MANCHESTER

Frequency:	Biannual
Subscription Cost:	£3.50 p.a.
Single Issue:	£2.00
Back issue price:	£2.00
Cheques/PO Payable to:	Sean Boustead
Overseas subs:	Same as UK
Payment Details:	By cheque to the editorial address

Description
Bi-annual poetry magazine / review; as many international poets and subscribers as national (India, Australia, USA., Germany, Denmark, Rep. of Ireland), Translations of European writers.

Addresses

Editorial:	13 Napier Street, Swinton, Manchester,M27 0JQ
Reviews:	As above
Subscriptions:	As above
Payment terms to contributors:	2 copies of the relevant issue
Accept/Rejection approximate times:	Up to 1 month
Inserts accepted:	No
Price per 1000:	£1125-00
Circulation:	940 (growing)

POETRY NOTTINGHAM INTERNATIONAL

Frequency:	Quarterly
Subscription Cost:	£9 per annum
Single Issue:	£2.25
Back issue price:	£1.25 inc p&p
Cheques/PO Payable to:	Poetry Nottingham
Overseas subs:	£15 sterling
Payment Details:	

Description

44 pages - poems, letters, some short reviews, short (500 word) articles on issues in poetry.

Any style of poetry that is well-written and - if in a set form - technically correct. Unpublished poetry ONLY. I particularly look for originality of subject matter, poems that appeal to the emotions but are not sentimental, and upbeat poems/subtle humour to contrast with the serious poems.

Editor: Cathy Grindrod

Addresses

Editorial:	13 Bradmore Rise, Sherwood, Nottingham NG5 3BJ
Reviews:	As above
Subscriptions:	As above
Payment terms to contributors:	Complimentary copy
Accept/Rejection approximate times:	Average 2 months
Inserts accepted:	Yes
Price per 1000:	Will exchange with other magazine
Circulation:	275

POETRY NOW MAGAZINE

Frequency:	Quarterly
Subscription Cost:	UK £14.00
Single Issue:	£3.50
Back issue price:	£3.50
Cheques/PO Payable to:	Forward Press
Overseas subs:	£18.00
Payment Details:	Postal order, cheque, visa, mastercard, America express

Description

Poetry Now Magazine tries to publish a selection of poetry that covers the broadest range of poetry the magazine's readers are writing. We aim to give enjoyment to, and answer the needs of our readers. Every letter, poem and article that comes into the office makes a difference to the shape and direction of the magazine. This is the reason why it continues to change and grow. We hope that you will become a part of the driving force.

* Poems on a Theme
* Competition News, Views and Events
* Poetry Workshop
* Articles of interest to Poets
* Profiles on Poets
* A totally refreshing Poetry Magazine

Editor: Andrew Head

Addresses

Editorial:	1-2 Wainman Road, Woodston, Peterborough,PE2 7BU
Reviews:	As above
Subscriptions:	As above
Payment terms to contributors:	Poems between £5 - £10. Articles £5 per 500 words. Other payments negotiated,

Accept/Rejection

approximate times: 12-16 weeks
Inserts accepted: Yes
Price per 1000:   Free
Circulation: 2000

POETRY REVIEW

Frequency:	Quarterly
Subscription Cost:	£23
Single Issue:	£5.95
Back issue price:	Varies
Cheques/PO Payable to:	The Poetry Society
Overseas subs:	£31 USA $56
Payment Details:	Sterling and US Dollar only, Eurocheques, Visa & Mastercard

Description
Poetry Review publishes new poems, reviews and features on contemporary poetry. Each issue has a theme illuminating tendencies and controversies. Work by the leading poets of today is published alongside the most promising new poets.

Addresses

Editorial:	The Poetry Society, 22 Betterton Street, London WC2H 9BU
Reviews:	As above
Subscriptions:	As above
Payment terms to contributors:	-
Accept/Rejection approximate times:	-
Inserts accepted:	Yes
Price per 1000:	£100
Circulation:	5000

POETRY WALES

Frequency:	Quarterly
Subscription Cost:	£10 a year (4 issues), £15 institution
Single Issue:	£2.50 plus 50p p&p
Back issue price:	£2.50 plus 50p p&p
Cheques/PO Payable to:	Poetry Wales Press Ltd
Overseas subs:	£15 a year; £20 institutions
Payment Details:	Payment in sterling only

Description

Established in 1965 to provide a platform for Welsh poets and poets living in Wales, Poetry Wales also maintains an International outlook with poetry, criticism and reviews by and about writers from all over the world. R.S Thomas, Les Murray, Dannie Abse and Fleur Adcock are regular contributors, but we also encourage new writers. We are one of the few poetry magazines to publish long poems, and we are interested in seeing formal poetry, as well as good quality free verse. We also publish translations, mainly from Welsh, but also from other European languages up to 6 poems should be submitted, with an SAE or IRCs for reply. Proposals for articles (2000-2500 words) should be sent to the Editor, potential reviewers should send a sample review to the reviews Editor in the first instance, all potential contributors are advised to read a recent issue of the magazine before submitting.

Addresses

Editorial:	Richard Poole, Poetry Wales, First Floor, 2 Wyndman Street, Bridgend, Mid Glamorgan, CF31 1EF
Reviews:	Amy Wack, 20 Denton Road, Canton, Cardiff, CF5 1TE
Subscriptions:	Clare Collett, Poetry Wales, First Floor, 2 Wyndham Street, Bridgend, Mid Glamorgan, CF31 1EF
Payment terms to contributors:	By arrangement
Accept/Rejection approximate times:	4 weeks
Inserts accepted:	Yes
Price per 1000:	Price per 700: £50 plus VAT
Circulation:	800

PQR (Poetry Quarterly Review)

Frequency:	4 times a year
Subscription Cost:	£5.00 (annual)
Single Issue:	£1.50
Back issue price:	£1.25 (No. 1)
Cheques/PO Payable to:	Odyssey Poets
Overseas subs:	Europe £8.00, USA £10.00 (airmail)
Payment Details:	Sterling only

Description

PQR was launched in Autumn 1995. It is a broadsheet (A4) magazine providing in depth reviews of both main stream and small press poetry publishing. Features include:* Reviews of poetry books and collections* Work from a FEATURED POET in each issue* Articles and essays on related topics* LISTINGS: Analysis of current poetry magazines* Editorial comment on the poetry scene* NEW VOICES: promising list collections* FRONT PAGE: major new books

Addresses

Editorial:	Coleridge Cottage, Nether Stowey, Somerset, TA5 1NQ
Reviews:	As above
Subscriptions:	As above
Payment terms to contributors:	Free copy to reviewers. Agreed fee to feature poet
Accept/Rejection approximate times:	4 weeks
Inserts accepted:	No
Price per 1000:	Advertising at reasonable rates (£3.00 - £40.00)
Circulation:	c 500

PREMONITIONS

Frequency:	Annual
Subscription Cost:	£10.00 (UK only) for 4 issues
Single Issue:	£2.50 (UK only)
Back issue price:	£2.50 (UK only)
Cheques/PO Payable to:	Tony Lee
Overseas subs:	Send SAE/IRC for details
Payment Details:	Pay by IMO in sterling

Description
The magazine anthology of science fictional horror stories, poetry and art.
PREMONITIONS publishes original stories, genre poetry, and artwork - in the form of
unique 'graphic poems'. PREMONITIONS covers exceptionally broad range of themes:
from futuristic urban shockers and mature 'space adventure', to 'mood' fiction, dark
satire, psychological terrors and surrealistic tales. PREMONITIONS is quality in
quantity with a dozen short stories in each issue!.

Addresses
Editorial:	Tony Lee, Pigasus Press, 13 Hazely Combe, Arreton. Isle of Wight, PO30 3AJ, England.
Reviews:	As above
Subscriptions:	As above
Payment terms to contributors:	None
Accept/Rejection approximate times:	Approx. one month
Inserts accepted:	No
Price per 1000:	N/A
Circulation:	Unknown

PRESENCE

Frequency:	2 issues per year minimum
Subscription Cost:	£5 / 2 issues
Single Issue:	£2.50
Back issue price:	£2.50
Cheques/PO Payable to:	Martin Lucas
Overseas subs:	£5 or $10 (US) per 2 issues
Payment Details:	

Description

PRESENCE is a Haiku magazine publishing Haiku, Senryu, Tanka, Renku and related forms in English. Other short poetry is accepted, if compatible. We are also happy to receive artwork/haiga suitable for reproduction in black/white. Books for review, and relevant announcements (publications, events) are welcome. We are also keen to publish articles on any aspect of Haiku poetry, whether relating to the Japanese tradition or to contemporary practice in English. Our minds are open.

Addresses

Editorial:	1 Eastview, Galgate, Lancaster LA2 0JT
Reviews:	As above
Subscriptions:	As above
Payment terms to contributors:	Free issue of magazine
Accept/Rejection approximate times:	Varies, generally very swift, (1 week)
Inserts accepted:	Yes
Price per 1000:	
Circulation:	110

PRINCESS SPIDER ZINE

Frequency:	Fitful
Subscription Cost:	No subscriptions
Single Issue:	£2
Back issue price:	£2
Cheques/PO Payable to:	No cheques or POs
Overseas subs:	$4
Payment Details:	Cash only

Description

The Zone is dedicated to and about Princess Spider, the notorious Hungarian Sadist. It contains work by the princess and work dedicated to her by her various slaves, sycophants and admirers.

Addresses

Editorial:	Princess Spider Zine, TY Fraen, The Park, Blaenavon, Gwent, UK, NP4 9AG
Reviews:	As above
Subscriptions:	
Payment terms to contributors:	None
Accept/Rejection approximate times:	Undefined
Inserts accepted:	
Price per 1000:	
Circulation:	250

PRINTER'S DEVIL THE

Frequency:	Twice a year
Subscription Cost:	£15.00
Single Issue:	£5.99
Back issue price:	£4.99 / £5.99 from issue 9
Cheques/PO Payable to:	The Printer's Devil
Overseas subs:	£25
Payment Details:	Mail order from top offices 13A Western Road, Hove, BN31AE

Description

We commission the best in new writing and accept some unsolicited material, but only if it suits our profile we publish interviews, essays, polemic, short fiction and poetry. We are particularly interested in the interface between culture and politics. We have included interviews with Jeffrey Archer / Helena Kennedy / Christopher Hampton and articles by Richard Gott, Marina Warner, Ronan Bennett.

Addresses

Editorial:	Top Offices, 13A Western Road, Hove,BN3 1AE
Reviews:	As above
Subscriptions:	As above
Payment terms to contributors:	£50 per thousand, poems £25
Accept/Rejection approximate times:	Up to three months
Inserts accepted:	No
Price per 1000:	
Circulation:	1500

PSYCHOPOETICA

Frequency:	4 issues per year and occasional 'theme' anthologies
Subscription Cost:	£10.00 inc. p&p
Single Issue:	£2.50 plus p&p
Back issue price:	£2.00
Cheques/PO Payable to:	G Lowe
Overseas subs:	$20
Payment Details:	In dollar notes or sterling

Description
We prefer short, experimental, unrhymed poetry - preferably under 30 lines. But since we also like to compile a large varied selection of poetry (traditional, rhymed and unrhymed, light verse, haiku, visual poems, etc.), we will read and consider any style and format. We're not too keen on self-indulgent, therapeutic poetry (unless it's very good and original), nor sweetly inspirational 'patience strong' stuff. We like poetry that has some (or all) of the following: humour, vivid imagery, powerful feelings, guts and substance, originality, creative style, boundary-shifting, punch or twist, word-play, craftsmanship....etc....Relevant artwork and graphics are frequently used; contributors are invited to experiment with various fonts and presentational effects. All submissions should be legible, typed or printed and ideally in clean, camera ready format (preferably titled in CAPITALS with author's name at the bottom plus hometown in brackets beneath). If preferred, authors may send camera ready work after acceptance. Good, clean photocopies are OK. All submissions should include self-addressed stamped envelope or IRCs for foreign mail.

Addresses

Editorial:	Geoff Lowe, Department of Psychology, University of Hull, Hull, HU6 7RX, OR Trevor Millum, Fern House, High Street, Barrow-on- Humber, DN19 7AA
Reviews:	As above
Subscriptions:	Geoff Lowe, address as above
Payment terms to contributors:	Under negotiation / contributors copy
Accept/Rejection	

approximate times:	Within 1 month normally
Inserts accepted:	Yes
Price per 1000:	£60 per 300 (or exchange deal)
Circulation:	300+

PSYCHOTROPE

Frequency:	Semi-Annually (approx.)
Subscription Cost:	£7.50 for 4 ($20)
Single Issue:	£2.10 ($4.25)
Back issue price:	£2.50 ($4.25)
Cheques/PO Payable to:	Psychotrope
Overseas subs:	See above
Payment Details:	

Description

Psychotrope is an illustrated magazine of Psychological horror, mad love and surreal short stories from new and established small press writers. Psychotrope attempts to explore the dark and disturbing underworlds of madness, obsession, secrecy and the subconscious with a unique mix of traditional and experimental prose. I am always on the lookout for good, inventive new stories for publication, but tend to avoid tales of gothic horror, the supernatural all out science fiction or 'dwarf and wizard' fantasy. The emphasis is on harsh, modern settings although occasionally I don't mind bending the rules for something surprising and fresh, assuming it fits somewhere under the banner of 'psychological horror, mad love and surrealism' Submissions of manuscripts of between 500 and 5000 words should always be accompanied by an SAE - sorry but no SAE no reply. Slightly shorter or longer pieces will always be considered if exceptional. All submissions will be replied to within 2 months and rejections are accompanied by helpful and constructive criticism. Alas, Psychotrope is not able to pay contributors in money, although they will receive a complimentary copy of the magazine. A free small Ad. section is available for books and magazines dealing with Horror / Sci Fi / fantasy / slipstream, and ads of up to 150 words should be sent to the editorial address.

Addresses

Editorial:	Flat 6, 17 Droitwich Road, Worcester,WR3 7LG
Reviews:	As above
Subscriptions:	As above
Payment terms to contributors:	Contributors copy of magazine only
Accept/Rejection	

approximate times: 1-2 months
Inserts accepted: Yes
Price per 1000:
Circulation:

PULSAR

Frequency:	Quarterly
Subscription Cost:	£10
Single Issue:	£2
Back issue price:	£2
Cheques/PO Payable to:	Ligden Publishers
Overseas subs:	Europe £10 equivalent USA $30
Payment Details:	By cheque - will accept $ dollar cheques (otherwise sterling)

Description

Pulsar- and Ligden Poetry Society (LPS) were formed by Ligden Publishers in December 1994 with the aim of encouraging the writing of poetry for pleasure and possible publication in Pulsar - (published quarterly). We seek interesting and stimulating work - thoughts, comments and observations; genial or sharp. LPS is non profit making; funds received help cover the cost of printing, distribution etc. LPS/Pulsar - are run by poetry enthusiasts for poetry enthusiasts; are not a business or corporate concern.

Addresses

Editorial:	34 Lineacre, Grange Park, Swindon, Wiltshire SW5 6DA
Reviews:	As above
Subscriptions:	As above
Payment terms to contributors:	Free copy of magazine
Accept/Rejection approximate times:	
Inserts accepted:	Yes
Price per 1000:	200/£10
Circulation:	200 and rising

PURGE

Frequency:	Occasional, usually one issue per year
Subscription Cost:	
Single Issue:	Variable
Back issue price:	£2 per issue
Cheques/PO Payable to:	R.G Hampson
Overseas subs:	
Payment Details:	

Description

PURGE is an occasional magazine of linguistically innovative poetry. It has appeared once a year - 3 issues to date; next one due in 1996. Issues are themed - or concept - based; accordingly, CONTRIBUTIONS ARE ALMOST ALWAYS BY INVITATION. PURGE accepts no responsibility for unsolicited submissions.

Addresses

Editorial:	11 Hillview Court, Hillview Road, Woking, GU22 7QN
Reviews:	Not usually included
Subscriptions:	N/A
Payment terms to contributors:	No payment
Accept/Rejection approximate times:	1 - 2 months
Inserts accepted:	No
Price per 1000:	N/A
Circulation:	200 / 300 copies

PURPLE PATCH

Frequency:	From 3 to 4 issues per year
Subscription Cost:	£3.50 for 3 issues
Single Issue:	£1.25
Back issue price:	£1.25
Cheques/PO Payable to:	G Stevens
Overseas subs:	North America $5 Europe £2 per issue
Payment Details:	

Description

Established 20 years ago, Purple Patch retains its individuality, being A4 photocopied & side - stapled it takes good poetry, preferring unrhymed copy or rhymed poetry, that satisfies the rules of the genre. Very short prose, fiction or essays, is also considered. Short reviews and a gossip column are included. The magazine is read in UK, USA, Australia, New Zealand, Germany, Spain, Mexico, USA & Canada and taken by The Poetry Library, London and libraries in the USA. Editor Geoff Stevens. Now in A5 format.

Addresses

Editorial:	8 Beaconview House, Charlemont Farm, West Bromwich, B71 3PL, England,
Reviews:	As above
Subscriptions:	As above
Payment terms to contributors:	None
Accept/Rejection approximate times:	One month
Inserts accepted:	Yes
Price per 1000:	100 - 200 free on acceptance
Circulation:	Varies

Q.W.F.

Frequency:	Quarterly (Dec, March, June, Sept)
Subscription Cost:	£12 for 4 issues
Single Issue:	£3.75
Back issue price:	£2.00
Cheques/PO Payable to:	JM Good
Overseas subs:	£15 Europe, £20 rest of the world
Payment Details:	Sterling cheques or money orders

Description

QWF aims to provide a platform for new women writers and to present a showcase of first class fiction for the discerning reader. A5 magazine around 72 pages with a glossy cover publishes about 12 short stories per issue plus articles (Against all odds' where writers tell us about their struggle for success) and a readers' letter page and editorial. Looking for original short stories which don't fit the mould; a thumping good yarn; gritty realism; a thought - pooking read, strong fresh images, forthright female characters; a story which reflects women's issues and stays in the mind long after it has been put aside. Accepts stories of less than 3000 words with covering letter, story must be previously unpublished.

Addresses

Editorial:	80 Main Street. Linton, Nr Swadlincote, Derbyshire, DE12 6QA
Reviews:	As above
Subscriptions:	As above
Payment terms to contributors:	£10 per short story, £5 per article. £5 for star letter (or a years free sub)
Accept/Rejection approximate times:	One month
Inserts accepted:	Yes
Price per 1000:	Prefer a swap or £30
Circulation:	300 subscribers and rising (1200 copies sold per year)

QUEER WORDS

Frequency:	Quarterly
Subscription Cost:	£17.95 per year
Single Issue:	£5.95
Back issue price:	£2.50
Cheques/PO Payable to:	Queer Words
Overseas subs:	£5 Europe £10 Rest of World
Payment Details:	Cheques in sterling only

Description

Queer Words (founded 1995) is the quarterly magazine of new lesbian and gay writing. Partly funded by the Arts Council for Wales, we publish both new and established writers. Contributors have included Alan Sinfield, Michael Carson, ET AL. The majority of the work we publish comes to us via our £1000 new writing prize. Fiction, non fiction and poetry all published.

Addresses

Editorial:	P.O. Box 23, Aberstwyth, Wales SY23 2AA
Reviews:	As above
Subscriptions:	As above
Payment terms to contributors:	Usually complimentary copies
Accept/Rejection approximate times:	3-6 months
Inserts accepted:	Yes
Price per 1000:	£25 non profit organisation. £50 business
Circulation:	1000

RAINBOW BRIDGE

Frequency:	Quarterly
Subscription Cost:	£6.50
Single Issue:	£2 incl. p & p
Back issue price:	£1.50 incl. p & p
Cheques/PO Payable to:	Rainbow Bridge
Overseas subs:	£10 incl. p & p
Payment Details:	Cheque/postal order

Description

Rainbow Bridge (Founded Summer 1996) is a compilation of information received by editor, and singer songwriter, Tricia Frances during meditation after a Near Death Experience in 1991. This information has lead to the founding of the International Light Foundation, a care organisation working with the long term and terminally sick and special needs children.The magazine features articles on world events, stories, poems, self awareness, healing, Wolf Wisdom, astrology, and other related subjects. Each edition features a guest poem or story and other related articles are published to back up the information received by Tricia. All profits from the magazine go towards the work of the ILF.

Addresses

Editorial:	Rainbow Bridge, The Editor, P.O. Box 136, Norwich, Norfolk NR3 3LJ
Reviews:	As above
Subscriptions:	As above
Payment terms to contributors:	Free magazine + Advertising Voucher/subscription by agreement
Accept/Rejection approximate times:	1 month
Inserts accepted:	Yes
Price per 1000:	Single A5 sheet £20
Circulation:	International. New magazine. Subscribers unknown at present. Increasing daily.

REACH

Frequency:	Quarterly
Subscription Cost:	£8
Single Issue:	£2
Back issue price:	£1.50
Cheques/PO Payable to:	Cherrybite Publications
Overseas subs:	£10 or £2.50
Payment Details:	Sterling/travellers cheque

Description

A non genre poetry magazine dedicated to helping poets into print. Readers' letters, poems, advice. A5 card cover 40 pages.

Addresses

Editorial:	Linden Cottage, 45 Burton Road, Little Neston, S. Wirral L64 4AE
Reviews:	As above
Subscriptions:	As above
Payment terms to contributors:	Copies only
Accept/Rejection approximate times:	2 weeks
Inserts accepted:	Yes
Price per 1000:	Reciprocal
Circulation:	150

RED HERRING

Frequency:	2-3 per annum
Subscription Cost:	£1 per issue
Single Issue:	£1
Back issue price:	£1
Cheques/PO Payable to:	Northumberland County Council
Overseas subs:	£1
Payment Details:	IMO, sterling cheques, postal order

Description
Red Herring is a poetry sheet which publishes new poetry of all kinds. It is distributed free through Northumberland libraries thereby reaching a wide membership, though contributors do not have to live in Northumberland to be accepted. Each issue includes a neglected classic poem taken from the English Poetry database maintained by the Northern Poetry Library. It is copublished by Northumberland County Council Amenities Division and Mid Northumberland Arts Group.

Addresses
Editorial:	Arts Section, County Library HQ, The Willows, Morpeth, Northumberland NE61 1TA
Reviews:	Does not publish reviews
Subscriptions:	As above
Payment terms to contributors:	Free copies of Red Herring
Accept/Rejection approximate times:	3-6 months
Inserts accepted:	No
Price per 1000:	N/A
Circulation:	3000 distributed

REFLECTIONS

Frequency:	Quarterly
Subscription Cost:	£5.00 Annually (inc. p&p)
Single Issue:	95p plus 30p p&p
Back issue price:	50p plus 30p (subject to availability)
Cheques/PO Payable to:	Reflections
Overseas subs:	Europe £6.20 (inc. p&p) other on application.
Payment Details:	Sterling only

Description
Mainly poetry, some short pieces of prose, regular black and white photography and art work. Reflections provides an outlet for those interested in using the creative arts to share positive ideas and emotions. Many contributors choose to do this by offering appreactions of beauty, work which has a healing influence, or communicates aspects of their spiritual life, in the broadest sense of this term. Much of the poetry in Reflections adopts a traditional stance towards rhyme, rhythm and melody, although the editorial team welcomes both formal verse and free verse. Potential contributors should keep in mind that whatever its merits, work which focuses on the mundane, or has an overall negative tone is likely to fall outside of Reflections limit. Reflections is not aligned to any political, social or religious movements. Work can only be returned if accompanied by suitable SAE work may be offered anonymously.

Addresses

Editorial:	Reflections, PO Box 178, Sunderland, SR1 1DU
Reviews:	As above
Subscriptions:	As above
Payment terms to contributors:	None
Accept/Rejection approximate times:	2 months
Inserts accepted:	No
Price per 1000:	N/A
Circulation:	150 - 200

RETFORD WRITERS

Frequency:	4 per annum
Subscription Cost:	£5
Single Issue:	£1.25
Back issue price:	£1
Cheques/PO Payable to:	Retford Writers
Overseas subs:	-
Payment Details:	-

Description
Retford Writers is a quarterly publication consisting of work by members and postal subscribers. Short pieces of poetry, short stories of factual accounts.

Addresses

Editorial:	3 Welham Road, Retford, Notts DM22 6TN
Reviews:	As above
Subscriptions:	As above
Payment terms to contributors:	Nil
Accept/Rejection approximate times:	-
Inserts accepted:	No
Price per 1000:	N/A
Circulation:	25

RHYME ARRIVAL

Frequency:	Quarterly
Subscription Cost:	£12
Single Issue:	£3.25
Back issue price:	£3.25
Cheques/PO Payable to:	Forward Press Ltd
Overseas subs:	£18.00
Payment Details:	P/order, Visa, Cheque, Switch, Delta, American Express

Description

The aim of Rhyme Arrival is to be a relaxed and enjoyable magazine. The emphasis is on poetry for pleasure and, as its title suggests, a good deal of rhyme. The magazine is good reading for all, regardless of age or beliefs, therefore will not include any poem or article that would be considered offensive or that contains foul language. Each issue includes:

* 'Snap', poems about a photograph.
* 'Inspirations', poems with description of inspiration.
* 'Poetry Arrivals', poems on any subject.
* 'Giggles', humorous poems.
* 'Expressions', religious faith poetry.
* 'Themes', various to each issue.
* 'Young Arrivals', 8-16 year olds poetry.
* 'Post Bag', news, views, gripes and grumbles.
* 'Articles', previously unpublished articles of interest to poets.

Editor: Tim Sharp

Addresses

Editorial:	1/2 Wainman Road, Woodston, Peterborough, PE2 7BU
Reviews:	As above
Subscriptions:	As above

Payment terms to contributors:	Poems £2, Articles £15, Other payments negotiated
Accept/Rejection approximate times:	12-14 weeks
Inserts accepted:	Yes
Price per 1000:	Free
Circulation:	2400

RIALTO THE

Frequency:	3 times a year
Subscription Cost:	£10 a year (£8 for those on low income)
Single Issue:	£3.90
Back issue price:	
Cheques/PO Payable to:	The Rialto
Overseas subs:	Europe £12, USA £16, Australia / Japan £17
Payment Details:	Sterling only

Description

The Rialto carries editorials and an occasional essay, but is otherwise all poetry. Generous in size (A4), it is illustrated in black and white. Recent covers have been by artists of international reputation, including Victor Pasmore, Kitaj, Paula Rego, Ana Maria Pacheco. Deliberately eclectic, The Rialto publishes poems on any subject, in any form, that work in their own terms. We place poems by major writers from all over the world alongside those of talented newcomers. Jenny Joseph's 'In Honour of Love,' Forward's 'best individual poem' of 1995, first appeared in Rialto 31 (summer 1995)

Addresses

Editorial:	32 Grosvenor Road, Norwich, NR2 2PZ,
Reviews:	No reviews
Subscriptions:	As above
Payment terms to contributors:	£10 per poem
Accept/Rejection approximate times:	4-8 weeks
Inserts accepted:	No
Price per 1000:	N/A
Circulation:	1100

RUSTIC RUB

Frequency:	Biannual
Subscription Cost:	£5
Single Issue:	£3
Back issue price:	N/A
Cheques/PO Payable to:	J. Woodman
Overseas subs:	£7 (or $10 cash)
Payment Details:	Cheques in sterling only to J. Woodman,

Description
Poetry and Art magazine - includes interviews. Emphasis on international flavour / net working sometimes includes reports on what's going on. No reviews. Always good value for money.

Addresses

Editorial:	Jay Woodman, 14 Hillfield, Selby, North Yorkshire, YO8 0ND
Reviews:	N/A
Subscriptions:	As Editorial
Payment terms	
to contributors:	Complimentary copy
Accept/Rejection	
approximate times:	Usually straight away - longer if undecided.
Inserts accepted:	Yes
Price per 1000:	By special arrangement only
Circulation:	300 - 400

SACCADE

Frequency:	Three yearly
Subscription Cost:	£6 - 4 issues
Single Issue:	£1.75
Back issue price:	£1.75
Cheques/PO Payable to:	R. Gill
Overseas subs:	£8
Payment Details:	Cash, cheque, postal order, IMO

Description

Saccade aims to publish new and original horror, fantasy and science fiction stories, although we also publish other genres such as crime, humour etc. The main body of the magazine is devoted to fiction, but we have also published poetry, artwork, interviews, reviews and non-fiction articles. Again these are of a similar nature to the fiction. Past subjects have included Porphrya and psychology.

Addresses

Editorial:	93 Green Lane, Dronfield, Sheffield S18 6FG
Reviews:	As above
Subscriptions:	As above
Payment terms to contributors:	Free copy of magazine
Accept/Rejection approximate times:	Based on quality of submission only
Inserts accepted:	Yes
Price per 1000:	£1
Circulation:	Increasing

SALOPEOT

Frequency:	Quarterly
Subscription Cost:	£10
Single Issue:	£2.50
Back issue price:	£1.50
Cheques/PO Payable to:	Salopian Poetry Society
Overseas subs:	£10 plus additional postage
Payment Details:	Annual in advance - cheque, postal order, IMO

Description

Salopeot, founded in 1976, publishes poetry of members only.* Current membership is around 150. The magazine is published quarterly, the poems published being chosen by a panel of six committee members from poetry submitted by members. The Society runs two competitions per year - an open competition and one for members only.* The winning poems of the open competition are published each year in our Christmas Edition. Poetry reading evenings are held monthly at various members' homes.

Addresses

Editorial:	Mr R.A. Hoult, Magazine Secretary, 5 Squires Close, Madeley, Shropshire TF7 5RU
Reviews:	Mr. Allister Fraser MBE - President, 5 Cordingley Way, Donnington, Shropshire, TF2 7LW
Subscriptions:	Mrs Mollie Bolt, Treasurer, 29 Christime Avenue, Wellington, Shropshire TF1 2DY
Payment terms to contributors:	No payments made
Accept/Rejection approximate times:	2 months
Inserts accepted:	Yes
Price per 1000:	No charge currently
Circulation:	150

SAMHAIN

Frequency:	Bi-monthly
Subscription Cost:	£9/$20 (5 issues)
Single Issue:	£2.50 (cover price) £2 if ordered direct
Back issue price:	£2 each or full set (1.58) for £50
Cheques/PO Payable to:	Samhain
Overseas subs:	£10 (Europe) $20 (US)
Payment Details:	US Orders in cash only - no US cheques

Description

Britain's longest running horror film magazine includes features, interviews, reviews etc. relating to the world of horror films and fiction. We are always on the look out for new contributors, especially reviewers and feature writers. In October we celebrate our tenth anniversary (59 issues).

Addresses

Editorial:	77 Exeter Road, Topsham, Exeter, Devon EX3 0LX
Reviews:	As above
Subscriptions:	As above
Payment terms to contributors:	Free issues of the magazine
Accept/Rejection approximate times:	-
Inserts accepted:	Yes
Price per 1000:	N/A
Circulation:	Increasing

SCHEHERAZADE

Frequency:	3 yearly
Subscription Cost:	£8.50 (4 issues)
Single Issue:	£2.50 (£3.25 overseas)
Back issue price:	£2
Cheques/PO Payable to:	Scheherazade
Overseas subs:	£10 (sterling only)
Payment Details:	As above

Description

Scheherazade magazine is principally a story telling magazine,with particular interest in fantasy and science fiction short stories. We also publish author interviews and other features. We do not publish poetry reviews. The magazine was originally started in response to the prevalence of 'Cyberpunch' and other hard/masculine SF in most other British magazines. We wanted to provide an alter for writers of short story fantasy and the 'Softer' more human aspects of science fiction.

Addresses

Editorial:	Elizabeth Counihan, St. Ives, Maypole Road, East Grinstead, West Sussex RH19 1HL
Reviews:	No
Subscriptions:	As above
Payment terms to contributors:	Nominal fee to fiction works, always complimentary copy
Accept/Rejection approximate times:	3-4 months
Inserts accepted:	Advert swaps welcome
Price per 1000:	N/A
Circulation:	Approx. 300

SCIENCE OF THOUGHT REVIEW

Frequency:	Bi-monthly
Subscription Cost:	£6 annually
Single Issue:	£1.10
Back issue price:	50p (including postage)
Cheques/PO Payable to:	Science of Thought Review
Overseas subs:	£9 Australia/N.Z. $24 USA $20 Canada
Payment Details:	By cheque

Description

Based on the teaching of Henry Thomas Hamblin, a practical English mystic, it is devoted to the Spiritual life, rather than the 'religious' one and applied right thinking. First hand experiences that lend a positive note to the reader looking for spiritual solace are popular. It covers complimentary medicine, meditation, some poetry and has a good Book review section. Has been in existance since 1921!!

Addresses

Editorial:	Stephanie Sorrell, Science of Thought Review, Bosham House, Bosham, Chichester, W. Sussex PO18 8PJ
Reviews:	As above
Subscriptions:	As above
Payment terms to contributors:	None - copy of magazine
Accept/Rejection approximate times:	2-4 weeks
Inserts accepted:	No - only subscribers can have a 'Notice'
Price per 1000:	N/A
Circulation:	2500 (including 200 abroad)

SCRATCH

Frequency:	2 a year
Subscription Cost:	£7.00
Single Issue:	£4.00
Back issue price:	£2.00
Cheques/PO Payable to:	Scratch
Overseas subs:	£15.00
Payment Details:	

Description

Scratch publishes poetry and criticism of new poetry it uses work by both new and established writers, and tends to writing which is engaged but not dogmatic, accessible but not simplistic, expansive in form but not pointlessly experimental, it leans to the left, and is keen to publish long poems, and sequences.

Addresses

Editorial:	9 Chestnut Road, Eaglescliffe, Stockon - on - Tees, TS16 0BA
Reviews:	As above
Subscriptions:	As above
Payment terms to contributors:	By negotiation - usually 2 free copies
Accept/Rejection approximate times:	6 weeks
Inserts accepted:	Yes
Price per 1000:	£25
Circulation:	

SCRIPTOR

Frequency:	Once a year
Subscription Cost:	£2.99 + 50p p&p
Single Issue:	£2.99 + 50p p&p
Back issue price:	£1.99
Cheques/PO Payable to:	Scriptor
Overseas subs:	N/A
Payment Details:	Cheques and Postal Orders only

Description

SCRIPTOR is a new magazine of writing from the South-East (Kent, Surrey, Sussex, Essex and London). Published by The Providence Press (Whitstable) it aims to provide a new opportunity for writers of poetry, short stories and essays. SCRIPTOR One was published in October 1996 and contained the work of over 30 regional writers, including that of its editors. SCRIPTOR Two will appear at the end of October 1997, and the last date for submissions is April 30th 1997.

Contributors' guidelines are available directly from the publishers (please enclose SAE). Only work from writers living/working in the South-East, as indicated above, will be considered. SCRIPTOR'S content is intentionally diverse, reflecting the nature of the work of its contributors. All submission are given careful consideration. The magazine is not merely sold back to successful contributors, but marketed extensively through small press outlets such as book-fairs, mail-order etc.

Addresses

Editorial:	Scriptor, The Providence Press Whitstable, 22 Plough Lane, Swalecliffe, Whitstable, Kent,CT5 2NZ
Reviews:	N/A
Subscriptions:	As above
Payment terms to contributors:	Discounted copies available to contributors - free to 'best' in genre
Accept/Rejection approximate times:	Approx. 6-8 weeks

Inserts accepted: No
Price per 1000:   N/A
Circulation: N/A

SEAM

Frequency:	2 yearly
Subscription Cost:	£6
Single Issue:	£3
Back issue price:	£3
Cheques/PO Payable to:	Seam
Overseas subs:	£7 p.a.:
Payment Details:	-

Description

Edited by widely published poets David Lightfoot and Robert Etty. Distinctive A6 format fits conveniently in pockets. Up to 80 pages of contemporary poetry from a wide range of writers, established and aspiring, and reviews by Sam Gardiner, winner of National Poetry Prize 1993. Sequences especially favoured. Seam has published poems by Annemarie Austin, Connie Bensley, James Brockway, V.A. Fanthorpe, Sophie Hannah, John Harvey, James Keery, Mimi Khalvati, John Latham, Vernon Scannell, Hugo Williams, and many others. Unpublished poets are encouraged to submit.

Addresses

Editorial:	David Lightfoot & Robert Etty,1 Horncastle Road, Louth LN11 9LB
Reviews:	82 Milton Road, Grimsby DN33 1DE
Subscriptions:	1 Horncastle Road, Louth LN11 9LB
Payment terms to contributors:	1 free copy
Accept/Rejection approximate times:	2-3 weeks
Inserts accepted:	Yes
Price per 1000:	Free, by reciprocal agreement
Circulation:	250

SEPIA

Frequency:	3 Times a year
Subscription Cost:	£2
Single Issue:	75p
Back issue price:	75p
Cheques/PO Payable to:	Kaqabata Press
Overseas subs:	$5 (USA)
Payment Details:	In dollar bills or via agent in UK cheque but not US cheques!

Description
No rhymes - avoid strict metre, avoid clichés - believe in the poem or story; poems normally up to 80 lines;stories normally up to 2500 words, reviews; artwork.

Addresses

Editorial:	SEPIA - Kawabata Press, Knill Cross House, Knill Cross, Millbrook, Nr Turpoint, Cornwall, PL10 1DX
Reviews:	As above
Subscriptions:	As above
Payment terms to contributors:	- None - only free copy
Accept/Rejection approximate times:	2 weeks
Inserts accepted:	Yes
Price per 1000:	Usually do as a swap
Circulation:	100

SHEFFIELD THURSDAY

Frequency:	Twice a year
Subscription Cost:	£7.00 pa. (plus £1.00 p&p)
Single Issue:	£3.50 (plus 48p. p&p)
Back issue price:	£3.50 (plus 48p. p&p)
Cheques/PO Payable to:	Sheffield Hallam University
Overseas subs:	£10 pa.
Payment Details:	Subscription. Cheque. Sterling cheque. P.O.

Description

Sheffield Thursday is a literary and arts magazine, edited by E.A. Markham from the school of Cultural Studies, Sheffield Hallam University. This international publication, appearing twice a year 'manages to be lively, informative and entertaining'. Poetry, art, essays, fiction and reviews give a feel of what's contemporary in the arts, and the interview with a major artist / arts worker is a prominent feature. Interviewees have included Margaret Drabble, Michelle Roberts, Malcolm Bradbury, Alastair Niven and (in the form of a questionnaire) assorted short story writers. As well as a forum for local and regional talent the magazine allows generous space in its 150-200 pages to work from the widest possible field: The first issue features Quatrains from Iranian-born poet, Mimi Khalvati: an article on the challenge of finding a notation for performance or 'dub' poetry, by West Indian poet and critic Mervyn Morris; and Greek poet Alexis Lykiard playfully urging us to eat meat. Other issues have maintained the international thrust with work from Europe, the Americas, Asia......

Addresses

Editorial:	School of Cultural Studies, Sheffield, Hallam University, 36 Collegiate Crescent, Sheffield, SIO 2BP
Reviews:	As above
Subscriptions:	As above
Payment terms to contributors:	By negotiation
Accept/Rejection approximate times:	3 months and getting better
Inserts accepted:	Yes

Price per 1000:   By negotiation
Circulation: 750

SIERRA HEAVEN

Frequency:	3-4 / year
Subscription Cost:	£14 / 4 issues
Single Issue:	£2.95 + 55p postage (or A4 SAE)
Back issue price:	£3.95 (inc. p&p)
Cheques/PO Payable to:	Alex Bardy
Overseas subs:	£4.50 Europe, $8 US
Payment Details:	Overseas payment should be in UK funds or $ cash

Description

SIERRA HEAVEN is a magazine of fantasy, horror, and science fiction for the layman! We make no outlandish claims of pushing forward any boundaries, cutting-edge experimental fiction, or such-like, but we do promise good, quality fiction (up to 20,000 words) accompanied by excellent illustrations from a superb collection of artists. Our artists regularly produce story- specific material for the magazine, both full and half-page work, and are proud to be associated with the format. Similarly, this is one of the attractions for a great many would-be contributions. SIERRA HEAVEN rarely published poetry, but is in constant need of potential features, articles, interviews etc. Whether they be about favourite artists, authors, perhaps a favourite trilogy of books, or a superbly realised alien / fantasy world, etc. The editorial policy of the magazine is thin to say the least, but basically the editor will publish genre material which he personally finds interesting, humorous, rather novel, or otherwise intriguing. Our shorts inc. section comprises genre material from over 15 different authors, these short shorts have a maximum wordage of just 250 and are incredibly popular with author and readers alike, as well as being devilishly difficult to write. SIERRA HEAVEN is 50 + A4 pages of solid reading, although at time of going to press we're considering an increase to 64-72 pages due to the wealth of the material regularly receive. The editor respectfully believes the magazine can best be described as a black & white version of two excellent US fiction magazine: Science Fiction Age and Realms Of Fantasy; and is constantly striving to achieve such a status within the UK! Amen.

Addresses

Editorial:	29 Harrier Way, Evelyn Mews, Beckton, London, E6 4YP
Reviews:	As above

Subscriptions:	As above
Payment terms to contributors:	Complimentary copy for material / artwork published (excludes letters and short
Accept/Rejection approximate times:	We are very proud of a turn around time of approx. 14 days
Inserts accepted:	Yes
Price per 1000:	£15 / 500
Circulation:	450 approx.

SKALD

Frequency:	3 yearly
Subscription Cost:	£3.50 including postage
Single Issue:	£1
Back issue price:	£1
Cheques/PO Payable to:	Skald Community Magazine
Overseas subs:	£6
Payment Details:	Cheque in sterling, postal order

Description

Skald is an old Norse word for a poet, but this magazine features all forms of creative writing. It is based in North Wales and aims to reflect that area to some extent. To that end, a proportion of the writing is in Welsh, though fresh and original writing from elsewhere is always welcome. Artwork is also published if it is easily reproducible, and need not necessarily be illustration to accompany text.

Addresses

Editorial:	2 Greenfield Terrace, Menai Bridge, Anglesey N. Wales LL59 5AY
Reviews:	As above
Subscriptions:	As above
Payment terms to contributors:	Free copy of magazine
Accept/Rejection approximate times:	6 weeks
Inserts accepted:	-
Price per 1000:	-
Circulation:	300

SMITHS KNOLL

Frequency:	3 issues per year
Subscription Cost:	£8 for 3 issues
Single Issue:	£3
Back issue price:	£2 - £3.00
Cheques/PO Payable to:	Smiths Knoll
Overseas subs:	£10
Payment Details:	Sterling only

Description

Founded in 1992 and named after the North Sea lightship, it aims at readability. Particularly attractive to would-be contributors are its two-week turnaround time for submissions and the editors' willingness to offer constructive criticism when they are interested in a poem. It showcases a wide range of poetry from different kinds of writers-established, up and coming, and complete first timers. It prints only previously unpublished new poetry, well-presented and perfect bound.

Addresses

Editorial:	49 Church Road, Little Glemham, Woodbridge, Suffolk, IP13 0BJ
Reviews:	None printed
Subscriptions:	As above
Payment terms to contributors:	£5 + complimentary copy
Accept/Rejection approximate times:	Less than two weeks
Inserts accepted:	Sometimes, by previous arrangement
Price per 1000:	Depends on postage cost
Circulation:	300

SMOKE

Frequency: Twice yearly
Subscription Cost: £2 for 3 issues
Single Issue: 50p + post
Back issue price: 50p + post
Cheques/PO Payable to: Windows Project
Overseas subs: £5/3 issues
Payment Details: -

Description
Smoke is one of the highest selling small poetry magazines in the country. Smoke can introduce you to new writing, poetry and graphics by some of the best established names, alongside new work from Merseyside, from all over the country and from abroad

Addresses
Editorial: 40 Canning Street, Liverpool L8 7NP
Reviews: -
Subscriptions: As above
Payment terms
to contributors: Comp. copy
Accept/Rejection
approximate times: 2 weeks
Inserts accepted: Yes
Price per 1000:   On exchange basis
Circulation: 500-1000

SOL MAGAZINE

Frequency:	Twice yearly
Subscription Cost:	2 / £3.50, 4 / £6.50
Single Issue:	£1.80
Back issue price:	£1 each
Cheques/PO Payable to:	Sol Publications
Overseas subs:	US 2 /$10 or 4 / $20
Payment Details:	Equivalent in cash - no foreign cheques

Description

Sol is chiefly a poetry magazine, tied to no particular school of writing, preferring instead simply to publish the best poems that it receives from its contributors. Since it was established in 1969 it has published work by Roger McGough, David Halliwell, Thomas Land, Andrew Darlilngton, Frederic Vanson, Susan Fromberg Schaeffer, Margot K. Juby, Michael Daugherty, David Jaffin, John Whitworth, Gavin Ewart, Ian McMillan, and many others. We also publish articles about literature, philosophy and politics and short stories up to 5000 words.

Addresses

Editorial:	24 Fowler Close, Southchurch, Southend-on-Sea Essex, SS1 2RD
Reviews:	As above
Subscriptions:	As above
Payment terms to contributors:	£1 per page
Accept/Rejection approximate times:	3 months
Inserts accepted:	Yes
Price per 1000:	35p per 100g
Circulation:	250

SOUTH

Frequency:	April & October
Subscription Cost:	£6.00 annually £10.00 biannually
Single Issue:	£3.00
Back issue price:	£3.00
Cheques/PO Payable to:	Wanda Publications
Overseas subs:	£6 + p&p
Payment Details:	Sterling

Description

South was launched in 1990 as a poetry magazine for the Southern counties. Its editorship travels the region in a cycle then takes next issues to completion, and is undertaken by a different group of poets each time. South prefers celebration to competition, giving poets time to grow rather than putting them under pressure to conform. As well as poetry, each issue includes space for criticism, news of poetry events and extracts form recent publications. Poets published in each issue are invited to take part in a reading of their poems at an event which launches the editorial group of the next issue on their bash. South is published twice a year in April and October and contributions should reach Wanda Publications by 30th November and 31st May respectively.

Addresses

Editorial:	Wanda Publications, (South Magazine), 61 West Borough, Wimborne, Dorset, BH21 1LX
Reviews:	As above
Subscriptions:	As above
Payment terms to contributors:	Free copy of magazine if poem printed
Accept/Rejection approximate times:	Up to six months
Inserts accepted:	No
Price per 1000:	N/A
Circulation:	

SOUTHFIELDS

Frequency:	Annual
Subscription Cost:	£13.00 for 2
Single Issue:	£7.00
Back issue price:	£6.00
Cheques/PO Payable to:	Southfields Press
Overseas subs:	£10.00 per issue
Payment Details:	PO/cheque/cash only/sterling only

Description

A cultural review with emphasis on the cultures of Scotland and of London, publishing poetry of a wide range of styles and commitments. Southfields has an interest in aesthetics, social criticism and pleasure. Would-be contributors should read an issue before submitting work.

Addresses

Editorial:	R.Price, 8 Richmond Road, Staines TW18 2AB
Reviews:	As abvove
Subscriptions:	As above
Payment terms to contributors:	Complimentary copy
Accept/Rejection approximate times:	3 months
Inserts accepted:	Yes
Price per 1000:	Negotiable
Circulation:	300

SPANNER

Frequency:	Irregular
Subscription Cost:	£12 Sterling
Single Issue:	£5
Back issue price:	£5
Cheques/PO Payable to:	Spanner
Overseas subs:	Surface mail - sterling only as above
Payment Details:	

Description
Art and Literary magazine usually dedicated to one artist or poet or group. Includes interviews or working documents. Presentation is rough and ready and almost instant. No unsolicited manuscripts.

Addresses

Editorial:	14 Hopton Road, Hereford, HR1 1BE, England,
Reviews:	As above
Subscriptions:	As above
Payment terms to contributors:	Negotiated
Accept/Rejection approximate times:	Not applicable
Inserts accepted:	No
Price per 1000:	Not applicable
Circulation:	Varies, under 500 copies

SPECTRUM

Frequency:	Twice yearly
Subscription Cost:	£6 incl. p & p
Single Issue:	£3 incl. p & p. £2.50 otherwise
Back issue price:	£2.50 incl. p & p.
Cheques/PO Payable to:	Spectrum
Overseas subs:	£8
Payment Details:	Cheque, postal order, IMO

Description

Founded 1990 by Stuart A. Paterson (poet) it's editor. Recently began to receive S.A.C. subsidy after braving the financial storms of an independent publication's lot for 6 years. Main emphasis is on publishing poetry and short stories by new and established writers, the promotion of the former being of utmost importance. Poetry accepted varies in form, though there is, if anything, a slight bias towards formal verse. Work accepted from all over. Pleased (but not proud) to be Scottish, but not parochial. Average issue: 68 pages, A5, laminated cover, 8-12 line-drawn illustrations, 2-3 short stories, editorial, news, few reviews, but more writing.

Addresses

Editorial:	c/o Stuart A. Paterson, 2A Leslie Road, Kilmarnock, Ayrshire KA3 7RR
Reviews:	As above
Subscriptions:	Amanda Fergusson, 1 Hemphill, Moscow, By Galston, Ayrshire KA4 8PS
Payment terms to contributors:	1 contributor's copy
Accept/Rejection approximate times:	Up to 8 weeks - but usually much quicker if poss!
Inserts accepted:	Yes
Price per 1000:	Varies - usually on a 'swap' basis though (or goodwill)
Circulation:	300-600 (subscribers/public sales)

SPINSTER'S ALMANACK THE

Frequency:	4 times a year pub. Jan, April, July, October
Subscription Cost:	£7.60
Single Issue:	£1.60
Back issue price:	Various - half price
Cheques/PO Payable to:	The Spinster's Almanack
Overseas subs:	£8.50 surface, £11.00 airmail
Payment Details:	Sterling or US bills

Description

THE SPINSTERS ALMANACK is published four times a year in January, April, July and October. It is edited by Rowena Edlin-White and Dee Duke who aim to produce a friendly but useful magazine with instructional articles, letters and reviews, Guild news, patterns and recipes. We research our material thoroughly but try not to take ourselves too seriously and we find that it is this approach which had made readers world-wide, in Great Britain, Eire, America, Australia, Canada and beyond and this makes for a good cross-fertilisation of ideas. NEW WRITERS: We have a number of regular contributors but are always interested in new ones. If you would like to offer an article, send for our Guidelines for Contributors from the address below, enclosing a stamped addressed envelope, please.

Addresses

Editorial:	Rowena Edlin - White, 'The Grebes' 89 Morley Avenue, Mapperley, Nottingham, NG3 5FZ,Tel: 0115 9604240.
Reviews:	As above
Subscriptions:	Dee Duke, 23 Vaughan Avenue, Papplewick Lane, Hucknall, Nottingham, NG15 8BTTel: 0115 9635538
Payment terms to contributors:	£5 per article + complimentary copy, we do not pay for reviews, recipes, letters
Accept/Rejection approximate times:	3 - 4 weeks

Inserts accepted:	Yes
Price per 1000:	For 250, £15
Circulation:	250 (subs) but reaches many more through spinsters, weavers Guilds.

SPLIZZ

Frequency:	Quarterly
Subscription Cost:	£5
Single Issue:	£1.30
Back issue price:	£1.30
Cheques/PO Payable to:	Amanda Morgan
Overseas subs:	£2.30 or equivalent per issue
Payment Details:	Cheques in sterling, postal orders

Description

Splizz was founded in 1993. It features poetry, prose and pictures alongside extensive reivews of contemporary music. Splizz started off as a bi-monthly publication, but now appears quarterly. New features are frequently introduced; most recently, 'Scribblers' where we aim to provide a background on our poetry contributors. We are always seeking a helping hand, and welcome your contributions at anytime.

Addresses

Editorial:	4 St Marys Rise, Burry Port, Carmarthenshire SA16 OSH
Reviews:	As above
Subscriptions:	As above
Payment terms to contributors:	N/A
Accept/Rejection approximate times:	2-3 weeks
Inserts accepted:	Yes
Price per 1000:	Negotiable
Circulation:	Ever increasing

STAND MAGAZINE

Frequency:	Quarterly
Subscription Cost:	£11.95
Single Issue:	£3.75
Back issue price:	£3.75
Cheques/PO Payable to:	Stand Magazine
Overseas subs:	£13.50 or $25
Payment Details:	Cheque / Credit Card

Description

A literary journal established in London in 1952 by the poet Jan Silkin. It is a registered charity that provides a platform for new unpublished poetry, fiction, criticism, reviews and translation. It alternates a poetry competition, thus 1996 = poetry competition, and 1997 = short story competition, send SAE or IRCs for details.

Addresses

Editorial:	Stand Magazine, 179 Wingrove Road, Newcastle on Tyne NE4 9DA
Reviews:	As above
Subscriptions:	As above
Payment terms to contributors:	£25.00 a poem unless under 20 lines.
Accept/Rejection approximate times:	1-2 months
Inserts accepted:	Yes
Price per 1000:	4,500 = £250 + VAT
Circulation:	4,500

STAPLE

Frequency:	3 issues, and first editions (collection) supplement
Subscription Cost:	Annually £12.00
Single Issue:	£3.50
Back issue price:	Two for £3.00
Cheques/PO Payable to:	STAPLE
Overseas subs:	£14 Europe for surface, overseas £17.50
Payment Details:	Institutions add £5.00 to above rates sterling or US dollars only.

Description

The magazine is entirely open, and sets little or no store by reputation or writers - or lack of one. The editors try not to have preconceptions and , other things being equal, will favour writers whose work they don't know over those they do. Staple does not carry work over from one issue to the next, so , in spite of the fact that the quantity of work received vastly exceeds that which can be used, material is always needed for the next issue. The disadvantage is that the editors decision may be quick or slow depending on when the typescript was sent. The most effective times to send to Staple are normally: March (for July publication): June (for December publication): November (for March publication).The poetry is 'main-stream' - i.e. Staple will consider poems which are either free in form or written in not - too - obvious traditional modes. The fiction is non-genre. There are exception to every rule, but in general Staple is unlikely to take detective stories, sci-fi, gothic etc. - or parodies thereof. The work published tends to have a bias towards the documentary.

Addresses

Editorial:	Bob Windsor, Gilderoy East, Upperwood Road, Matlock, Bath, Derbys DE4 3PD
Reviews:	Staple does not review
Subscriptions:	Donald Measham, Tor Cottage, 81 Cavendish Road, Matlock, Derbys DE4 3HD

Payment terms to contributors:	£5 per poem, £10 per story

Accept/Rejection
approximate times: See above for optimum submission times
Inserts accepted: Yes on exchange or payment basis
Price per 1000:   £20 per 500
Circulation: 500 - special issues 750+

STICK TWO FINGERS

Frequency:	Approx every 6 weeks - 2 months
Subscription Cost:	N/A
Single Issue:	30p
Back issue price:	40p incl p & p (Except issues)
Cheques/PO Payable to:	Mick Sinclair (blank postal orders as I have no Bank Account)
Overseas subs:	N/A...yet
Payment Details:	Blank postal orders or better still cash

Description

Humourous funzine of extremely anarchic and non conformist nature. Rude, crude, offensive, self opinionated, abusive..., and humourous. Although most of the articles, normally gig and record reviews, views on life and society and a selection of cartoons are written and compiled by the editor (Mick a.k.a. 'Dark Punk') any contributions are welcomed. Anything that's ararchic and absolutely no trendy stuff. Make it as shocking as possible! Issue 23, out in November will feature 'Fare Dodgers Utd,' 'Anti-Copper; Anti Pig.' 'Punk Diary - Edinburgh City of Punk Rock 1996' '20 years of British Punk Pt. 3' and 'Attitude Problem Man.' Most handwritten stuff with the articles rarely, if ever, typed.

Addresses

Editorial:	Mick, 54 Bekesbourne Tower, Wichling Close, Orpington, Gtr. London, England
Reviews:	As above
Subscriptions:	Not in process yet, but any enquiries - see above address
Payment terms to contributors:	Free copy of magazine
Accept/Rejection approximate times:	3 weeks before edition is due out
Inserts accepted:	Yes
Price per 1000:	£1
Circulation:	Increasing

STONE SOUP

Frequency:	Quarterly
Subscription Cost:	£15 a year
Single Issue:	£7
Back issue price:	£5
Cheques/PO Payable to:	Stone Soup
Overseas subs:	Europe £18; Elsewhere £21
Payment Details:	cheques/postal orders in sterling

Description

Stone Soup (founded 1994) is an international magazine for new writing, publishing mainly poetry, theory and interview. It aims 'to provide a fluent dialogue between small and established national literatures, and first two issues are printed bilingually in English and the languages of former Yugoslavia. Edited by British poet Ken Smith and Bosnian poet Igor Klikovac, Stone Soup is 'the effective combination of poetry, fiction, philosophical and political writing,' favouring writing concerned with the problems of modern European society, problems of language and exile. The first three issues include the exclusive materials by Umberto Eco, Jean Beudrillard, Alain Bosquet, Noam Chomsky, Slavoj Zizek, Hanif Kureishi, Juan Goytisolo, Arseny Tackovsky and James Pillinszky. The magazine works largely on a commission basis; unsolicited mss must have an sae supplied.

Addresses

Editorial:	37 Chesterfield Road, London W4 3HQ
Reviews:	As above
Subscriptions:	As above
Payment terms to contributors:	Payment by arrangement
Accept/Rejection approximate times:	60 days
Inserts accepted:	Yes
Price per 1000:	£1
Circulation:	2000

STRIDE

Frequency:	Occasional
Subscription Cost:	N/A
Single Issue:	Last issue £5.95
Back issue price:	£3.95
Cheques/PO Payable to:	Stride
Overseas subs:	$10 bill only
Payment Details:	-

Description

An occasional arts magazine, featuring literature, music, visual arts alongside reviews and new writing. Recent issues have included Sun Ra, William Burroughs, Jeremy Reed, Grail Marws, Brian Eno, King Crimson, Biba Kopf etc. 'Perversely eclectic, well written and highly impressive' (Ramroid Extraordinaire) Informed and accessible writing well worth investigating' (Ribberneck)

Addresses

Editorial:	Stride, 11 Sylvan Road, Exeter, Devon EX4 6EW
Reviews:	As above
Subscriptions:	As above
Payment terms to contributors:	Nil
Accept/Rejection approximate times:	1 week
Inserts accepted:	No
Price per 1000:	N/A
Circulation:	2000

SUPER TROUPER

Frequency:	3-4 yearly
Subscription Cost:	£10 - for four
Single Issue:	£3
Back issue price:	£3
Cheques/PO Payable to:	Andrew Savage
Overseas subs:	$25 for 4
Payment Details:	Money orders or cash

Description

Super Trouper is a small press magazine that is recorded onto tape. We use poetry, music, comedy, short interviews and short reviews. Anyone is more than welcome to submit material for consideration, but all submissions should be recorded on tape. Super Trouper is played on community radio stations in the USA and mainland Europe, and so provides an exciting platform for all who participate. Sales are also quite good and we have a wide and varied audience.

Addresses

Editorial:	35 Kearsley Road, Sheffield S2 4TE
Reviews:	As above
Subscriptions:	As above
Payment terms to contributors:	A copy of the issue they appear in
Accept/Rejection approximate times:	2-4 weeks
Inserts accepted:	Yes
Price per 1000:	By special arrangement
Circulation:	100+

SWAGMAG

Frequency:	Twice yearly
Subscription Cost:	£3 + 50p postage
Single Issue:	£1.50 + postage
Back issue price:	£1.50 + postage
Cheques/PO Payable to:	SWAG, Swansea Writers' and Artists' Group
Overseas subs:	On request
Payment Details:	-

Description

The magazine of Swansea's writers and artists. Edited by Peter Thabit Jones, it publishes poetry, prose, features, interviews and reviews. Cartoons/photos/artwork. Includes work in the Welsh language too (editor for Welsh, Dafydd Rowlands). Recent issues include interview with Adrian Mitchell, features on Paul Peter Piech, international artist and anglo-welsh poet Harri Webb

Addresses

Editorial:	Dan-y-bryn, 784 Cwm Level Road, Brynhyfryd, Swansea, SA5 9DY
Reviews:	-
Subscriptions:	-
Payment terms to contributors:	Free copy of magazine
Accept/Rejection approximate times:	3 months
Inserts accepted:	Yes
Price per 1000:	On request
Circulation:	Increasing

SWANSEA REVIEW THE

Frequency:	Twice yearly
Subscription Cost:	£5
Single Issue:	£2.50
Back issue price:	£2
Cheques/PO Payable to:	The Swansea Review
Overseas subs:	£6
Payment Details:	Cheque preferred, sterling if possible

Description
A journal of poetry, criticism and prose (including fiction). Occasional musical scores. Features including interviews (e.g. Helen Vendlar, Les A. Murray, Denise Levertor), poetry (e.g. John Heath-Stubbs, Charles Tomlinson, Mimi Khalvati, John Greening) and critical essays (e.g. Nicholas Potter, M. Wynn Thomas, Fred Beake).

Addresses

Editorial:	Glyn Pursglove, Dept. of English, University of Wales, Swansea, Singleton Park, Swansea SA2 8PP
Reviews:	As above
Subscriptions:	As above
Payment terms to contributors:	5 free copies
Accept/Rejection approximate times:	3 months
Inserts accepted:	No
Price per 1000:	N/A
Circulation:	500

T.O.P.S. - THE OLD POLICE STATION

Frequency:	Quarterly
Subscription Cost:	£4 p.a.
Single Issue:	£1
Back issue price:	£1
Cheques/PO Payable to:	A. Cooney
Overseas subs:	£10
Payment Details:	Sterling cheques/dollar bills

Description
Poetry magazine - no prose. Three sections:The Toadbird, Free Verse, Canto, Measured verse, Rhyme pattern, Stanza pattern, Platform, Reviews, readers' letters.

Addresses
Editorial:	Rose Cottage, 17 Hadassam Grove, Lark Lane, Liverpool, L17 8XH
Reviews:	As above
Subscriptions:	As above
Payment terms to contributors:	Copy of issue
Accept/Rejection approximate times:	3 months
Inserts accepted:	No
Price per 1000:	N/A
Circulation:	200

TABLA

Frequency:	Annual
Subscription Cost:	N/A
Single Issue:	£2.75 (incl.p & p)
Back issue price:	£2
Cheques/PO Payable to:	Tabla
Overseas subs:	N/A
Payment Details:	-

Description

Founded in 1991, Tabla Poetry Magazine publishes work from a tie-in competition alongside poems by more pranchent authors. Non-established writers thus attract a wider audience than is usual for competition anthologies. The poets whose entries are selected from the competition for publication are invited to contribute poems to subsequent issues and have a collection reviewed in Tabla. A different judge assists the editorial decisions each year. Poets we have helped to promote include Julia Copus and Tobias Hill. We have also published work by Charles Smuc, Peter Redgrove, Kathleen Raine, Lee Harwood, George Szirtes, Pauline Staher, Judith Kazantzis, Medbh McGuckian and others. A new poem by Seamus Heaney is in the 1997 issue. Tabla Has been widely praised for its content, and for its elegant design. It sells well in bookshops as well as by post (See Peter Finch, Writers' Monthly, October 1995: 'Best new little magazine so far this year. It makes a real change to find a magazine that cares...about its content, with every contribution read and measured before publication and the layout clean and clear, a joy to read!')

Addresses

Editorial:	Stephen James, Tabla, 7 Parliament Hill, London NW3 2SY
Reviews:	As above
Subscriptions:	As above

Payment terms to contributors:	Free copy of magazine; cash prizes/books to competition winner and 3 runners up

Accept/Rejection
approximate times: All poems judged and selected for anthology during
                       September/October
Inserts accepted: -
Price per 1000:   -
Circulation: 300 copies

TAK TAK TAK

Frequency:	Occasional
Subscription Cost:	Variable
Single Issue:	Variable
Back issue price:	Variable
Cheques/PO Payable to:	Tak Tak Tak
Overseas subs:	Variable
Payment Details:	Cheque, IMO, postal order or registered cash

Description
Formed in 1986 Tak Tak Tak is a publishing house and label dedicated to the experimental in writing, music and other media. Publications have taken various forms. We are not currently accepting unsolicited contributions.

Addresses

Editorial:	N/A
Reviews:	N/A
Subscriptions:	BCM Tak ,London WC1N 3XX
Payment terms to contributors:	Copies or royalty by negotiation
Accept/Rejection approximate times:	N/A
Inserts accepted:	No
Price per 1000:	N/A
Circulation:	Variable

TANJEN NOVELLAS

Frequency:	6 yearly
Subscription Cost:	£3 (for 8)
Single Issue:	£4.99
Back issue price:	£4.99
Cheques/PO Payable to:	Tanjen Ltd.
Overseas subs:	£46
Payment Details:	IMO, cheque, postal order

Description
Founded 1996 - specialising in sci-fi, fantasy and horror of between 20,000 to 60,000 words. We distribute to shops as well as through mail order. Each issue perfect bound, colour cover and over 100 A5 pages.

Addresses

Editorial:	52 Denman Lane, Huncote, Leicester LE9 3BS
Reviews:	As above
Subscriptions:	As above
Payment terms to contributors:	5% royalties
Accept/Rejection approximate times:	About 1 in 20
Inserts accepted:	Yes
Price per 1000:	£10
Circulation:	2000

TEARS IN THE FENCE

Frequency:	2/3 issues annually
Subscription Cost:	£9
Single Issue:	£3.50
Back issue price:	£3.50
Cheques/PO Payable to:	Tears In the Fence
Overseas subs:	$15 cash US £12 sterling elsewhere
Payment Details:	IMO, sterling cheques, dollars in cash

Description
An international literary magazine that combines new writing with criticism and reviews. Recent contributors include Lee Harwood, Fred Voss, Joan Jobe Smith, Martin Stannard, John Freeman, K.M. Dersley, June Ella Harris, Mary Maker, Donna Hilbert and Mandy Pannett.

Addresses
Editorial:	38 Hod View, Stourpaine, Blandford Forum, Dorset DT11 8TN
Reviews:	As above
Subscriptions:	As above
Payment terms to contributors:	One copy of magazine
Accept/Rejection approximate times:	2/3 weeks
Inserts accepted:	Yes
Price per 1000:	£10
Circulation:	1500

THIRD ALTERNATIVE THE

Frequency:	Quarterly
Subscription Cost:	£9.00
Single Issue:	£2.50
Back issue price:	Sold Out
Cheques/PO Payable to:	TTA Press
Overseas subs:	USA $6/$22 Europe £3/£11 rest of world £3.50/£13.00 All o/seas airmail
Payment Details:	Foreign currency cheques accepted, IMO, Eurocheque No foreign cash.

Description

Award winning magazine of modern horror, fantasy, science fiction and slipstream fiction, poetry and artwork. Specialising in borderline horror/fantasy. Publishes talented newcomers alongside award-winning authors. Unsolicited manuscripts welcome if accompanied by appropriate return postage. Read by 'best-of' editors: huge number of honourable mentions and a couple of reprints. Litho printed onto glossy artboard and art paper, 60 pages. 'TTA Press' imprint also publishes books and the magazine 'Zene'. Please study the magazine before submitting work.

Addresses

Editorial:	Andy Cox, 5 Martins Lane, Witcham, Ely, Cambs CB6 2LB
Reviews:	No reviews currently (one 'profile' per issue on a single author)
Subscriptions:	As above
Payment terms to contributors:	Negotiable
Accept/Rejection approximate times:	One month average
Inserts accepted:	Yes
Price per 1000:	Negotiable
Circulation:	1,000

THIRD HALF LITERARY MAGAZINE THE

Frequency:	As often as possible
Subscription Cost:	£4.95; £5.50 by post;
Single Issue:	£4.95 £5.50 by post
Back issue price:	£4.95
Cheques/PO Payable to:	K.T. Publications
Overseas subs:	£7
Payment Details:	

Description

The Third Half is an illustrated literary magazine. Send contribution to the editor with a sae.

Addresses

Editorial:	Kevin Troop, 16 Fane Close, Stamford, Lincs. PE9 IH9
Reviews:	
Subscriptions:	As above
Payment terms	
to contributors:	Free copy per issue
Accept/Rejection	
approximate times:	As soon as humanly possible
Inserts accepted:	Occasionally - as negotiated
Price per 1000:	Negotiated - usually distribute flyer free with mailing
Circulation:	Worldwide

THUMBSCREW

Frequency:	3 issues annually
Subscription Cost:	£10 p.a.
Single Issue:	£3.50
Back issue price:	£3.50
Cheques/PO Payable to:	Thumbscrew
Overseas subs:	IR £12.50 USA $26, all other currency the equivalent of £20
Payment Details:	Cheque/postal order

Description

Thumbscrew is an independent poetry journal publishing work by internationally renowned writers, alongside exciting new poets and critics. Important contributions include Ted Hughes on Sylvia Plath, recently-discovered stories by Louis Macneice, and Charles Simic on the art of invective - as well as work from Paul Muldoon, Fleur Adcock, Craig Raine and others.Thumbscrew also sets out to provoke critical debate with a series of essays re-evaluating the reputations of several 'major' contemporary poets.

Addresses

Editorial:	P.O. Box 657, Oxford OBX2 6PH
Reviews:	As above
Subscriptions:	As above
Payment terms to contributors:	Two free copies
Accept/Rejection approximate times:	2-3 months
Inserts accepted:	Yes
Price per 1000:	£50
Circulation:	500 (increasing)

TIME HAIKU

Frequency:	Twice yearly
Subscription Cost:	£5.50 p.a. including two newsletters
Single Issue:	£2.50
Back issue price:	£2.50
Cheques/PO Payable to:	K.K. Facey
Overseas subs:	£7 Europe £10 other
Payment Details:	Sterling cheques, foreign currency must allow for commission

Description

Time Haiku is a magazine (founded 1995) which publishes haiku, tanka and short poems in English. Short essays are published and there are articles on various aspects of haiku. The main intention of the magazine is to make haiku more accessible and popular and to provide a place where all types of haiku can be found. Works by new writers are just as welcome as that of established haiku writers. The magazine is intended to appeal both to experts and those just curious about haiku. A newsletter is also published twice a year to give information about haiku and other poetry events. Past contributors have been Gavin Ewart, John Light, Chris Sykes, Douglas Johnson, Dan Rugh and so on!!

Addresses

Editorial:	105 Kings Head Hill, London E4 7JG
Reviews:	As above
Subscriptions:	As above
Payment terms to contributors:	-
Accept/Rejection approximate times:	About 1 in 5 acceptances
Inserts accepted:	Yes
Price per 1000:	£1
Circulation:	Increasing

TOCHER

Frequency:	Bi-annual
Subscription Cost:	£6.00 for 2 issues
Single Issue:	£3.50
Back issue price:	Issues 2-24 75p / 26-43 £1.00 / 44 £2.00
Cheques/PO Payable to:	Tocher
Overseas subs:	$18 for 2
Payment Details:	

Description

Tocher - the name was chosen because of its fairly common use in both Scots and Gaelic, meaning dowry - contains some of the riches stored in the archives of the School of Scottish Studies. That archive now contains about 10,000 tapes, as well as a large number of video recordings. Transcriptions of some of those have been issued in Tocher since 1971. There are stories and legends, songs, items on customs, children's rhymes, proverbs, riddles, the occasional recipe, and reminiscences of daily life from Shetland to the Borders. Items in Gaelic are translated into English, and glossaries are added to Scots items when that is thought appropriate.

The production of the magazine is entirely done by the staff of the School of Scottish Studies, and it is printed in the University of Edinburgh.

Tocher 51 (Winter 1995) is given over to excerpts from class work by students of Scottish Ethnology. No 52 is now nearing printing stage.

Addresses

Editorial:	Miss Morag MacLeod, School of Scottish Studies, 27 George Square, Edinburgh EH8 9LD
Reviews:	As above
Subscriptions:	Mrs Fran Beckett (As above)
Payment terms to contributors:	N/A
Accept/Rejection approximate times:	N/A
Inserts accepted:	No

Price per 1000:   N/A
Circulation: 800

TOUCHPAPER

Frequency:	Variable: 2/3 issues yearly
Subscription Cost:	£1.50 for 5 issues
Single Issue:	Free for SAE/IRC
Back issue price:	N/A
Cheques/PO Payable to:	Tony Lee
Overseas subs:	2 x IRC per issue
Payment Details:	-

Description

The science fiction newsletter of polemics and review. Touchpaper is an irregular newsletter of commentary, review and other matters of interest to anybody concerned with the science fiction genre. Readers, writers, critics, academics and publicists are all welcome to send us their opinions and views (relevant or irrelevant) about science fiction. Please study our guidelines for contributers (available for sae/IRC) before submitting nonfiction writings. Like many other (similar or not) genre publications of today, the contents of Touchpaper may be subject to editorial vagaries and whim. There isn't a fixed policy or schedule. All writings will be considered, so long as the material fits in with the newsletter's basic theme. Contributors have free rein to say whatever they want but libellous stuff will go straight in the rubbish bin.

Addresses

Editorial:	Tony Lee, Pigasus Press, 13 Hazely Coombe, Arreton, Isle of Wight PO30 3AJTel. 01983-865668
Reviews:	
Subscriptions:	
Payment terms to contributors:	Copies only
Accept/Rejection approximate times:	Approx 1 month
Inserts accepted:	Yes
Price per 1000:	Free
Circulation:	Unknown

TREE SPIRIT

Frequency:	3/4 annually
Subscription Cost:	£10 waged £6.50 unwaged
Single Issue:	£1.50
Back issue price:	£1
Cheques/PO Payable to:	Tree Spirit
Overseas subs:	£15
Payment Details:	Cheque, postal order, foreign currency

Description

The magazine of Tree Spirit, charity 801511, includes news and views on all matters related to trees; poems, drawings, stories and articles which are tree orientated. Tree Spirit's aims are to protect trees and woodlands, to create new woods, to promote a greater understanding, awareness and affection for trees, woods and the natural environment.

Addresses

Editorial:	Tree Spirit, Hawkbatch Farm, Arley, Nr. Bewdley, Worcs. DY12 3AH
Reviews:	As above
Subscriptions:	Glennie Kindred, Appletree Cottage, Dale End, Brassington, Matlock, Derbyshire DE4 4HA
Payment terms to contributors:	Free copy of magazine
Accept/Rejection approximate times:	1 month from receipt
Inserts accepted:	No
Price per 1000:	N/A
Circulation:	350-500

UNDERSTANDING MAGAZINE

Frequency:	2 yearly or one double issue
Subscription Cost:	£6 for 2 issues
Single Issue:	£3
Back issue price:	£2.50
Cheques/PO Payable to:	Dionysia Press Ltd.
Overseas subs:	£8
Payment Details:	Sterling cheque, Visa

Description

Understanding magazine includes poems, short stories, parts of plays or whole plays if they are small and book reviews. Understanding magazine was founded by Denise Smith in 1989.

Addresses

Editorial:	20A Montgomery St. Edinburgh EH7 5JSEditor Denise Smith, Associate Editor Thom Nairn.
Reviews:	As above
Subscriptions:	Same address
Payment terms to contributors:	Free copy of magazine
Accept/Rejection approximate times:	6 months
Inserts accepted:	Yes
Price per 1000:	£100 per page, a flyer £25
Circulation:	400 increasing

UNIVERSAL MIND THE

Frequency:	Biannual
Subscription Cost:	£4.50
Single Issue:	£2.50
Back issue price:	None available
Cheques/PO Payable to:	Carl Thomas
Overseas subs:	£5 for EEC/$10 for USA
Payment Details:	Postal orders, sterling cheques. Foreign currencies must allow for exchange

Description

The Universal Mind is a new magazine which seeks to explore the unusual in all its forms, with stories of horror, science fiction and fantasy. Poetry and illustrations are also sought, please send examples. The first edition featured stories by Nicholas Royle, Ramsey Campbell, J.N. Williamson and Simon Clark. The response to the first edition has been unexpectedly good. To quote: 'Thank you very much for The Universal Mind. My God! The magazine took me by surprise!A small press magazine with glossy paper and extremely professional in appearance? I was brought up on a diet of ink duplicated magazines with dodgy print, haphazard stapling and certainly no photographs. Seriously though, your magazine is a delight to the eye in both content, design and production; and I'm proud to be part of it on its debut issue.' (From Simon Clark, author of Nailed by the Heart and Blood Crazy); 'I've seen a copy of your excellent first issue of TUM' (From D.F. Lewis, author of 900 stories); 'Thanks for sending me my copy of The Universal Mind. I was very impressed with the quality of the magazine as a whole, very professionaly typset, striking colour cover and some very enjoyable and varied stories.' (Andrew Hook); 'Thank you for issue 1 of The Universal Mind. I was pleasantly surprised when I ripped open the envelope to find an A4 glossy with very professional production values and nice artwork (especially the front cover). I began reading, and found an excellent mix of top quality, thoughtful and exciting fiction.' (Tom Bellon). 'I just received my copy of The Universal Mind and I am very impressed. It's one of the best looking short story magazines I've ever seen, and for a new venture and a first issue!' (Caroline Campbell).

Addresses

Editorial: Carl Thomas, 4 Baptist Street, Rhos, Wrexham LL14 1RH

Reviews:	As above
Subscriptions:	As above
Payment terms to contributors:	Free copy of magazine
Accept/Rejection approximate times:	Hard to say
Inserts accepted:	Yes
Price per 1000:	£40
Circulation:	Quickly increasing

URTHONA

Frequency:	Twice yearly
Subscription Cost:	£6.50
Single Issue:	£3.50
Back issue price:	£3
Cheques/PO Payable to:	Urthona
Overseas subs:	Air mail £11.50 Surface £8.50
Payment Details:	Sterling cheque drawn on UK Bank IMO (Sterling) postal orders

Description

Urthona (founded 1992) is dedicated to exploring the arts from a spiritual perspective. We see beauty in its widest sense as a tool for change - both personal and social. Urthona publishes contemporary poetry, short stories, reviews and indepth articles on artists (modern and 'old masters') whose work exhibits a dynamic spiritual vision. We are particularly inspired by the Buddhist Tradition of the east and by the work of Williana Blake - 'Urthona is his arche typal spirit of the Imagination.

Addresses

Editorial:	3 Coral Park, Henley Road, Cambridge CB1 3EA
Reviews:	As above
Subscriptions:	As above
Payment terms to contributors:	All cotributions are voluntary
Accept/Rejection approximate times:	1 month
Inserts accepted:	Yes
Price per 1000:	-
Circulation:	700

VARIOUS ARTISTS

Frequency:	1 annually
Subscription Cost:	£3
Single Issue:	£1
Back issue price:	£1
Cheques/PO Payable to:	A Lewis James
Overseas subs:	$5
Payment Details:	Cash

Description
Various Artists Bristol's premier poetry magazine. We also accept good graphics. Recent issues have included work by R.L. Cook, Sophie Hannah and Mary Maher. We like good, well-written poems up to 40 lines. No misogynist, racist or anti-minority stuff pleace.

Addresses
Editorial:	65 Springfield Avenue Bristol BS7 4QS
Reviews:	As above
Subscriptions:	As above
Payment terms to contributors:	1 complimentary copy
Accept/Rejection approximate times:	10 days-2 weeks
Inserts accepted:	Yes
Price per 1000:	-
Circulation:	250

VELVET VAMPYRE THE

Frequency:	3 or 4 times a year
Subscription Cost:	£16.00
Single Issue:	£2.60
Back issue price:	£2.60
Cheques/PO Payable to:	The Vampyre Society
Overseas subs:	£24.00
Payment Details:	English/sterling cheque/PO

Description

Vampyre based A5 glossy black/white spot colour magazine. With news, reviews on books, films, occasional music. Stories fiction, horror, vampyre, romantic gothic. Illustrations, photos, articles on Vampyre Society events. Fashion, accessories, product information. Small ads. Hoping to expand to include more lifestyle and home interest.

Published by The Vampyre Society (founded in 1987 by Carole Bohanan).

Addresses

Editorial:	PO Box 68, Keighley, West Yorkshire BD22 6RW
Reviews:	As above
Subscriptions:	As above
Payment terms to contributors:	None - free copy of magazine
Accept/Rejection approximate times:	6 months
Inserts accepted:	Yes
Price per 1000:	£80
Circulation:	700 - 1000

VIGIL

Frequency:	2 p.a.
Subscription Cost:	£5.50
Single Issue:	£2.80
Back issue price:	£1.20 - £1.80
Cheques/PO Payable to:	Vigil Publications
Overseas subs:	£7
Payment Details:	

Description

Exploration of relationship through poetry and fiction from writers around the world. An international journey into what it means by human amidst daily threats to freedom from political oppression, the tyranny of hunger and poverty or the chains of technological control systems.Affirmation of the sanctity of the human spirit through the beauty of heart and soul expression in poems and stories of highest endeavour. Above all fellowship in the craft of words to promote greater consciousness of our humanity rejoicing in our cultural diversity yet coming together in the common cause of our inspiration.

Addresses

Editorial:	Vigil Publications, 12 Priory Mead, Bruton, Somerset, BA10 0PZ
Reviews:	As above
Subscriptions:	As above
Payment terms to contributors:	Currently 2 free copies/under review as an eventual move towards cash payment
Accept/Rejection approximate times:	6 weeks - we're aiming to shorten the time period.
Inserts accepted:	Yes
Price per 1000:	25
Circulation:	250

WEARWOLF

Frequency:	Sporadic
Subscription Cost:	£3 for 5 issues
Single Issue:	2 x 26p stamps
Back issue price:	On request
Cheques/PO Payable to:	Wolfs Head Press
Overseas subs:	On request
Payment Details:	Strictly CWO

Description

Wearwolf is published sporadically and tends to change direction faster than Tony Blair, but without the sound bytes, and mad staring eyes. Well, without the sound bytes anyway. Poetry submissions should be no longer than 10 lines in length and to be considered must include the words 'autotelic,' 'Pelaglanism' and 'uzzard. 'Fiction submissions must include a number of compulsory characters, list supplied on request.

Addresses

Editorial:	Wolfs Head Press, P.O. Box 77, Sunderland SR1 1EB
Reviews:	-
Subscriptions:	-
Payment terms to contributors:	No, no, you pay us!
Accept/Rejection approximate times:	Within a generation
Inserts accepted:	Yes
Price per 1000:	Negotiable
Circulation:	Variable

WEST COAST MAGAZINES

Frequency:	3 per year
Subscription Cost:	£10 (four issues)
Single Issue:	£2.50 includes post and package
Back issue price:	£2.50 includes post and package
Cheques/PO Payable to:	West Coast Magazine
Overseas subs:	£15 if paid in sterling - £20 if other
Payment Details:	Sorry, but due to many let downs in the past we cannot send subs, current issues

Description

West Coast Magazine consists of: short fiction, poetry, articles, essays and reviews. Our aim is always to be a platform for mainly new and up and coming, as well as the established writers. The editors of West Coast Magazine demand a high quality in the standard of work we publish. We like to see works from writers who enjoy a challenge - the quirky and offbeat usually sit well with us. As ever space is a deciding factor when selecting material and for that reason we like to try and keep things to around 3,500 words. We will, though, publish bigger pieces if we like them enough, buy they would need to be quite special. We like sequences of poems, or groups of poems that compliment each other, though that is not strictly necessary. Single poems are welcome also. As for articles, we will publish anything of interest, preferably literary interest, but not necessarily so - in the past we have published articles on football, music, French cinema, public sector housing and contemporary art among others. Please always send a SAE with contributions or no reply, and don't overload the envelope 2 or 3 short stories max. and 5-6 poems (unless, and only if , they are a larger sequence). Like most mags cash is in short supply, but we do always try to pay a small ` fee.

Addresses

Editorial:	Top Floor, 15 Hope Street, Glasgow G2 6AB
Reviews:	As above
Subscriptions:	As above
Payment terms to contributors:	Small fee when we can, usually after publication.

Accept/Rejection
approximate times: Please allow 8 weeks for reply
Inserts accepted: Yes
Price per 1000:   £50 (1000 only)
Circulation: 850

WEYFARERS

Frequency:	3 times a year
Subscription Cost:	£5.00
Single Issue:	£2.00
Back issue price:	£1
Cheques/PO Payable to:	Guildford Poets Press
Overseas subs:	£6.00 (sterling)
Payment Details:	If in foreign draft add £6.00 equivalent.

Description

An independent magazine founded in 1972 which now travels world-wide. Poetry serious and humorous, rhymed / metred and free verse. Three issues per year: different editors take turns, giving variety. Payment for contributors is a free copy and good company of new and established poets, and widely read. Copyright remains with poet. SEE A COPY BEFORE SENDING POEMS Linked to annual competition with prizes. Free Newsletter to subscribers tells of poetry events, other mags, books etc. Our accepted poems are largely mainstream / modern. Current Editors are Margaret Pain, Martin Jones, Jeffrey Wheatley.

Addresses

Editorial:	1 Mountside, Guildford, Surrey GU2 5JD
Reviews:	As above
Subscriptions:	9 White Rose Lane, Woking, Surrey GU22 7JA
Payment terms to contributors:	1 free copy only
Accept/Rejection approximate times:	Up to 4 months depending on when received, deadlines end May / September / January
Inserts accepted:	Yes but very limited by prior arrangement
Price per 1000:	See above
Circulation:	300

WHISTLE HOUSE THE

Frequency:	Quarterly
Subscription Cost:	£2.50
Single Issue:	None (annual only)
Back issue price:	Negotiable
Cheques/PO Payable to:	The Whistle House
Overseas subs:	£6 sterling Europe/America
Payment Details:	IMO, sterling cheque, postal order

Description

A 'flaucing' literary magazine promoting the Interiorist approach to poetry, and condemning both the 'ancien regime' of Oxford/London publishers and the slick approach of the Huddersfield/Newcastle brigade. Poetry, prose (under 1500) reviews and controversial articles. The Whistle House is dedicated to blowing the whistle on contemporary poetry! No Arts Council grant, no back-scratching, just flagrant raspberry-blowing!

Addresses

Editorial:	4 Hamilton Road, Windle, St. Helens, Merseyside WA10 6HG
Reviews:	As above
Subscriptions:	As above
Payment terms to contributors:	Single copy
Accept/Rejection approximate times:	3 weeks average. For survival purposes, subscribers are preferred!
Inserts accepted:	Yes
Price per 1000:	Swop for own flyers, other mags. only
Circulation:	New magazine (unknown)

WINDLESORA

Frequency:	Annually
Subscription Cost:	-
Single Issue:	£2
Back issue price:	£2 + p & p 35p
Cheques/PO Payable to:	Windsor Local History Publications Group
Overseas subs:	-
Payment Details:	-

Description

Windlesora is the local history journal for the town of Windsor and its surrounding villages. Articles should only be submitted if they have been written following research into original sources or are memories of people who have lived in the town. We do not want re-hashes of already published work or articles about the Castle or Eton College. Most contributions come from local people but we are particularly interested in contacting experts on various topics who can write about the Windsor aspect of their interest. In this way we have already published an article on some of Windsor's historic pillar boxes. We are also interested in family historians who have traced their family back to Windsor. We review appropriate books, museums and exhibitions. Articles of 2500 words are required down to 100 word fillers. We print black and white photographs and drawings. Windlesora 15 is due to be published in November 1996 and copy for No 16 is required by August 1997.

Addresses

Editorial:	256 Dedworth Road, Windsor SL4 4JR
Reviews:	
Subscriptions:	
Payment terms to contributors:	Free copy
Accept/Rejection approximate times:	2 weeks
Inserts accepted:	No
Price per 1000:	N/A
Circulation:	500

WORDS WORTH (Journal of Language Arts)

Frequency:	Irregular
Subscription Cost:	For 3 issues Individual £12; Institution £20
Single Issue:	Individual £4.50; Institution £8
Back issue price:	As above (Issue 2: 1 OP)
Cheques/PO Payable to:	Words Worth Books
Overseas subs:	Same as above but £3.50 p& p to USA
Payment Details:	Sterling or double total price to cover Bank charges

Description

Editor: Alaric Sumner. Various Guest Editors incl. Paul Buck, Richard Tabor. founded 1977. Publishes innovative work related to language including: visual, found and performance texts, text sound compositions, linguistically-innovative work. Writers/artists have included Susan Hiller, Ernst Jandl (TRS Michael Hamburger), Bernard Noel, Mac Wellman, Richard Kostelanetz, Dom Sylvester Houedard (dsh), Carlyle Reedy, cris cheek, Henri Chopin. Building a reputation despite erratic publication history. Issue Vol 2 No. 2 (2:2) Performance. Issue 2:3 New technology. (in pre-formative stages). Editors seek work that surprises and amazes them by its unconventional content and form.

Addresses

Editorial:	B.M. Box 4515, London WC1N 3XX
Reviews:	As above
Subscriptions:	As above
Payment terms to contributors:	2 copies of magazine
Accept/Rejection approximate times:	Various - definite rejection often by return!
Inserts accepted:	Yes (Advertising rates available)
Price per 1000:	-
Circulation:	Print run 300 at present

WORKING TITLES

Frequency:	Annual
Subscription Cost:	£4.50 for 3
Single Issue:	£1.50
Back issue price:	£1.50
Cheques/PO Payable to:	C. Williamson
Overseas subs:	$8 or equivalent
Payment Details:	Cash

Description
Working Titles does not accept any work which is racist, misogynistic or any other anti-minority material.

Addresses
Editorial:	5 Hillside, Clifton Wood, Bristol BS8 4TD
Reviews:	As above
Subscriptions:	As above
Payment terms to contributors:	1 magazine
Accept/Rejection approximate times:	1 month
Inserts accepted:	Yes
Price per 1000:	
Circulation:	250

WORKS

Frequency:	One or two per year
Subscription Cost:	£5 x two issues
Single Issue:	£2.50, From issue #11
Back issue price:	Sold out
Cheques/PO Payable to:	Works
Overseas subs:	
Payment Details:	

Description

I prefer stories that are slightly off - tilt, but they should have some form of logic or foundation. I favour stories that are really different, but don't try to be different for its own sake. I don't want stories of over 5000 words. Subjects preferred are SF, Surreal, Speculative, and will occasionally consider Horror. Ideally you should get a copy of Works as that is the real way you'll get any idea of what I like. I like poetry with strong imagery, in a industrial, isolation, deserted landscapes, etc. If you mange to get any of these icons in your prose you're half way there. No more that 50 lines. non-fiction articles from 500-4000 words. As long as they're related to SF, publishing small press etc., if you have any ideas send a synopsis to me and we can maybe see it through. I'm open to any ideas. I'm always interested in artwork. I usually forward the artist a story to illustrate. If you're an artist, send me a few pages of your work and we'll take it from there. All stories, poetry, artwork and articles should have your name on each page. I prefer stories to be double spaced. I really insist on a covering letter though, because if you can't be bothered to talk to me, how do you expect me to talk to you? A SAE should be enclosed for the return of acceptance / rejection or ms. Finally whilst I do take care over manuscripts I can't be held responsible once Postman Pat has them, so NEVER send originals

Addresses

Editorial:	12 Blakestones Road, Slaithwaite, Huddersfield, HD7 5UQ
Reviews:	As above
Subscriptions:	As above
Payment terms	
to contributors:	Complimentary copy

Accept/Rejection
approximate times: One to three weeks
Inserts accepted: Negotiable
Price per 1000:
Circulation: 4000

WORSHARE

Frequency:	As and when sufficient suitable writing comes in
Subscription Cost:	Nil
Single Issue:	N/A
Back issue price:	-
Cheques/PO Payable to:	-
Overseas subs:	-
Payment Details:	-

Description

Creative writing magazine Wordshare welcomes contributions from disabled people, and people past retirement age. It is an A4 format magazine funded by the Eastern Arts Board.

Addresses

Editorial:	John Wilkinson, 8 Bodmin Moor Close, North Hykham, Lincoln LN6 9BB
Reviews:	-
Subscriptions:	-
Payment terms to contributors:	No payment. One copy for every submission; two copies for those accepted
Accept/Rejection approximate times:	-
Inserts accepted:	No
Price per 1000:	N/A
Circulation:	4000

WRITER'S GUIDE AND FICTION FOCUS

Frequency: Alternate months
Subscription Cost: £10 inc.
Single Issue: £1.80 inc.
Back issue price:
Cheques/PO Payable to: G Carroll
Overseas subs:
Payment Details:

Description
This magazine publishes market and media information for freelance journalists and hobby writers, including short story authors, latest news about consumer, professional, business, independent and small press publications and their requirements. Competitions and other opportunities for beginners and the more experienced. News welcomed but not normally acknowledged until used preliminary suggestions advised for articles.

Addresses
Editorial: 11 Shirley Street, Hove, East Sussex, BN3 3WJ
Reviews: As above
Subscriptions: As above
Payment terms
to contributors: £1 per 100 words minimum more where justified
Accept/Rejection
approximate times: By return
Inserts accepted: Yes
Price per 1000:   By negotiation
Circulation: Small Ads - 5p a word TITLE: Display Ads - Camera ready A5 page £10 TITLE: Half page horizontal £7

WRITERS FORUM

Frequency:	Quarterly
Subscription Cost:	£14.50 (£18.00 overseas)
Single Issue:	£3.35
Back issue price:	£2.00
Cheques/PO Payable to:	Writers Forum
Overseas subs:	£18.00 Europe / £21 rest of world
Payment Details:	Cheques / POs / (sterling cheques preferred)

Description

Writers Forum is a quarterly magazine designed to help, guide and inspire the new and semi-professional writer along the sometimes rocky path to publication. It carries regular articles on the art, craft and business of writing, covering all specialisms, from poetry and short fiction to playwriting and novels. Foto Forum is now a regular feature: plus two pages of market information - articles and photographs and a full page of writing competition news in each edition. Edited by Hugh Graham, Foto Forum will guide newcomers from first principles to professional-quality darkroom techniques while helping experienced photographers to improve their skills. Writers Forum also organises annual Open Writing Competitions, the winners of which, in addition to substantial cash prizes, see their entries published during the following year.

Addresses

Editorial:	John Benton, 9/10 Roberts Close, Moxley Wednesbury, West Midlands, WS10 8SQ
Reviews:	As above
Subscriptions:	As above
Payment terms to contributors:	£8 - £10 per 1000 words published
Accept/Rejection approximate times:	Six - eight weeks
Inserts accepted:	Yes
Price per 1000:	£20
Circulation:	1000+

WRITERS OWN MAGAZINE

Frequency:	Quarterly
Subscription Cost:	£8 per year
Single Issue:	£2
Back issue price:	£1.75
Cheques/PO Payable to:	Mrs E.M. Pickering
Overseas subs:	£2.75 Single, £11.00 per year
Payment Details:	Sterling (money orders preferred payable to E.M Pickering)

Description
Includes short stories (max 1,500 words), Articles (max 800 words), Poetry (max 32 lines)- on most subjects, but must be in good taste. Market information and competitions, Letters pages, a quarterly competition with small money prizes and booklet, plus critique/score points. Now in its 16th year of publication.No payment except in copy of the magazine in which work appears, or extension of subscription.

Addresses

Editorial:	121 Highbury Grove, Clapham, Bedford, Bed's
Reviews:	Same as above
Subscriptions:	Same as above
Payment terms to contributors:	Copy of magazine
Accept/Rejection approximate times:	2 weeks
Inserts accepted:	Yes
Price per 1000:	£3 per 100
Circulation:	200

WRITERS VIEWPOINT

Frequency:	Quarterly
Subscription Cost:	£12 Posted
Single Issue:	£3.00 Posted
Back issue price:	£3.00 Posted
Cheques/PO Payable to:	Viewpoint Manuscript Service
Overseas subs:	European £15 USA $22
Payment Details:	

Description

We publish short-short stories, articles and poems. We prefer the punchy and provocative, but, in fact, publish a whole range of material. Some of our contributors are well known while others are just starting their careers.We also run open competitions for adults childrens short stories, articles and poems with closing dates of March 31st, May 31st, September 30th and December 31st every year. Prizes and gifts total £1,000. There's an optional critique service at £1 per entry- typed. This service has been much praised, we run a postal workshop.
In folio form, currently there are five.

Addresses

Editorial:	Viewpoint Manuscript Service, P.O Box 514,Eastbourne, East Sussex, BN23 6RE
Reviews:	
Subscriptions:	
Payment terms to contributors:	None
Accept/Rejection approximate times:	24 hours normally
Inserts accepted:	Yes
Price per 1000:	Negotiable
Circulation:	1,000

WRITERS' EXPRESS

Frequency:	Quarterly
Subscription Cost:	£10
Single Issue:	£2.50
Back issue price:	£2.50
Cheques/PO Payable to:	Cherrybite Publications
Overseas subs:	£11 or £3 single issue
Payment Details:	Sterling or travellers cheque

Description
Dedicated to helping writers into print. Short stories, articles, advice, readers' letters. A5, card cover, 40 pages

Addresses

Editorial:	Linden Cottage, 45 Burton Road, Little Neston, S. Wirral L64 4AE
Reviews:	As above
Subscriptions:	As above
Payment terms to contributors:	Copies only
Accept/Rejection approximate times:	2 weeks
Inserts accepted:	Yes
Price per 1000:	Reciprocal
Circulation:	150

WRITING WOMEN

Frequency:	Bi annually
Subscription Cost:	£7.50 for 2 issues
Single Issue:	£4, £4.50 overseas
Back issue price:	£2.50 (inc postage) £2 overseas
Cheques/PO Payable to:	Writing Women
Overseas subs:	£14 including airmail
Payment Details:	Cheque or P.O

Description

Writing Women publishes poetry and prose by women. The aim is to demonstrate the high quality and the diversity and creative achievement amongst women writers. Our prose contributions, are generally less than 3000 words in length. We only accept six poems at a time. An S.A.E is essential. We do not have a narrow ideological approach- we are interested in innovative work of all kinds.

Addresses

Editorial:	PO Box 111, Newcastle Upon Tyne NE3 1WF
Reviews:	Same as above
Subscriptions:	Same as above
Payment terms to contributors:	£10 per 1000 words £10 per poem + free subscription
Accept/Rejection approximate times:	2-4 Months
Inserts accepted:	Yes
Price per 1000:	Done on exchange basis
Circulation:	1000

XENOS

Frequency:	Bi-monthly
Subscription Cost:	£16.50
Single Issue:	£3.45
Back issue price:	£3.45
Cheques/PO Payable to:	Xenos
Overseas subs:	EEC Same as UK. Rest of the World £22.50
Payment Details:	UK cheque or postal order. Overseas Sterling only: Either cheque drawn on UK Bank or international money order.

Description

Established 1990, Xenos is the premier short story magazine for both readers and writers. Submissions welcomed of all genres except blood and gore, gratuitous violence, pornography of the purely romantic. We publish short stories only (i.e. no poetry, plays, articles reviews etc.) Please submit only one story at a time. We give honest, constructive criticisms on nearly all material received, and suggest ideas for revising at no charge. Good, clear presentation and an acceptable knowledge of English spelling and grammar are essential. Suitably stamped s.a.e. or sufficient IRCs must be included for reply. Our turn round time is normally no more than 4 weeks. Word lengths: upper limit 10,000, lower limit 2000. Each issue of Xenos carries 6-7 excellent and varied stories. The evaluation section allows readers to give constructive criticism on the stories in the previous issue. We have been publishing Xenos for over 6 years and every issue has appeared on time. We have a loyal readership of all ages, both nationally and internationally. Our continuing aim is to help and advise writers of all abilities.

Addresses

Editorial:	29 Prebend Street, Bedford MK40 1QN
Reviews:	N/A
Subscriptions:	As above
Payment terms to contributors:	Complimentary copy of magazine. Annual competition awards cash and subscription

Accept/Rejection
approximate times: -
Inserts accepted: No
Price per 1000:   N/A
Circulation: Continually increasing

YELLOW CRANE THE

Frequency:	Quarterly
Subscription Cost:	£7
Single Issue:	£1.50
Back issue price:	£1.50
Cheques/PO Payable to:	The Yellow Crane
Overseas subs:	£10
Payment Details:	IMO, cheque, postal order

Description
Interesting new poems from South Wales and beyond...

Addresses

Editorial:	J. Brookes, Flat 6, 23 Richmond Crescent, Roath, Cardiff CF2 3AH
Reviews:	As above
Subscriptions:	As above
Payment terms to contributors:	2 copies of magazine
Accept/Rejection approximate times:	Goodness knows
Inserts accepted:	No
Price per 1000:	N/A
Circulation:	Growing

YORKSHIRE JOURNAL

Frequency:	Quarterly
Subscription Cost:	£12 p.a.
Single Issue:	£2.95
Back issue price:	£2.95
Cheques/PO Payable to:	Smith Settle Ltd.
Overseas subs:	Add £2 Europe and £4 Rest of the world
Payment Details:	Postal order, cheque, Visa, Access

Description
Yorkshire Journal contains in-depth features about Yorkshire, short stories, poetry, photographs and drawings. The magazine is attractively designed and well produced. It covers topics such as Yorkshire history, culture, landscape, customs, art, people, current events, architecture and literature.

Addresses

Editorial:	Ilkley Road, Otley, West Yorkshire LS21 3JP
Reviews:	As above
Subscriptions:	As above
Payment terms to contributors:	Complimentary copy of magazine plus payment to article and short story writers
Accept/Rejection approximate times:	As soon as possible, usually within a month
Inserts accepted:	Yes
Price per 1000:	£20
Circulation:	3000

ZENE

Frequency:	Quarterly
Subscription Cost:	£7
Single Issue:	£1.95
Back issue price:	Sold out
Cheques/PO Payable to:	TTA Press
Overseas subs:	USA $4.50/$16.60. Europe £2.60/£9.50
Payment Details:	Foreign cheques accepted/Eurocheque/ No Foreign Cash

Description

Every Issue features many detailed contributors guidelines of international small press and semi-professional publications-Magazines, anthologies, novels, comics, varied authoritative articles, news, views, reviews and interviews. Unsolicited articles/ideas welcome with appropriate return postage. Aspects of publishing, editing, illustrating, and especially writing. All genres, poetry and fiction Zene is litho printed onto glossy art paper, 36 pages from TTA press, the publishers of 'The Third Alternative'.

Addresses

Editorial:	Andy Cox, 5 Martins Lane, Withcham, Ely, Cambs CB6 2LB
Reviews:	Same as above
Subscriptions:	Same as above
Payment terms to contributors:	Negotiable
Accept/Rejection approximate times:	One month average
Inserts accepted:	Yes
Price per 1000:	Negotiable
Circulation:	Up to 1,000

ZONE THE

Frequency:	Irregular 2-3 Issues a year
Subscription Cost:	£10
Single Issue:	£2.50
Back issue price:	£2.00
Cheques/PO Payable to:	Tony Lee
Overseas subs:	Write for details, enclosing I.R.C
Payment Details:	

Description

The Zone is the last word in science fiction magazines; with excellent short fiction, big name interviews, insightful criticism and incisive articles - plus complete coverage of SF in the media, with illustrated review colums in every issue . . .

The Zone publishes original SF stories alongside genre poetry and experimental or stylist prose of the highest quality. Nonfiction is of vital importance too, and so The Zone features interviews, articles, essays and regular review columns - covering all manner of relevant (and irrelevant) science fictional topics and themes in the media. Unsolicited mss are welcome. We are looking for high quality, speculative fiction, with plenty of ideas and imagination - but it does not have to be 'hard-SF'. We are not interested in 'epic fantasy quest sagas' (with wizards and warriors, etc.) or any traditional or contemporary horror (satanism, werewolves/needless gore of serial killers, respectively). However, subtle SF-fantasy may be acceptable.

Fiction for The Zone should be of approx 1000 to 5000 words. SF poetry is published in The Zone, by invitation only. The work of one genre poet will be featured in the magazine's poetry showcase. Nonfiction: original articles on any aspect of science fiction (retrospective or topical), will be considered. Please write first, outlining your idea. Several special projects are ongoing and others are in development - send an SAE/IRC if you want details of these. Length of any nonfiction works, by arrangement with the magazine's editors, but articles of 1000 to 5000 words (or longer if serialised), will be considered. Book reviews (approx: 250 to 500+ words) by arrangement with editors. Send samples of your published reviews and list of your favourite SF authors. Designed for the discerning readers of SF fandom. The Zone aims to please the lifetime enthusiast and genre newcomers alike.

Addresses

Editorial: PIGASUS PRESS, 13 Hazely Combe, Arreton, Isle of Wight, PO30 3AJ

Reviews: As above

Subscriptions: as above

Payment terms
to contributors: Token payment (currently £5.00 / $10.00) plus free copy, paid on publication.

Accept/Rejection
approximate times: Varies from 2-5 weeks

Inserts accepted: No

Price per 1000: N/A

Circulation: No figures available

A CHANGE OF ZINERY
Address: Peter Cox, 58 Pennington, Orton Goldhay,
                        Peterborough PE2 0RB
Accept: SF. fantasy, horror. Peterborough Area
                        contributors only

- 0 -

A WAY OF LIFE
Address: Andy Farr, 4 Firbeck, Birch Green, Skelmersdale,
                        Lancashire WN8 6PW
Accept: Music Interviews, reviews, articles

- 0 -

ACTIVE IN AIRTIME
Address: Ralph Hawkins & John Muckle, 53 East Hill,   Colchester,
                        Essex CO1 3QY
Accept: Poetry

- 0 -

ADVENTURE PROBE
Address: Barbara Gibb, 52 Burford Road, Liverpool
                        L16 6AQ
Accept: Computer games, Information, Fiction, Reviews,
                        Poetry

- 0 -

AKLO
Address: Mark Valentine, 10/12 Castle Gate, Clitheroe,
                        Lancs. BB7 1AZ
Accepts: Journal of the Fantastic

ALBEDOL

Address: 2 Post Road, Lusk, Co. Dublin, Ireland
Accepts: Science fiction, fantasy, horror

- o -

ALFRED DAVID EDITIONS

Address: 3a Palace Road, London SW2 3DY
Accepts: Poetry

- o -

ALL HALLOWS

Address: Barbara Roden, Ashcroft, 2 Abbotsford Drive, Penyffgordd,
                Chester CH4 0JG
Accepts: Magazine of the Ghost Story Society

- o -

ALTERNATIES

Address: Mark Rose, 39 Balfour Court, Station Road, Harpenden,
                Herts AL5 4XT
Accept: SF.Fantasy, Horror, Articles, Fiction, Poetry

- o -

ALTERNATIVE WORLDS

Address: Michael Morton, 19 Bruce Street, Rodbourne,
                Swindon,
                Wilts. SN2 2EL
Accept: Alternative history, Articles, Fiction, Artwork, Maps

- o -

ANARCHIST ANGEL

Address: Liz Berry, 5 Aylesford Close, Sedgley, Nr. Dudley, West
                Midlands DY3 3QB
Accepts: Youth poetry

- o -

AND NOW FOR SOMETHING COMPLETELY DIFFERENT

Address: James Gent, 1 Pond Meadow, Milford Haven, Dyfed, Wales
                SA73 1HB
Accepts: Monty Python: Reviews etc.

- o -

ANTHEM

Address: Howard Roake, 36 Cyril Avenue, Bobbers Mill,
                Nottingham
                NG8 5BA
Accepts: Poetry

- o -

APOTHEOSIS OF THE HAMBURGER

Address: Andy Butler, English Department, Hull University,
                Hull
Accepts: SF research

- o -

AREOPAGUS

Address: Julian Barritt, 27 Old Gloucester Road, London
                WC1N 3XX
Accepts: Christian oriented fiction, poems, articles

ASTARTE

Address: V H Monks, Muchaxo, Mont es Croix, Beauport, St.
                Brelade, Jersey JE3 8EN

Accepts: Romantic & Classical: Poetry, short fiction

- o -

AT LAST

Address: 16 Ramsay Lane, Kincardine-on-Forth, Fife
                FK10 4QY

Accepts: Poems, stories, articles

- o -

AUGURIES

Address: Nik Morton, 48 Anglesey Road, Alverstoke,
                Gosport, Hampshire PO12 2EQ

Accepts: Subscribers only: SF Poetry, Fiction, Art

- o -

AWAZ

Address: Zohra Jabeen, 1 Ferndown Green, Llittle Horton,
                Bradford W. Yorkshire BD5 9QT

Accepts: BENGALI, HINDI, PUNJABI,URDI: Women Writers

- o -

BANSHEE THE

Address: Rachel Fones, 16 Rigby Close, Waddon Road,
                Croydon CRO 4JU

Accepts: Small press magazine for writers, artists & musicians

BARDONNI/STOPGAP/SONGS

Address: Peter E Presford, Rose Cottage, 3 Tram
             Lane, Buckley, Clwyd
Accepts: Poetry

- o -

BARE BONES

Address: Brian Tasker, 16 Wren Close, Frome,
             Somerset BA11 2UZ
Accepts: Haika and short poetry only

- o -

BASICALLY INSANE

Address: Gary Greenwood & Others, Number 20
             Publications, 48 St Davids Crescent, Newport,
             Gwent NP9 3AW
Accepts: Creative writing

- o -

BATS AND RED VELVET

Address: Jo 47 Cavendish Place, Newcastle upon Tyne
             NE2 2NE
Accepts: Gothic, Horror, Poems, articles, stories

- o -

BAZAAR

Address: South Asian Arts Forum 237 Bon Marche
             Blng 444, Brixton Road, London SW9 8EJ
Accepts: News, reviews, poetry, artwork

BESTINGS

Address: 19 Southminster Road, Roath, Cardiff
                           CF2 5AT

- o -

BETE NOIRE

Address: John Osbourne, American Studies, The
                           University, Collingham Road, Hull HU6 7RX
Accepts: Reviews, Interviews, Stories, Paintings,
                           Poetry

- o -

BEYOND

Address: David Riley, 130 Union Road, Oswaldwistle,
                           Lancashire BB5 3DR
Accepts: Fantasy, SF, stories

- o -

BEYOND THE BRINK

Address: Ed Hackett, PO Box 493, Sheffield S10 3YX
Accepts: Poetry, fiction, articles

- o -

BEYOND THE BOUNDARIES

Address: John Sheppard, 87 Station Street, Barry,
                           South Glamorgan, CF63 4LX
Accepts: Speculative fiction and poetry

THE BIG ISSUE

Address: John Bird, 4 Albion Place, Galena Road,
                  Hammersmith, London W6 0LT
Accepts: Social issues: features, humour, fiction

- o -

THE BIG SPOON

Address: The Editors, 32 Salisbury Court, Belfast,
                  BT7 1DD
Accepts: Irish poetry

- o -

BINDWEED

Address: Janet Goldsborough-Jones, 38 Cranworth
                  Road, Worthing, W Sussex BN11 2JF
Accepts: Anglosaxon Studies: articles, occasional
                  poems

- o -

BLACK ARTS IN LONDON

Address: 28 Shacklewell Lane, London E8 2EZ
Accepts: News, articles

- o -

BLACK LITERATURE PROJECT

Address: 12 St Georges Square, Huddersfield
                  HD1 1FJ
Accepts: News for black writers

BLACK TEARS
Address: Adam Bradley, 28 Treaty Street, Islington,
                  London N1 0SY
Accepts: Horror, stories, articles, interviews, art

- o -

BLEEDING EYESORE
Address: Paul Harrison, 1 Prince William Court,
                  Featherstone, W Yorkshire WF7 5PH
Accepts: Radical, progressive: music, film, fiction

- o -

BLITHE SPIRIT
Address: Jackie Hardy, Farnley Gate Farmhouse,
                  Riding Mill, Northumberland NE44 6AA
Accepts: Haiku, senryu, renga, tanka etc.

- o -

BLUDGEONED MAGAZINE
Address: Dean Standerwick, 48 Ingleside Road,
                  Kingswood, Bristol BS15 1JD
Accepts: Music, Occasional Poetry

- o -

BLUE CAGE
Address: Paul Donnelly, 98 Bedford Road, Birkdale,
                  Southport, Merseyside PR8 4HL
Accepts: Innovative Verse, prose, reviews, graphics

BOGG

Address: George Cairncross, 31 Belle Vue Street,
                  Filey, Yorkshire YO14 9HU
Accepts: Poetry, Short Storkes, Art, Reviews

- o -

BOGGERS ALL

Address: George Cairncross, 31 Belle Vue Street,
                  Filey, Yorkshire YO14 9HU
Accepts: All Poetry, fiction, reviews

- o -

THE BOUND SPIRAL

Address: Mario Petrucci, 72 First Avenue, Bush Hill
                  Park, Enfield EN1 1BW
Accepts: Poems, short Stories, Reviews, Art, Articles

- o -

BRIXTON POETS

Address: 2 Lorn Court, Lorn Road, London SWI OAA
Accepts: Poetry

- o -

BUTTERFLY STOMACH

Address: Sam, 5 Barlleydale Road, Barrowford, Nr. Nelson,
                  Lancashire BB9 6AD
Accepts: Poetry

- o -

CANAL AND RIVERBOAT

Address: Norman Aldborough, Stanley House, 9 West Street, Epsom, Surrey, KT18 7RL

Accepts: Waterway boating: articles, stories

- o -

CANDIS

Address: Eleanor Jones, Newhall Publications, Newhall Lane, Hoylake, Wirral L47 4BU

Accepts: Family general interest: articles, short fiction

- o -

THE CANDYMAN'S TRUMPET

Address: Kevin Cadwallender, 42 Christchurch Place, Peterlee, Co. Durham SR8 2NR

Accepts: Poetry

- o -

CARESS

Address: The Write Solution, Flat 1, 11 Holland Road, Hove, E Sussex BN3 1JF

Accepts: Markets, reviews, news of erotic fiction

- o -

CARNIVAL

Address: Carl Burness, 693 Chester Road, Erdington, Birmingham B23 5TH

Accepts: New Realist Writing

CHILLS

Address: Peter Coleborn, 46 Oxford Road, Acocks
                  Green, Birmingham, B27 6DT
Accepts: Dark Fantasy, Horror Fiction

- o -

CHRISTOIC MAN

Address: 47 Athol Street, Gorton, Manchester M18 7JP
Accepts: Christian heroic: Poetry, Prose

- o -

CLOWNS KILLING PEOPLE

Address: CKP Box 32, 52 Call Lane, Leeds LS1 6DT
Accepts: Fiction, Articles, Art, Reviews

- o -

THE CRACK

Address: c/o Crick-Crack Office, Interchange Studios,
                  Dalby St. London NW5 3NQ
Accepts: Poems, Stories, Reviews, Interviews

- o -

CRIMSON

Address: Phill White, 82 Rip Croft, Portland, Dorset
                  DT6 2EE
Accepts: Vampires: Poems, articles, stories, reviews,
                  art, music

CRITICAL QUARTERLY
Address: Programme in Literary Linguistics, University
of Strathclyde, Glasgow G1 1XH

Accepts: Poetry

- o -

THE CRYSTAL GATE
Address: c/o P. Page, Sharkti Laureate, 104 Argyle
Gardens, Upminster, Essex RM14 3EU

Accepts: New Renaissance Poetry and fantasy

- o -

CURLEW
Address: The Curlew Press, Hare Cottage, Kettlesing,
Harrogate HG3 2LR

Accepts: Poetry

- o -

CYBERSPACE
Address: Keith Cosslett, 12 Crowsbury Close,
Emsworth, Hampshire PO10 7TS

Accepts: SF; News, articles

- o -

DADAMAG
Address: W. Walker, P.O. Box 472 Norwich NR3 3TS

DARK HORIZONS

Address: Phil Williams, 8 Milton Close, Severn
Meadows, Shrewsbury SY1 2UE

Accepts: Fantasy, Horror, Fiction, Articles

- o -

THE DARK HORSE

Address: Gerry Cambridge, 19 Cunninghamhead
Estate, By Kilmarnock, Ayrshire KA3 2PY,

Accepts: Poetry

- o -

THE DARK SIDE

Address: Stray Cat Publishing, PO Box 146, Plymouth
PL1 1AX

Accepts: Interviews, Imaginative Fiction

- o -

THE DARNED THING

Address: Jean Thomas, 24 Moore Road, Granary Way,
Horsham, West Sussex RH12 1ZS

Accepts: Horsham Writers Circle Magazine

- o -

DASKHAT

Address;   Seema Jeena, 90 Dunstable Road, Luton,
Beds. LU1 1EH

Accepts;   South Asian: Poetry, Fiction, Criticism

DIAL 174
Address: Joseph Hemmings, 8 Highham Green,
Fairstead, Kings Lynn, Norfolk PE30 4RX

Accepts: Poetry, short stories, articles

- o -

DISTAFF
Address: J. Brice, London Women's Centre, Wesley
House, 4 Wild Court, Kingsway, London WC2

Accepts: Writing women

- o -

DOG
Address: David Crystal, 32b Breakspears Road,
London SE4 1UW

Accepts: Poetry

- o -

DRAKES DRUM
Address: c/o Hargreaves Close, Kings Tatterton,
Plymouth PL5 2UB

Accepts: SF, Articles, Fiction, Comics

- o -

DRAKULA KISS
Address: 3 Chapel Mews, Bridgehouse Gate, Pately
Bridge, Harrogate N. York HG3 5HG

Accepts: Strange poetry, short stories, artwork,
reviews, essays

DREAMS FROM THE STRANGERS' CAFE

Address: John Gaunt, 15 Clifton Grove, Clifton,
Rotherham, South Yorkshire S65 2AZ

Accepts: A magazine for connoisseurs of the strange

- 0 -

DREAMS FROM WITHIN

Address: Paul Rance, 17 Farrow Road, Whaplode
Drove, Spalding, Sth Lincs. PE12 0TS

Accepts: Music

- 0 -

ECO-RUNES

Address: 68b Fivey Road, Drones,
Ballymoney, N Ireland BT53 8JH

Accepts: Poetry, Prose, Art

- 0 -

EDIBLE SOCIETY

Address: Peter Godfrey, 10 Lincoln Street, Brighton,
East Sussex BN2 2UH

Accepts: Poetry, art, fresh air

EPOCH

Address: Neil Mathers, The Corbie Press, 31 Market
Street, Montrose, Angus DD10 8NB

Accepts: Politics, poetry, philosophy, art, folk music

EROTIC STORIES MAGAZINE

Address: Portland Publishing, PO Box 381, 4 Selsden
                Way, London E14 9GL
Accepts: Erotic fiction, 2500-4000 words

- o -

ESCAPE

Address: Weavers Press Publishing, Tregeraint
                House, Zennor, St. Ives, Cornwall TR26 3TB
Accepts: Career change: Articles, Poetry

- o -

EXUBERANCE

Address;   J Smith, 13 Roman Gardens, Kings Langey,
                Herts WD4 8LG
Accepts: SF, F. Horror. Fiction

- o -

40000 REASONS FOR LIVING

Address: Rob Callen, 15 Sparrow Square, Eastleight.
                Hants.SO5 3LB
Accepts;   Punk: poetry, art

- o -

FANS ACROSS THE WORLD

Address;   17 Mimosa, 29 Avenue Road, Tottenham
                N15 5JF
Accepts: SF Newsletter

FANTASYNOPSIS

Address: Paul J Brown, 1 Bascraft Way,
                Godmanchester, Huntingdon, Cambridge,
                PE18 8EG
Accepts: Film, video, articles, reviews, interviews

- o -

FATCHANCE

Address: Louise Hudson, Elm Court, East Street,
                Sheepwash, Devon EX21 5NL
Accepts: Poems

- o -

FICTION FURNACE

Address: John Williams, 17 Ankermoor Close, Shard
                End, Birmingham B34 6TF
Accepts: SF Fantasy, Gothic, Horror, Detective Short
                stories, features, art

- o -

FIRE

Address: Chris Ozzard & Jeremy Hilton, 3 Holywell
                Mews, Malvern, Worcs. WR14 1LF
Accepts: Experimental: Articles, prose, poems, visuals

- o -

FIRING SQUAD

Address: Geoff Stevens, 8 Beaconsview House,
                Charlemont Farm, West Bromwich B71 3PL
Accepts: Poetry

FLICKERS AND FRAMES
Address: c/o John F Peters, 299 Southway Drive,
                    Southway, Plymouth, Devon PL6 6QN
Accepts: SF. Horror, Reviews, interviews, film, fiction,
                    music

- o -

FOOLSCAP
Address: Judi Benson, 78 Friars Road, East Ham,
                    London E6 1LL
Accepts: Poetry, Prose

- o -

FORTNIGHT
Address: Edna Langley, 7 lower Crescent, Belfast
                    BT7 1NR
Accepts: Reviews, current affairs, poetry

- o -

FRACTAL REPORT
Address: Reeves Telecommun. Lab's Ltd. West Towan
                    House, Porthtowan, Truro TR4 8AX
Accepts: Computer art

- o -

FRAGMENTE
Address: 8 Hertford Street, Oxford OX4 3AJ
Accepts: Poetry

FREEDOM ROCK

Address: Mike Coleman, 18 Sunningdale Avenue,
                Sale, Cheshire M33 2PH

Accepts: Nice mix of humour, philosophy, poetry and
                prose

- o -

FREELANCE MARKET NEWS

Address: Freelance Press Services, Cumberland
                House, Lissadel Street, Salford M6 6GG

Accepts: News of magazine etc. markets

- o -

FREELANCE WRITING AND PHOTOGRAPHY

Address: Weavers Press Publishing, Tregartaint
                House, Zennor, St Ives, Cornwall, TR26 3DB

Accepts: Short Stories, Poems, Articles, Photos

- o -

FRICTION MAGAZINE

Address: 2 Postbrooke Road, Portsmouth, Hants
                PO4 8JJ

Accepts: Fiction & visuals

- o -

FRONT COVER

Address: Danny Fleskwater, 68b Fivey Road, Drones,
                Ballymoney, N. Ireland BT53 8JH

Accepts: Comment, Articles, Essays

FUGUE

Address: Peter Hawkins & Paul Fairbairn, 9 Aynsley
Terrace, Consett, Co. Durham DH8 5NF

Accepts: Poetry, Short Stories

- o -

FULL MOON

Address: Barbara Parkinson, Church Road, Killbyecs,
Co. Donegal, Eire

Accepts: Poetry broadsheet

- o -

GAIJIN

Address: Steve Green, 33 Scott Road, Olton, Solihull
B92 7LQ

Accepts: SF fanzine news

- o -

GAIRFISH

Address: 34 Gillies Place, Broughty Ferry, Dundee
DD5 3LE

Accepts: Poetry, Literary & Cultural Criticism

- o -

GARUDA

Address: Ulli Freer, 74 Lodge Lane, London N12 8JJ

GET CONNECTED

Address: Ali, 37 Rowley Street, Stafford, ST16 2RH
Accepts: Small presses and personal: markets, adverts

- o -

GOWN

Address: John Brown and Martin Crawford, Student
                Union, Queen's University, Belfast
Accepts: Reviews, poetry

- o -

GRANITE

Address: Alan M Kent, South Voew, Wheal Bull,
                Foxhole St.Austell, Cornwall PL26 7UA
Accepts: Cornish poetry

- o -

GRANTA

Address: 2/3 Hanover Yard, Noel Road, Islington,
                London N1 8BE
Accepts: Fiction

- o -

GREENSCENE

Address: Sean McElherron, Parkdale, Dunham Road,
                Altrincham, Cheshire WA14 4QG
Accepts: Vegetarian: articles, short stories

GRILLE
Address: Simon Smith, 53 Ormonde Court, Upper
                            Richmond Road, London SW15 6TP
Accepts: Avante-garde: Poetry

- o -

GRIM HUMOUR
Address: Andrea Parsons & Richard Johnson, PO Box
                            63, Herne Bay, Kent, CT6 6YU
Accepts: Underground music: Articles

- o -

GROTESQUE
Address: David Logan, 39 Brook Avenue, Barn Road,
                            Carrickfergus,Co. Antrim N.I. BT38 7TE
Accepts: Horror, SF fantasy, speculative fiction

- o -

GROUND LEVEL
Address: Peter Pavement, Slab-o-concrete Press, PO
                            Box 148, Hove, BN3 3DQ
Accepts: Comics, interviews

- o -

THE HARDCORE
Address: J. Denny, PO Box 1893, London SW16 2ZB
Accepts: Cyberpunk

HEART THROB

Address: Mike Parker, 95 Spencer Street,
                    Birmingham B18 6DA

Accepts: Poetry, Fiction from West Midlands area

- o -

HEAVENBONE

Address: AK Distribution, 3 Balmoral Place, Stirling,
                    Scotland FK8 2RD

Accepts: Articles, Fiction

- o -

HERE AND NOW

Address: Mike Peters, PO Box 109, Leeds, West
                    Yorkshire LS5 3AA

Accepts: Anarchist politics, culture, arts, articles

- o -

IDENTITY MAGAZINE

Address: Pete Kalu, Cheetwood House, 21 Newton
                    Street, Manchester M1 1FZ

- o -

ILLUMINATIONS

Address: Stephen Lewis, Radley College, Abingdon,
                    Oxon OX14 2HR

Accepts: Poetry, translations

IMMEDIATE ARTS
Address: James Morrison, 26 Lyndhurst Gardens,
                Glasgow G20 6QY
Accepts: Independent & Small Press Listings

- o -

INTERACTIONS
Address: Diane M Moore, PO Box 250, St Helier,
                Jersey JE4 8TZ
Accepts: Multilingual: Poetry and art

- o -

ISSUE
Address: Jeremy Nuttall, 24 Eastwood Road, Basall
                Heath, Birmingham B12 9NB
Accepts: Reviews, Articles, Letters

- o -

JOE SOAP'S CANOE
Address: Martin Stannard, 30 Quilter Road, Felixstowe,
                Suffolk IP11 7JJ
Accepts: Poetry

- o -

KAMI KAZI PUBLICATONS
Address: 31 Belle Vue Street, Filey, East Yorks
                YO14 9HU

KENNEL GAZETTE
Address: Charles Colborn Kennel Club, 1-5 Clarges
                     Street, Piccadilly, London, W1Y 8AB
Accepts: Dogs: short stories

- o -

THE KEROUAC CONNECTION
Address: James Morton, 141 Maple Terrrace, East
                     Kilbride, Glasgow GT5 9EH
Accepts: Beat, Articles, Reviews

- o -

KRINO - the review
Address: Gerald Dawe & others, PO Box 65, Dun
                     Laughaire, Co Dublin, Ireland
Accepts: Irish-based, European orientated literary
                     review: poetry & fiction

- o -

KUNAPIPI
Address: Anna Rutherford, PO Box 20 Hebden Bridge,
                     West Yorks. HX7 5UZ
Accepts: International arts mag - literature of post-
                     colonial countries

- o -

LALLANS
Address: David Purves, 8 Strathalmond Road,
                     Edinburgh EH4 8AD
Accepts: Scots

LAUGH MAGAZINE

Address: Alan Forrest, Bradgate Press, 28 Stainsdale
                  Green, Whitwick, Leics LG67 5PW

Accepts: The quarterly British humour magazine,
                  featuring cartoons, poems etc.

- o -

LEGEND

Address: JP Reedman, 75 Melville Stret, Abington,
                  Northampton NN1 4HX

Accepts: Robin Hood: Fiction, Poetry

- o -

LEOPARD

Address: 27 Rose Street, Aberdeen

- o -

LINEAR A

Address: Johan de Wit, Flat 1, Sylva Court, 81 Putney
                  Hill, London SW15 3NX

Accepts: A Poetry, Review

- o -

LINES REVIEW

Address: Macdonald Publishing, Edgefield Road,
                  Loanhead, Midlothian EH20 9SY

Accepts: Poetry, Reviews

THE LINK

Address: David Pollard, Brumus Management, PO Box
                  317, Hounslow, Middlesex TW3 2SD
Accepts: Short fiction and poetry

- o -

LIT UP

Address: Jeremy Rogers, 8a Mill Street, Torrington,
                  Devon EX38 8HQ
Accepts: New writers, new writing

- o -

THE LITERARY REVIEW

Address: Auberon Waugh, 51 Beak Street, London
                  W1R 3LF
Accepts: Reviews, articles, interviews, short stories

- o -

THE LITTLE RED BOOK

Address:
                  B Dobson, PO Box 513, Bainber Bridge,
                  Preston, Lancs. PR5 6UZ
Accepts: Pagan: resources, poems, reviews

- o -

LIVING POETS - online ezine

Address: Sean Woodward, 11 Menin Road, Allestree,
                  Derby DE22 2NL
Accepts: Magazine of the Living Poets Society using
                  Worldnet & Fidonet

LONDON QUARTERLY
Address: John R Bradley, 63 Oakley Square, London NW1 1NJ

Accepts: Hospitable to poetry

- o -

THE LOST POET
Address: PO Box 136, Norwich, Norfolk NR3 3LJ
Accepts: Poetry

- o -

LYRICAL EXPRESSION
Address: PO Box 2, 315 Chapeltown Road, Leeds 7, Yorkshire

- o -

THE MAGPIES NEST
Address: B S Saini, 176 Stoney Lane, Sparkhill, Birmingham B12 8AN

Accepts: Poetry, short stories

- o -

MASQUE
Address: Wyrd Press, Rosewood Cottage, Langtoft, Driffield, E Yorks. YO25 OTQ

Accepts: Macabre, fantasy, surreal, horror: Stories, poems, Illustrations, reviews

MASSACRE

Address: BCM 16989, London WC1N 3XX
Accepts: Polemic fiction

- o -

MATRIX

Address: Jenny Glover, 16 Aviary Place, Leeds
                            LS12 2NP
Accepts: SF articles

- o -

MEDIEVAL HISTORY

Address: Judith Loades, PO Box 41, Bangor, Gwynedd
                            LL57 1SB
Accepts: Articles, some fiction

- o -

MIND YOUR OWN BUSINESS

Address: Bill Gledhill, 106 Church Road, London
                            SE19 2UB
Accepts: Small businesses, articles, light-hearted
                            fiction

- o -

THE MODERN DANCE

Address: D.W. Hughes, 12 Blakestones Road,
                            Slaithwaite, Huddersfield, Yorks HD7 5UQ
Accepts: Music reviews

MY LITTLE FANZINE

Address: Natasha, 26 Valley Close, Loughton, Essex
Accepts: Music reviews, interviews, cartoons, art,
                stories, poems, articles

- o -

MYSTIQUE

Address: Mike Chinn, 137 Priory Road, Hall Green,
                Birmigham B28 0TB
Accepts: Fantasy Fiction

- o -

THE NECKROSCOPE

Address: D Crow, Highfield House, 27 Little Green
                Lane, Farnham, Surrey GU9 8TF
Accepts: Gothic music, Reviews, Fiction, Poetry

- o -

THE NEW WELSH REVIEW

Address: Robin Reeves, Chapter Arts Centre, Market
                Road, Canton, Cardiff CF5 1QE
Accepts: Reviews, articles, poems, short stories

- o -

NOVOCAINE

Address: 22 Wilderness Road, Mannamead, Plymouth,
                Devon PL3 4RN
Accepts: Poetry-prose, reviews

NUTSHELL

Address: 8 George Marston Road, Binley, Coventry
                                 CV3 2HH

Accepts: Poetry, Short Stories, Letters, Reviews

- o -

THE OLAF ALTERNATIVE

Address: Ken Cheslin, 10 Coney Green, Stourbridge,
                                 West Midlands, DY8 1LA

Accepts: Articles, humorous fiction, cartoons

- o -

'O' MAGAZINE

Address: Una Deva, PO BOX 1426, Shepton Mallet,
                                 Somerset BA4 6HH

Accepts: Erotic Fiction,

- o -

OOH MY BRAIN HURTS

Address: Daniel Auty, 9 Andrew Close, Wokingham,
                                 Berkshire RG11 2HY

Accepts: Horror Reviews

- o -

ORE

Address: Eric Ratcliffe, 7 The Towers, Stevenage,
                                 Herts. SG1 1HE

Accepts: Poetry, Reviews, Articles

THE ORIENT EXPRESS
Address: c/o Astounding Comics, 61 Pyle Street,
                        Newport, Isle of Wight PO30 1UL
Accepts: Films

- o -

ORION
Address: 3 Bower Street, Reddish, Stockport SK5 6NW
Accepts: Speculative fiction, SF Horror

- o -

OSTINATO
Address: PO Box No. 522, London N8 7SZ
Accepts: Jazz-related poetry, stories, articles

- o -

OUT OF PRINT
Address: 27b Elswick Road, Lewisham, London
                        SE13 7SP
Accepts: Cassette Songs, Sketches, Drama, Demos.
                        Poetry

- o -

PANURGE
Address: John Murray, Crooked Holme Farm Cottage,
                        Brampton, Cumbria CA8 2AT
Accepts: Fiction

PASSPORT

Address: T McCarthy & M Gerard, 5 Parsonage Street, Wistow, Cambs. PE17 2QD

Accepts: Fiction, Non-fiction, poetry

- 0 -

THE PENNY DREADFUL

Address: Angela & Lee, 72 Fern Dene Road, Gateshead, Tyne & Wear NE8 4RX

Accepts: Gothic, vampire: Poems, essays, stories, reviews

- 0 -

PEN PALS

Address: Paul Ricketts, 43 Denbydale Way, Royton, Oldham, Lancs. OL2 5TN

- 0 -

PERIAKTOS

Address: John Gonzalez, 5 Sandhurst Avenue, Ipswich, Suffolk IP3 8DU

Accepts: Poetry

- 0 -

PHANTASY PROVINCE

Address: Misty Publishing, PO Box 6, Fraserburgh, AB43 5ZX

Accepts: Horror, Articles, Fiction

POETRY DIGEST

Address: The Editors, 28 Stainsdale Green, Whitwick,
                          Leics. LE67 5PW
Accepts: Poetry: Subscribers only, beginners and
                          seasoned writers

- o -

POETRY LONDON NEWSLETTER

Address: Persiflage Press, 26 Clacton Road, London
                          E17 8AR
Accepts: Poetry, articles, reviews

- o -

POETRY MATTERS

Address: 2 Kelly Gardens, Calstock, Cornwall
                          PL18 9SA
Accepts: Short Stories, Poems, Art, Members work
                          only

- o -

POMES

Address: Adrian Spendlow, Jane Publishing, 23 Bright
                          Street, York YO2 4XS
Accepts: Vocal Poetry Tabloid

- o -

POWERCUT

Address: BM Powercut, London WC1N 3XX
Accepts: Antisexist articles, poetry, cartoons

PROTOSTELLAR
Address: PO Box 491, Coulsdon, Surrey CR5 2UJ
Accepts: SF & F Short Stories, Reviews

- o -

PSYKLOPS
Address: 57 Tyndale Street, West End, Leicester
                  LE3 0QQ
Accepts: Comics

- o -

QUARTOS MAGAZINE
Address: Suzanne Riley, BCM-Writer, 27 Old
                  Gloucester Street, London WC1N 3XX
Accepts: Creative Writing

- o -

Q.W.F.
Address: Mrs M Good, 80 Main Street, Linton, Nr.
                  Swadlincote, Derbyshire DE12 6QA
Accepts   Fiction magazine for women

- o -

RAMRAID EXTRAORDINAIRE
Address: Kerry Sowerby, 2 Midland Road, Leeds
                  LS6 1BQ
Accepts: Poetry, short prose, graphics

RAPID EYE

Address: Simon Dwyer, 83 Clerkenwell Road, London
                EC1M 5RJ
Accepts: Journal of occulture - the dark side of popular
                culture

- o -

RATTLER'S TALE

Address: Anthony North, 2A Coronation Road, Walsall
                Wood, West Midlands WS9 9NG
Accepts: Articles, Imaginative Fiction, News

- o -

RAW NERVE

Address: Darren Floyd, 186 Railway Street, Splott,
                Cardiff, South Glamorgan CF2 2NH
Accepts: Dark Fiction

- o -

READ THIS

Address: Paul McDonald, 70 Walstead Road, Delves,
                Walsall,West Midlands WS5 4LX
Accepts: Poetry

- o -

THE REATOR

Address: Shane Rhodes, 1 Pilmar Lane, Roos, North
                Humberside HU12 0HP
Accepts: No flowers, just blunt chiselled poetry

REBEL INC.
Address: Kevin Williamson, 334 South Gyle Mains,
                  Edinburgh, EH12 9ES
Accepts   Poetry, Prose, Articles

- o -

THE RED SHOES
Address: Adrian Hodges, 3 Ashfield Close, Bishops
                  Cleeve, Cheltenham, Glos GL52 4LG
Accepts: An eclectic ragbag of poetry, fiction & essays

- o -

REM
Address: Arthur Straker, 19 Sandringham Road,
                  Willesden, London NW2 5EP
Accepts: F & SF long stories

- o -

THE REVIEW
Address: Bosham House, Bosham, Chichester, West
                  Sussex PO18 8PJ
Accepts: Spiritual life, Poetry, articles

- o -

REVOLTING
Address: PO Box 393, Kingston upon Thames, Surrey
                  KT2 5YR
Accepts: Revolutionary: Poems, articles

REZPONZEZ

Address: Tony Rollinson, 10b Riverside, Totnes,
             Devon TQ9 5JB
Accepts: Anonymous poetry

- o -

RHINOCEROS

Address: Patrick Ramsey & Kevin Smith, 120 Sondan
             Street, Belfast, BT12 6LD
Accepts: Poetry

- o -

RIVET

Address: Eve Catchpole, 74 Walton Drive,
             High Wycombe, Bucks HP13 6TT
Accepts: Short stories, articles, poetry

- o -

ROISIN DUBH

Address: Ty Fraen, The Park, Blaenavon, Gwent
             NP4 9AG
Accepts: Gothic: Poetry, artwork, reviews

- o -

ROMANTIC HEIR

Address: PGP Thompson, Precious Pearl, Pr. 71
             Harrow Crescent, Romford, Essex RM3 7BJ
Accepts: High Inspirational Romantic Poetry

RQC

Address: Gavin Wilson, 18 Worcester Drive, Didcot,
Oxfordshire OX11 8UP

Accepts: Sf short fiction

- o -

RUBBERNECK

Address: 21 Denham Drive, Basingstoke, Hampsire
RG22 6LT

Accepts: Music, News, reviews, fiction, articles

- o -

SAYLA

Address: Celia Stuart, Combehayes Farm, Buckerell,
Honiton, Devon, EX14 0ET

Accepts: Poems, Stories Illustrations

- o -

SCAR TISSUE

Address: Tony Lee, 13 Hazely Combe, Arreton,
Newport, Isle of Wight PO30 3AJ

Accepts: Market news, poems

- o -

SCARED TO DEATH

Address: Joe Rattigan, 1 Hill Farm Close, Fitton Hill, Oldham
OL8 2LL

Accepts: Horror, Articles, Fiction, Art

SCOTS GLASNOST

Address: Neal R MacCallum, 18 Redford Avenue,
Edinburgh EH13 0BU

- o -

THE SHARKTI VANGUARD

Address: c/o P Page, Sharkti Laureate, 104 Argyle
Gardens, Upminster, Essex RM14 3EU

Accepts: New Renaissance: Poems to 36 lines, prose
to 1000 words

- o -

SHEARSMAN

Address: Tony Frazer, 47 Dayton Close, Plymouth
PL6 5AX

Accepts: Poetry

- o -

SHIVERS

Address: Visual Imagination, PO Box 371, London
SW14 8JL

- o -

SHOES OF QUALITY

Address: Syd and Leu, PO Box 2267, West Mersea,
Essex CO5 8HF

Accepts: Poetry, photos, articles

SICKLE MOON

Address: c/o P. Page, Sharkti Laureate, 104 Argyle
                            Gardens, Upminster, Essex RM14 3EU
Accepts: Celtic New Renaissance, Poems, stories to
                            1000 words

- o -

THE SILVER ARROW

Address: Julie Phipps, 47 Cotswold Avenue, Dustan,
                            Northants NN5 6DP
Accepts: Robin Hood: Poetry, artwork, fiction, reviews

- o -

SILVER WOLF AND LITTLE PEOPLE

Address: 13 Sandyhill Gardens, Dublin 11, Ireland
Accepts: For writers and readers worldwide

- o -

SKELETON GIRLS

Address: Allison Burgess, 36 Rowley Street, Stafford
                            ST16 2TH
Accepts: Gothic goddesses: artwork, poetry, prose,
                            reviews, photos

- o -

SLOW DANCER

Address: John Harvey, Flat 2, 59 Parliament Hill,
                            London NW3 2TB
Accepts: Poetry, Fiction

THE SMALL HOURS

Address: Paul A Broome, 21 Ganton Way, Fixby,
                Huddersfield HD2 2ND
Accepts: Horror Fiction, Art, Films

- o -

SMALL PRESS MONTHLY

Address: 11 Ashburnham Road, Bedford MK40 1DX
Accepts: News, letters, articles

- o -

THE SMELL OF NAPALM

Address: W Clark, 12 Lyme Road, Ampthill, Beds
                MK45 2LB
Accepts: Films

- o -

THE SOCIETY OF CIVIL SERVICE AUTHORS

Address: Joan Hykin, 8 Bawtree Close, Sutton, Surrey
                SM2 5LQ
Accepts: Open to non civil servants

- o -

SODEM

Address: Tom O'Brien, 57 Cassiobury Road,
                Walthamstow, London E17 7JD
Accepts: Poems, articles, stories

THE SOLAR COURIERS

Address: c/o P. Page, Sharkti Laureate, 104 Argyle Gardens, Upminster, Essex RM14 3EU

Accepts: New Renaissance: Poems to 36 lines, prose to 500words

- o -

SOLAR PLANET EARTH

Address: c/o P. Page, Sharkti Laureate, 104 Argyle Gardens, Upminster, Essex RM14 3EU

Accepts: Young New Renaissance, Poems to 36 lines, prose to 1000 words

- o -

SONGS

Address: Pete Presford, Rose Cottage, 3 Tram Lane, Buckley, Clwyd, North Wales

Accepts: News, Poetry

- o -

SOUND AND LANGUAGE

Address: 85 London Road South, Lowestoft, Suffolk NR33 0AS

Accepts: Poetry

- o -

SPEAR

Address: Jacqueline Jones, 22 Fforest Road, Lampeter, Dyfed

Accepts: SF. Poetry

SPECTACULAR DISEASES
Address: Paul Green, 836 London Road,
Peterborough, Cambs.
Accepts: Poetry, Articles, Translations

- o -

SPHINX
Address: PO Box 417, London NW3 6YE
Accepts: Archetypal Psychology and The Arts, Poetry

- o -

SPLINTER
Address: K Jones, 40 Lark Hill, Hove, Sussex BN3 8PF
Accepts: Daffodil free poetry for the post-me
generation

- o -

SPOKES
Address: Alistair Winter, 319A Hills Road, Cambridge
CB2 2QT
Accepts: Poetry, Artwork

- o -

SPRINGBOARD
Address: Ann Froggatt, Flat A, 6 Heathfield Road,
Croydon, Surrey CRO1ES
Accepts: Poetry, prose, articles

STARBURST
Address: Visual Imagination, PO Box 371, London
                     SW14 8JL

- o -

THE STEEPLE
Address: Patrick Cotter, Three Spires Press, Killeen,
                     Blackrock Village, Cork City, Eire
Accepts: Ireland's new poetry magazine

- o -

STONED SOUL PICNIC
Address: Liv, 64 Hughendon Road, Norwich, Norfolk
                     NR1 2PY
Accepts: Poems, Stories, Indie Music Reviews

- o -

STORYTELLER
Address: Brian Lewis, 6 Church Street, Darfield, South
                     Yorkshire ST3 9LG
Accepts: Short stories

- o -

STRANGE ADVENTURES
Address: Tony Lee, 13 Hazely Combe, Arreton,
                     Newport, Isle of Wight PO30 3AJ
Accepts: Sf. Fantasy, Horror, Reviews, Artwork

STRANGE ATTRACTOR

Address: Rick Cadger, 111 Sundown Road, Houghton
                Regis, Dunstable, Beds. LU5 5NL

Accepts: Sf. Horror, Fantasy: No new work at present

- o -

STRING

Address: Borogore Productions, 97 St Peters Way,
                Warrington, Cheshire WA2 7BL

Accepts: SF stories

- o -

SUBSTANCE

Address: Paul Beardsley, 16 Blenheim Gardens,
                Denvilles, Havant, Hants PO9 2PN

Accepts: SF Fantasy: Fiction, articles, reviews

- o -

SUMMER BULLETIN

Address: Muriel Shackleton, 3 Northdale Mount,
                Bradford BD5 9AP

Accepts: Yorkshire dialect verse, news

- o -

SUNK ISLAND REVIEW

Address: Michael Blackburn, P.O. Box 74, Lincoln
                LN1 1QG

Accepts: Fiction, Poetry, Criticism

SWORD

Address: JP Reedman, 75 Melville Street, Abington,
                  Northampton NN1 4HX
Accepts: Sword and sorcery: Art, Fiction, Poetry

- o -

SYMPHONY

Address: PhillipTait, Betterton Press, 9 Hamilton
                  Gardens, London NW8 9PU
Accepts: Christian Poetry, Articles, Reviews

- o -

T 3 x 4

Address: J Mingay, 2 Henderson Street, Kingseat by
                  Dunfermline, Fife KY12 0TP
Accepts: Poetry

- o -

TALES FROM THE BROKEN DRUM

Address: S Halligan, 192 Stanbridge Road, Leighton
                  Buzzard, Beds. LU7 8QW
Accepts: Humorous SF Fiction

- o -

TALUS

Address: Dept. of English, King's College, Strand,
                  London WC2R 2LS
Accepts: Creative writing

TANDEM

Address: Michael J Woods, 13 Stephenson Road,
Barbourne, Worcs. WR1 3EB

Accepts: New and established writers

- o -

TARGET

Address: Bryn Fortey, 212 Caeleon Road, Newport,
Gwent NP9 7GC

Accepts: Poetry from Gwent and beyond

- o -

TASH

Address: Tommy, 42 Ava Drive, Belfast BT7 3DW

- o -

THE TEMPEST

Address: M Paraskos, The New Leeds Arts club, 4 Lifton
Place, Leeds LS2 9JZ

Accepts: Contemporary cultural issues: Articles,
poetry, prose

- o -

10TH MUSE

Address: Andrew Jordan, 33 Hartington Road,
Southampton, Hants SO14 OEW

Accepts: Poetry, Prose Graphics

TERRIBLE WORK

Address: Tim Allen, 21 Overton Gardens, Mannamead,
            Plymouth, Devon PL3 5BX
Accepts: Speculative poetry, art, fiction, articles

- o -

TERRITORIES

Address: c/o MC Nair, 65 Nidrie Road, Strathbingo,
            Glasgow, G42 8PT
Accepts: Slipstream: criticism

- o -

THINGUMMYBOB

Address: C Connor, Sildan House, Chediston Road,
            Wissett, Halesworth Suffolk IP19 ONF
Accepts: SF Personal: Articles

- o -

THREADS

Address: Geoff Lynas, 32 Irvin Avenue, Saltburn,
            Cleveland TS12 1QH
Accepts: SF Fantasy, Chilling, Fiction, Poetry

- o -

TOCHER

Address: Alan Bruford, School of Scottish Studies, 27
            Georges Square, Edinburgh EH8 9LD
Accepts: Folklore and oral history from Scots and
            Gaelic recordings

TOK

Address: A Richards, 17 Althorp Road, Northampton
NN5 5EF

Accepts: Poetry, fiction, essays

- o -

TONGUE TO BOOT

Address: Miles Champion, 5 Abbots Court, Thackeray
Street, London W8 5ES

Accepts: Poetry

- o -

TRANSACTIONS OF THE YORKSHIRE DIALECT SOCIETY

Address: 22 Aspin Oval, Knaresborough HG5 8EL

Accepts: Poetry, Prose, Reviews

- o -

TRANSIT

Address: Kevin Ring, 27 Court Leet, Binley Woods,
Coventry, CV3 2SQ

Accepts: Beat Poetry

- o -

TRANSITIONS

Address: 15 Queen Court, Queen Square, London
WC1N 3BB

Accepts: A twice-yearly anthology from the European
borderlands

TUBA
Address: Charles Graham, Tunley Cottage, Tunley, Nr.
Cirencester, Glos. GL7 6LW

Accepts: Poetry

- o -

TURKEY SHOOT
Address: Ian Sales, 56 Southwell Road East,
Mansfield, Notts NG21 0EW

Accepts: SF Reviews

- o -

TWISTED SOULS
Address: Lorraine Sinnott Paton, 10E Houston Street,
Renfrew, PA4 8NR, Scotland

Accepts: Horror Reviews

- o -

UNCOMPROMISING POSITIONS
Address: C Wilkinsin, 82 Staneway, Leam Lane,
Gateshead, Tyne & Wear NE10 8LS

Accepts: Popular poetry

- o -

UNDER SURVEILLANCE
Address: Eddie Hartiman, 60 Arnold Street, Brighton,
East Sussex BN2 2XT

Accepts: Poetry, artwork

UNICORN
Address: Alex Warner, 12 Milton Avenue, Millbrook,
               Stalybridge, Cheshire SK15 3HB
Accepts: Mainstream poetry magazine

- o -

THE UNNAMEABLE
Address: Paul Richardson, 37 Abingdon Grove,
               Walton, Liverpool L4 9UZ
Accepts: Horror: stories to 3000 w. articles

- o -

URBAN FANTASY
Address: Will Parker & Others, The Art Hive, 34 Castle
               House, 1 Overton Road, Sutton, Surrey
               SM2 6QE
Accepts: Creative writing

- o -

VALID
Address: Bradford Community Arts Centre, 17-21
               Chapel Street. L. Germany, Bradford
               BD1 5DT
Accepts: English & Asian languages, fiction, poetry by
               disabled women

- o -

THE VALLEY POETS
Address: Eugene Nowakowski, 123 Coedpenmaen
               Road, Pontypridd, S. Wales CF37 4LH
Accepts: Short stories, Poetry

VECTOR

Address: Catie Cary, 224 Southway Park Barn,
Guildford, Surrey GU2 6DN

Accepts: SF Reviews, articles

- o -

VERSE

Address: Dept. of English, The University, St. Andrews,
Fife, KY16 9AL, Scotland

Accepts: Poems, Interviews, Criticism, Reviews

- o -

VIOLENT SPECTRES

Address: Adam Bradley, 28 Treaty Street, Islington,
London, N1 0SY

Accepts: Intelligent horror: fiction to 3000w. poetry to 1
page

- o -

WALKING NAKED

Address: Sean Boustread, 13 Napier Street, Swinton,
Manchester M27 3JQ

Accepts: Poetry

- o -

WASAFIRI

Address: Susheila Nasta, English Department, QMW,
Mile End Road, London E1 4NS

Accepts: Caribbean, African, Asian Literature, film

WE KISS THROUGH GAS MASKS
Address: Paul, 517 Seven Sisters Road, Tottenham,
                        London N15
Accepts: SF Fantasy: Fiction, comics

- o -

WESTWORDS
Address: Dave Woolley, 15 Trelawney Road, Peverell,
                        Plymouth, PL3 4JS
Accepts: Poetry, Short Stories, Drawings, Photos,
                        Revs.

- o -

W.H. - Wider Horizons
Address: Anne Dobson, Ghyll Cottage, Ings, Kendal,
                        Cumbria LA8 9PU
Accepts: Creative work by the physically handicapped

- o -

THE WIDE SKIRT
Address: Geoff Hattersley, 1a Church Street,
                        Penistone, South Yorks S30 6AR
Accepts: Poetry

- o -

WINDLESORA
Address: Pamela Marson, 256 Dedworth Road,
                        Windsor, Berks SL4 4RL
Accepts: Journal of the Windsor local history
                        publications group

WINDOWS POETRY BROADSHEET
Address: Heather Brett & others, Nature Haven,
                        Legaginney, Ballinagh, Cavan, Eire
Accepts: The best contemporary literature from
                        authors everywhere

- o -

WIRE POETRY MAGAZINE
Address: Mal Cieslak, 1 Alanbrooke Close, Knaphill,
                        Surrey GU21 2RU
Accepts: Contemporary poetry by new and established
                        writers

- o -

WITANA GEMOT
Address: Guild of St George, Rose Cottage, 17
                        Hadassah Grove, Liverpool L17 8XH
Accepts: Philos, econs, history, theology, SF articles,
                        short stories

- o -

WITS END
Address: Jean Turner, 27 Pheasants Close, Winnersh,
                        Workingham, Berks RG11 5LS
Accepts: Magazine by aspiring writers

- o -

THE WIZARDS KNOB
Address: Spinneys, Post Office Road, Woodham
                        Mortimer, Maldon, Essex CM9 6SX
Accepts: Terry Pratchett fanzine: Articles, news etc.

THE WORD
Address: Lawrence Gertig, 31 Westfield Lane, South
                            Elmsall, Pontefract, Yorkshire
Accepts: Popular fiction

- o -

WORDS
Address: Shaun Peare, 37A Okehampton Road,
                            Kensal Rise, London NW10 3EE
Accepts: Stories, competitions, letters

- o -

WORKS
Address: D W Hughes, 12 Blakestones Road,
                            Slaithwaite, Huddersfield, Yorks HD7 5UQ
Accepts: Imaginative Fiction, Poetry, Artwork

- o -

WRITE ANGLES
Address: Yorks and Humberside Arts, 21 Bond Street,
                            Dewsbury, W. Yorks WF1 1AX
Accepts: News, markets

- o -

WRITE AROUND THE YEAR
Address: 2 Sycamore Road, Middlesborough TS6 6RA
Accepts: Cleveland only: Articles, stories, poems, revs.

WRITERS MONTHLY

Address: Alan Williams, 29 Turnpike Lane, London
                  N8 OEP
Accepts: Advice, interviews, comps.

- o -

WRITERS NEWS

Address: PO Box 4, Nairn, Scotland IV12 4HU
Accepts: Articles on writing

- o -

WRITERS REIGN

Address: Paul Ricketts, 43 Denbydale Way, Royton,
                  Oldham, Lancs OL2 5TN

- o -

WRITERS REPORTS

Address: Oakwood Publications, 23 Mill Crescent,
                  Kingsbury, Warwickshire BT8 2LX
Accepts: Markets, news

- o -

THE YONKLY

Address: Mike Dillon, 16 Angle Park Terrace,
                  Edinburgh EH11 2JX
Accepts: Poetry comment

ZENE
Address: 5 Martin's Lane, Witcham, Ely,
Cambridgeshire CB6 2LB
Accepts: Small Press Listings, guidelines, reviews,
articles

- o -

ZERO HOUR
Address: 20 Thorpe Green Drive, Leymoor,
Huddersfield, HD7 4QU
Accepts: Strange Art, Fiction

- o -

ZIMMERFRAME PILEUP
Address: Stephen Jessener, Loose Hand Press, 54
Hillcrest Road, Walthamstow, London
E17 4AP
Accepts: Articles, dreams, whatever

Organisations of Interest to Poets and Writers

ASSOCIATION OF LITTLE PRESSES
30 Greenhill
Hampstead High Street
London
NW3 5VA
Tel: 0171 435 1889

THE SOCIETY OF AUTHORS
84 Drayton Gardens
London
SW10 9SB
Tel: 0171 373 6642

Places that could help

The Poetry Library, South Bank Centre, Royal Festival Hall, (Level 5, Red side), London SE1 8XX. 0171 921 0943. Huge holdings of little mags and poetry titles. Issues current awareness lists of poetry publishers, organisations, magazines, and competitions.

The Little Magazines Collection and Poetry Store, Rare Books Room, University College, Gower Street, London WC1E 6BT. 0171 380 7796. Geoffrey Soar and David Miller's collection of more than 3500 poetry mags.

HMSO ORIEL's Magazine Subscription service. For £40 receive a different UK poetry small mag each month. The Friary, Cardiff CF1 4AA. 01222 395548

1998 Edition

Details for the 1998 Small Press Guide should reach us by 5th
September 1997. Entries should be addressed to Writers' Bookshop,
7-11 Kensington High Street, London W8 5NP. Forms for entries can
be obtained from the same address.